The Importance of disappointment

D0223623

This book explores the nature of identity in late modern society. The author, a sociologist and a psychoanalytic psychotherapist, brings together the insights of both disciplines to argue that 'late modern' society seems to present new possibilities of living that are in fact illusions. We come to believe that we can create ourselves; that we have 'rights' to aspects of life such as happiness, a 'fulfilling relationship', parents who love us unconditionally; we come to believe that we can find a 'real self' or alternatively we believe that we can be anything that we want to be as the occasion arises. Craib shows this through examining modern theories of death and mourning, contemporary ideas of masculinity, and notions of the self espoused by modern therapies.

Psychoanalysis too gets caught up in these illusions, offering ideals which are unrealisable, attempting to mould the personality in such a way that it fits late modern society, paradoxically reinforcing the conditions which lead people to seek help in the first place. Against this, Craib points to the 'negative' strands of psychoanalysis: Freud's insistence on 'normal human misery', Klein's insistence on envy and the death instinct, Lacan's insistence on the fragmented nature of the self and the emphasis in British psychoanalysis on helplessness, dependence and paradox. It is by drawing on such ideas that psychoanalytic therapy can become more than an ideology, offering genuine help to its patients and providing a real source of radical social criticism.

Ian Craib is Lecturer in Sociology at the University of Essex and a psychoanalytic group psychotherapist.

The importance of disappointment

Ian Craib

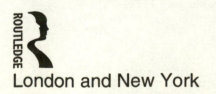

London and New York

First published in 1994
by Routledge
11 New Fetter Lane, London EC4P 4EE

Simultaneously published in the USA and Canada by
Routledge
29 West 35th Street, New York, NY 10001

© 1994 Ian Craib

Typeset in Baskerville by
NWL Editorial Services, Langport, Somerset

Printed and bound in Great Britain by
Mackays of Chatham PLC, Chatham, Kent

British Library Cataloguing in Publication Data
A catalogue record for this book is available from the
British Library

Library of Congress Cataloging in Publication Data
Craib, Ian, 1945–
    The importance of disappointment/Ian Craib.
        p.   cm.
    Includes bibliographical references and index.
    ISBN 0–415–09382–1: $50.00. –
    ISBN 0–415–09383–X (pbk.): $17.95
    1. Disappointment.   2. Psychoanalysis.   I. Title.
    BF575.D57C73   1994   94–5593
    150.19′5 – dc20   CIP

ISBN 0–415–09382–1 (hbk)
ISBN 0–415–09383–X (pbk)

Contents

Preface

The writing of this book was punctuated by a period of some four months during which I had to deal with a serious illness. I might anyway have moved the chapter on death and mourning from its original place near the end of the book, but in the event I had no hesitation in taking up a colleague's suggestion that I should do so. I had never before allowed myself to recognise the fear of death that must be common to us all, and neither had I properly understood its implication: that life is immensely precious and the links we have with other people, in all their dreadful complexity, are all that we have, and if there is such a thing as evil it lies in the deliberate breaking of those links.

This is not normally the ground trodden by sociologists; it should be, but it is all too often not, ground trodden by psycho-therapists. Sociology offers an ideology of social improvement, psychotherapy offers an ideology of individual improvement. The truth is that we will all die. The first duty of the human sciences is perhaps to hold on to both sides of the equation: that life can be good and made better, and that life ends in the ultimate disappointment of death. The argument in this book is that there is much about our modern world that increases disappointment and at the same time encourages us to hide from it: to act as if what is good in life does not entail the bad – for example, that we can love and be loved by another person without having to give up other aspects of our lives; that we can have children without sacrifice; that we can love without ambivalence and hatred; that we can take decisions about our lives without being bounded on all sides by the needs and actions of others; that we can grow without pain and loss, and in the end that we can grow without dying.

In this book I have tried to employ two very different ways of thinking about the world – the sociological and the psychoanalytic – to criticise each other and bring together both sides of the equation in the same place. Maybe up until 30 years ago the emphasis would have been on the possibility of making life better; at the moment I believe, we can only make life better if we can recognise and incorporate the dark side, the side of disappointment and death. Paradoxically, the more we deny this, the more difficult our lives become, the more we become involved in breaking the links between people.

Much of what is good and useful in this book comes from the help of others. First, I would like to take the opportunity to thank all those whose moral and practical support helped me through last summer. Second, many thanks to Ian Birkett, Andrew Samuels and John Walshe who read draft versions and spent their valuable time and energy in making helpful comments. My wife, Fiona Grant, also belongs in this group, but deserves special thanks for persevering with the task under my baleful gaze. Michael Roper read the chapter on masculinity and made me think. I would like to thank the students in my seminar in Sociology and Psychodynamic Processes – Heather Alston, Kathleen Cannings, Simon Ehlert, Jessica Evans, Marion Diederiks Hales, Terri Magee and Patricia Skirrow – for their encouragement and for a stimulating set of discussions on the themes of the book. The undergraduates on my Social Psychology course have provided a tolerant area for the development of many of my ideas over the last decade. Finally there are those I cannot name: members of my therapy and experiential groups over the years: sometimes I think they have taught me more than I could ever teach them, and the best I can do is offer my apologies.

And my son, Ben, and my step-children, Theo, Penelope (who offered particular encouragement at the beginning) and Chris, who between them provide me with a kaleidoscope of contradictory reasons for staying alive.

Chapter 1

Cutting out gingerbread people

This book is drawn from a range of experiences and ideas. On the one hand, there is my work as a group psychotherapist working with patient and client groups, student groups and groups of trainee counsellors. On the other, there is my work as a sociologist, as a teacher of and writer about modern social theory. It is a study of the nature of identity in contemporary society, and a critique of the place of psychotherapy in our society. It is also a defence of psychotherapy, against those who would dismiss it wholesale: for all its faults and problems, I will argue that it still has something important to offer, but that something often runs counter both to what people might hope to gain from psychotherapy and to a current of expectations and ways of thinking in the wider culture and society.

It is also a defence of a certain type of psychotherapy: that based within the psychoanalytic tradition. In Britain, therapy and counselling seem to be experiencing an unprecedented popularity: we have reached the stage where they figure in soap operas. This is reflected throughout the Western world and elsewhere, and over recent decades there has been a blossoming of different types of therapy that often claim to offer more than the traditional forms, more quickly and with fewer doubts and complications than can be found in the work that began with Freud. Psychoanalysis itself tends to get caught up in this, promising results that are competitive rather than realistic. So within the psychoanalytic tradition, I want to offer a defence of certain themes, in fact certain values, that I believe important to preserve. They can be summed up in words such as conflict, difficulty, work, failure, complexity, ambivalence, rationality, morality, restraint, judgement and many others, all of which I am lumping together under *disappointment*.

The popularity of psychotherapy and the growth of new forms of therapy is not something that just happens, nor is it necessarily a 'good thing', certainly not in any simple way. It is not necessarily part of the march of progress, a steady alleviation of the human condition and improvement of human relationships. I will argue that some aspects of this popularity can be dangerous, even destructive, and they can be intimately bound up with a loss of freedom and the development of a highly organised and controlled society. A society, a culture, is a complex entity and there will be, at any one time, a number of contradictory processes going on; nothing is ever simply 'good' or 'bad', and most things are at the same time good *and* bad. What I hope to do is not only to offer a defence of psychotherapy, to some degree against itself, but also to tease out and criticise certain aspects of our culture which seem to me to be threatening.

This should not be seen as some wholesale condemnation of the modern (or postmodern) world: I am only trying to identify some strands, albeit, I would argue, important strands, of our culture and think about them sceptically. These strands are bound up with large-scale social changes, and as they have developed, so ideas from psychotherapy and psychoanalysis have been drawn into them. I suspect that the present popularity of psychotherapy has more to do with these changes than with any virtues that psychoanalysis might possess on its own account; indeed it seems to me that *one* of the real virtues of psychoanalysis might be that it can protect the values that are threatened by the changes we are living through, but to do this it might have to reject its own popularity and stand back from it.

This book, then, will be about psychoanalysis and psychoanalytic ideas about psychotherapy and what we can and should expect from it, and the way in which it works; it will be about the place of both of these in our society; and it will be about what is happening to our society and the way that affects, for better or worse, the way we think about ourselves, the way we expect to live and work. It will be about what we might expect from our lives and from the society we live in.

I will often use the first person plural. Who is this 'we' I am talking about? Much of the time I am describing a normal human difficulty, so the 'we' is everybody. However, perhaps these difficulties are more pronounced for some than others. By 'we' perhaps I mean primarily people like myself. The social changes

I am concerned with affect most strongly those who might once have been called 'middle-class': the professions, those controlling and some of those working in the service industries, the 'caring' professions, the media; those of us who have a comparatively uncertain future, reasonable levels of education, who range from the comfortably off to the comparatively poor, but who are not entirely trapped. There are many who do not fall into this category: there are those who have been consistently disappointed, whose life does not often rise much above a matter of day-to-day survival and who have little material out of which to form choices for the future. Such people might be in the majority – their existence, I suspect, acts as a permanent threat to those of us who try to avoid disappointment.

Why disappointment? In common usage, and in the dictionary, we talk about disappointment as what happens, what we feel, when something we expect, intend, or hope for or desire does not materialise. One of the difficulties of living in our world is that it is perhaps increasingly less clear exactly what we might expect or hope for or desire. In fact, these words mean different things. The most basic is desire: it carries connotations of needing urgently, yearning, to the point almost of trying to will something into existence. Sometimes we desire something so completely that we revert to our infant selves and scream, metaphorically or in reality, in the hope that our desire may be realised – just as, if we were lucky, the milk used to appear in response to our screams from the cot. Sometimes we will break things, threaten to hurt, or actually hurt, ourselves or others in order to obtain our desire. From the outside, such behaviour is often seen as simply selfish: 'She's only doing it to get what she wants.' From the inside, it is more powerful, not simply a matter of wanting something but of needing it so urgently that without it, life seems unbearable. At those moments, we desire something with all our heart and soul, but go beyond the powerful yearning that is usually suggested by that phrase. In a lower key, the feeling seems to say: 'If I yearn hard enough, long enough, if I feel this pain sufficiently intensely, then my desire will be realised.'

Most of us will experience such feelings at times, some more than others. Most of us learn eventually to survive the disappointment of desire, often with a great deal of heartache. Sometimes we will take our desire for reality: after the death of somebody we love, we will see them walking ahead of us down the street, and run to catch up, before we remember. Usually, we can accept that what we desire does not always exist; that we can desire something without necessarily hoping for it and certainly without expecting it. But perhaps there might be areas in our lives where we can believe something to be the case because we desire it, and find ourselves unable to give up the idea whatever evidence we are presented with.

I am interested in these grey areas. In psychotherapy, there are many examples: the continued belief that a particular person is really the 'right one' for us; the hope that we can do something to change our relationship to our parents so that they will become the people that we've always wanted them to be. Such beliefs are clearly not 'mad' and not the reaction to some trauma but none the less they do not quite stand the test of 'reality'. My argument will be that there are certain social processes going on around us that make the reality testing more difficult and that perhaps encourage us to believe what we desire to be the case. In American and British society at the moment, for example, there are tendencies to encourage us to believe that we can achieve the personal fulfilment, the space for self-expression, the 'personal growth' which, in these societies, many people certainly desire.

Desire is not quite the same as hope. When we use the term 'hope', I suspect we are indicating that some thought has gone into the process of hoping; we are not quite so driven by basic forces as we are when we desire. To hope for something implies an acknowledgement that the hope may not be realised, that we have made some judgement about what reality can offer and we are testing it. But we can discover that we have unrealistic hopes and we find ourselves maintaining the hope against the evidence; it is not unknown to talk of the triumph of hope over experience.

There is something different in our experience of hope. We have desires whether we like it or not. On the whole, we like to have hopes, they are amongst the things that keep us going; the opposite of hope is hopelessness, despair, giving up. There might be periods in our lives, after the disappointment of hope, when we try to give up all future hopes, not being able to face again even the possibility of the pain of disappointment. Some people despair and do not return to hope; but many will despair in the hope that hope will return. Sometimes we fight hard, quite consciously with great energy, to maintain our hopes, the psychological equivalent, perhaps, of the stiff upper lip. There are times, perhaps, when hope seems to be everything, when to give up hope is to plunge into nothingness. And, in the same way that there are certain processes at work in our society encouraging us to desire the impossible, so there are processes which encourage us to hope for too much, not to surrender our hopes when they prove unrealistic or to surrender them, as far as possible, without experiencing the pain and despair that follow. The search for somebody or something to blame when hopes are frustrated can help to avoid the pain and has become intimately bound up with modern politics.

There is a connection here between hope and ideals – the way we would like the world to be and the sort of people we would like ourselves to be. It can seem that without our ideals, nothing is worth while; we need to hold onto them but at the same time we need to accept that our ideals are never likely to be realised. If we believe we can achieve our ideals, then we are back with blind desire, but of a more persecutory nature. If the world won't match up to our ideals, then we must try to force it; if we don't ourselves match up to our ideals, then we punish and try to force ourselves. Perhaps the dominant sense in which we have in the past talked about idealism, whether on a political or a personal level, has been in terms of altruism: of giving to other people, of restraining one's own desires and demands and often of creating a situation in which other people may do the same. It has been associated with morality, enforced on us by society and on ourselves by ourselves, through a sense of failure and guilt. Now, however, there is a tendency to equate morality with self-expression, with the satisfaction of our needs and wants; we often regard ourselves as having 'rights' to these things; they become our ideals. And when we fail to live up to them, it is not ourselves but society and other people that we punish.

Another way of putting all this is that we might change our desires, hopes, ideals, into intentions and expectations, things we actually set out to achieve in their fullness, rather than see them as distant goals that we will never achieve, yet still have to work towards, or as pleasant dreams that are, in reality, simply not on. It is a paradox of our existence that we have to be in both of these positions at the same time. Some part of us wants immediate satisfaction, wants it all and wants it now, and whilst we might try to rationalise this away with our knowledge that it is unreasonable, our gut reactions belie our heads. To occupy the second position as well, to make the compromises with reality, involves an ongoing, painful process that is rather like giving up part of ourselves. At a time when self-fulfilment and self-expression seem to be major cultural values, achieving this second position becomes more and more difficult. There are ways in which reality itself, our social reality and the natural world around us, becomes uncertain, obscure. We do not quite know what it is. And it is as if, in response to this immense uncertainty, we *have* to believe in the certainties of our own desires. The tangles and confusions that we get ourselves into when trying to maintain these certainties come to seem preferable to the pain of disappointment and uncertainty.

Alternatively we may try to give up our hopes, not in the despair that always lurks behind disappointment, but as a sort of abstention from areas of life where these difficulties most often manifest themselves. We might decide that because we cannot be absolutely certain of everything, then we cannot be certain of anything. We might decide that because we cannot be absolutely sure of what is right or good or beautiful, then nothing in particular is right or good or beautiful, and we save the energy of expending serious thought on these things. Our inner life becomes empty and our outer life a cynical manipulation of people and events for our own, usually modest, purposes.

Many of the things that frustrate us belong to the world outside, but in this book I am interested in the way we are inevitably frustrated by the social world and by our own psychological and physical make-up. It might sound odd to emphasise disappointment in a discussion of psychotherapy. The public face of psychotherapy and counselling is a comforting and understanding face, providing help and support, easing pain, sorting out difficulties and problems, resolving conflicts, enabling people to find themselves, take responsibility for themselves and satisfy their needs. Some of this is rooted in classical psychoanalytic theory, in Freud's criticisms of the repression of sexuality. Freud, however, was writing in a form of society where too much, rather than too little, repression seemed to be required and where many neuroses seemed to be the result of keeping too tight a rein on instinctual desires, particularly sexual desires. One of the ways in which psychoanalysis first entered popular culture was with the idea that we ought to be less repressed sexually.

Increasingly, 'repression' has come to gain as many negative connotations when it refers to internal, psychological processes as it has when it refers to external, political repression, although they are by no means the same thing. The removal of repression, the expression of needs, of desires, has become a theme of modern culture and of many post-psychoanalytic therapies, and it is not unusual to hear people claiming rights to self-expression, rights to have their needs met, not in the political sense of freedom of speech and reasonable standards of living, but in terms of personal relationships, where the meaning can be very different: I can say what I want to you, however much hurt and humiliation it causes; you must give me what I need, whatever its cost to you, or else. Often the 'or else' entails the end of the relationship, the satisfaction of needs triumphing over connections to other people. There is, of course, a matter of balance in all this: I am not suggesting that people should make themselves slaves to others, or refrain from voicing anger, but it often seems to me that the subtleties and difficulties of all this are ignored.

These claims are often bound up with a sense of omnipotence, and if they are refused, we rage against a world which will not be as we want it to be. The claim 'I have a right to control my own life', when made collectively by a subjugated people, has a very different meaning to that which it has when it is made by an individual. I spend my life surrounded by other people, who are more or less independent of me and constantly doing things on their own account. As a consequence, I have to adjust to them. If I am to control my own life, then I will first have to control the lives of all those around me. The rights I might have to do as I wish are certainly a political matter, but they are also a moral matter. I think it would be unacceptable for a society to outlaw extra-marital sexual activities. It would rightly be claimed that that is a matter for individual conscience. But if I were to claim that I have a right to engage in extra-marital sexual relationships, irrespective of the wishes and feelings of those who would be affected, I would be denying my conscience and duty to find reasonable ways of living with those around me. The very powerful ideas of self-expression that we can find in both the wider culture and the world of psychotherapy and counselling need careful examination.

I want to take my argument further and look at what we are doing if, as psychotherapists or counsellors or health professionals of any sort, we get caught in this denial of negative experience.

The cultural pressures, often normal pressures which have to do with wanting to help people, to ease suffering, to be effective, to be good at our jobs, make us vulnerable to the denial of the necessity and inevitability of certain forms of human suffering. We set out to cure and we construct blueprints of what people *ought* to be feeling, *ought* to be like, and we can too easily set about trying to manipulate or even force people into these blueprints. I will be arguing all the way through this book that we need to be aware of the complexity of situations and the narrowness of the various lines that we tread, and that it is too easy to get carried away in directions that often run counter to the values we believe in.

Patients, of course, can tell us this very clearly if we choose to listen. As a way of illustrating this, I want to take a vignette from my own practice: a therapy group that at the time consisted of seven members. The background to the particular incident was that some months previously I had returned to supervision, and I was now discussing this group regularly in my supervision. The group was not aware of this in any conscious way, but the inform-ation had clearly been conveyed unconsciously. This was made known to me through the metaphor of feelings about their parents, and the things that their parents expected of them. To feel bad, unhappy, depressed seemed to be taken by parents as a criticism or attack, parents assuming that it was their fault. This extended through feelings to actions and ways of living which seemed to hurt parents. When discussing why this should be the case, it was thought that an important part of it was that their behaviour was taken to reflect on their parents in the eyes of other family, neighbours, etc. 'If I am depressed, then my parents will feel that aunts and uncles will regard them as failures.'

The group was, of course, quite right; having joined a supervision group, I very much wanted my patient group to 'work', to do well, to be happy, to be cured, and I certainly felt that their failure to do this would reflect on my ability in the eyes of the aunts and uncles in the supervision group. To put it simply, I did not want to appear to be a bad therapist.

This theme had been around for several weeks. In the particular session I wish to discuss here, the group had been working away at a number of issues; the 'parent' theme was around but not especially prominent. I had said very little for the first hour of the session, although I had been aware that one woman, A, had been silent, often looking worried and distressed.

I had commented that I was very aware of her silence and I wondered what might be happening. She responded that she was thinking hard about what people were saying, and it was clear that she did not want to add anything more.

About ten minutes after this, another woman, B, produced a very powerful fantasy. After the previous week's session, when two of the men in the group had been talking about how they wanted to change, she had gone home and started to see everybody in the group as potential 'gingerbread men' (her words), put out on a tray and waiting to be cut into their proper, similar shapes (which would then, presumably, be hardened in the oven), This had been such a powerful and frightening fantasy for her that she had not been able to go to her kitchen drawer all day.

In the discussion that followed, I was presented with three different ways in which I was experienced as the cook, cutting them out into required shapes. The first came from a man who had joined the group, amongst other reasons, to learn to assert himself more. He had noticed in his first months that although I sometimes asked questions of other people, I did not ask him anything. He thought this was deliberate, a way of forcing him to join in on his own account. He was right that there was certainly a deliberate sense about it on my part, but as I thought about it afterwards, this seemed fair enough. This was for two reasons: firstly, it left him to do something he wanted to do – to learn how to join in on his own account; and secondly – and importantly – I had left the choice to him. He did not have to join in, and indeed many people don't, remaining comparatively silent for many months. In this case, I felt, I was not wielding the cutter to force him into a shape I desired; he had chosen the shape and he had the choice of using the cutter himself.

The second example came when I was roundly criticised for trying to draw A into active participation in the group. It was rightly pointed out that if A wanted to remain silent than she had every right to do so. To her credit, it seems to me, she continued to exercise that right. But here I had been acting the fussy, anxious parent that wanted the child to 'be all right' or 'do well', and for at least a minute or two had forced her participation, which had in fact been one which had reassured me that she was OK, just thinking hard. Here it was my concern about her possible distress which had led me into an intervention which had, possibly, led her to deny it, and I have to ask myself whether it was my desire to deny her suffering that had led me into the intervention. Here, I was certainly wielding the cutter.

The third example is very complex and has to do with B herself and her desire to protect her symptoms. These were briefly a recurrent experience of paralysis followed by self-inflicted injury which brought her relief and enabled her to carry on. Psychoanalytic theory can offer a number of possible explanations of why she should want to protect the symptom. My own preference would be that under the threat of immense anxiety which could lead to psychosis, a split-off part of the ego produced the symptoms as a way of maintaining contact with reality and enabling her to continue with her life. Certainly, the self-injury was experienced as a relief and sort of freeing: 'It just makes me feel better.'

B was clearly ambivalent in her attitude towards her difficulty: the fear was, I think, that if she was stopped from injuring herself she would not be able to fend off the anxiety; this was experienced consciously as the fear that she would become somebody she did not like – somebody less sensitive, harder, even cruel and proud. This was the shape she feared I would compel her to be. She felt her presence in the group was the result less of her desire to change and more because other people – her family, her doctor, her psychiatrist – could not tolerate her symptoms, endorsing Rickman's comment that madness is being unable to find anybody who can stand you.

I am interested in the moral dilemma that this presents me as a therapist. B might be quite right, although perhaps unconsciously so, that her behaviour stands between her and a complete loss of touch with reality, and that there is no other alternative. There is no way I can say whether she is right or wrong about that and it would be arrogant and presumptious of me even to attempt to decide. I could, of course, being horrified by her self-injury and even more by the real childhood suffering that lay behind it, attempt to 'do something about it'. Clearly this was the desire of her doctor and her family. If I decided this, I would be wielding the cutter, quite possibly clumsily and with disastrous results. It seems to me that as therapists, or as helpers or healers of any sort, we need to respect symptoms, in fact respect madness, and what might be the impossibility of 'cure', even of significant improvement. If there is a therapeutic aim involved in this it would be, at least to begin with, and perhaps for ever, to respect her symptom, where others refused to allow it; to respect her suffering, as a choice which might be, in context, her best choice. Yet if we deny disappointment, if I try to *make* her better, then I am failing in my work.

The denial of disappointment is then, double-sided; I might deny it first because I cannot stand the suffering of others, most probably because if I accepted the suffering of others, then I would have to accept my own suffering; and secondly because I cannot tolerate the thought of my own 'failure', my inability to achieve what I set out to do, which is to alleviate suffering. If I cannot accept any of this, then I engage in the business of cutting out gingerbread men, trying to form people into a shape which would make me, the family, the GP and the rest of society happy.

In the course of this book, I will be looking at the social developments, some taking place over centuries, others much more recent, that have contributed towards a society in which disappointment and the necessity of disapointment are denied, and the way such a society implicates psychotherapy in its workings, to create the sort of person – the gingerbread persons – that it seems to need. I will also be looking at areas where the avoidance of disappointment seems to me most socially dangerous: the area of human relationships, friendship, marriage, sexual relationships; the area that sociologists refer to as 'gender identity', our sense of ourselves as men and women. One of the more dramatic symptoms of the change since Freud was writing is in the way in which, in much psychotherapy and counselling literature, loss and death are turned into 'positive' things, denying the dimension of disappointment that they involve. Yet even in situations where changes might be expected to be entirely positive, both by individuals and by the culture, disappointment is implicated. Having a baby, getting married, getting promotion at work often bring unexpected feelings of loss and depression – which are in many cases quite appropriate, since they involve the loss of situations and relationships that will never return. If apparently 'positive' movements bring the experience of loss, then there are many more experiences which are clearly negative – divorce, redundancy, for example – yet which in the wider culture can be portrayed as potentially positive experiences. Perhaps the most striking example is contemporary ways of thinking about death and mourning.

Chapter 2

The organisation of mourning

When the British feminist journalist Jill Tweedie contracted motor neurone disease, a particularly vicious, unrelenting and incurable paralysing illness likely to kill her within the next three years, the *Guardian* (14 September 1993) published the news in the form of an article/interview by her friend Polly Toynbee. Tweedie was indeed, in the words of the headline, 'raging against the dying of the light', rejecting all the platitudes and false hopes that are sometimes offered in such situations. Four days later (18 September) a handful of letters appeared in the same paper, several of which questioned her reaction – some clearly drawing on current therapeutic ideas about death and dying. I think it is useful to ask what is going on in a world in which we can question a person's reaction to the prospect of her or his own, imminent death.

Many of the themes that will recur through this book stand out most dramatically in relation to changing conceptions of death, grief and mourning. Changes in the way we live in the modern world produce a set of difficulties to which we respond by denying the difficult, painful adjustments that we have to make, attempting to transform painful experience of loss into a creative experience, as if the loss could be shrugged off. The psychoanalytic theory of mourning has lost its original depth and complexity and been drawn into the practice of 'bereavement counselling', which often has a very clear idea of what the mourner should do and be. Mourning itself has been increasingly pathologised – regarded as an illness, and, of course, if there is an illness, we need a body of professionals to treat that illness, and those professionals have to establish that they are effective. Reactions such as rage and inconsolable grief are not normally associated with effective professional practice.

Psychoanalysis has always been concerned with an understanding of the process of grief and mourning, increasingly as a way of understanding reactions to other losses we experience in the course of a lifetime. It is arguable now that mourning has become a central concern of our culture because of the increasingly rapid speed of social change. This has undermined the traditional, socially sanctioned forms of mourning, and these are being replaced by a set of abstract guides to the process. If we consider the human relationships that we form and move on from in the course of a lifetime, the increasing attention to mourning becomes intelligible. Geographical and social mobility might vary from class to class, but both the notion of career and the increased flexibility of the labour market make it likely that fewer and fewer people will stay in one place with a stable network of family, friends and acquaintances for a large part of their lives. For many people, life will consist of regular movement, relinquishing old relationships and forming new ones; serial monogamy replaces the 'till death do us part' of marriage, and I wonder if the increase in the numbers of couples who choose not to get married illustrates a conscious or unconscious reluctance to commit oneself to a prospect of permanence when one's knowledge and/or intuition of the world indicates that permanence will not be possible.

It is a commonplace to say that death is hidden away, that it has become the 'last great taboo', replacing the taboo on sex of a century ago. Certainly a great deal has happened to support such an idea. The growing effectiveness of medicine has lengthened life expectancy and led to a substantial decrease in infant and child mortality and in the number of women who die in childbirth. All this means that death – the death of somebody close, a parent, brother or sister, spouse – is no longer quite the everyday event that perhaps it once was; generally the first death that is now experienced is that of a grandparent. And death takes place in special places, hospitals and hospices, away from home. The experiences of being with somebody who is dying, on a day-to-day basis, of being present at or near a death, of keeping the body in the home – these are more rare. Along with this the socially sanctioned, traditional habits of mourning have faded. Wearing black at a funeral is no longer required, let alone the wearing of black for a shorter or longer period after the death of a loved one. It seems difficult now to talk about death; frequently it is still the case that people with terminal illnesses are not told, and it is a common experience for the recently bereaved to find themselves avoided in the street, or engaged in awkward and embarrassed conversations with people desperately trying to avoid the topic of their bereavement. There is little 'social space' for grieving – often it seems the funeral is supposed to mark the end of the process.

Those who write about death and mourning often present their concerns as running counter to this dominant trend. There is, I think, a degree of truth in this. Modernism placed its faith in the development of science, and it was medical science that hived off death from our everyday life, putting it in hospitals and dealing only with its physical aspects. Perhaps the hope was that somehow science could eventually abolish death. The concern with death and mourning is often presented as involving a critique of science and medicine, and a return to a variety of more humane and traditional ways of thinking about people.

There is, however, another way of looking at it. It can be argued that death is not such a taboo subject as it is claimed; in fact, over recent decades more and more has been written about death. Each year when I lecture my second- and third-year students on these issues, a sizeable number seize the opportunity to write long and often passionate essays on the topic, and I find that whenever the end of an experiential group of trainees approaches, members are willing to use death as a metaphor for ending; sometimes, I suspect, *too* willing, as if the idea is almost comfortable. I wonder if what is going on in all this is similar to what Foucault (1984) argues went on in the latter part of the nineteenth century in relation to sex. Far from being a period when sex was a taboo subject, it was one when more was written about sex than during any other period in history. It was written by a variety of 'experts' – medical, psychological and others. Sexuality was brought into the orbit of the developing professions; it was organised, categorised, different aspects were assigned to different disciplines. It was a period when sexuality was brought into social control as exercised through the professions – it became organised and integrated into the systemic structure of society itself.

If this is what is happening to death and mourning, we are not witnessing a dramatic transformation in attitudes, but the continuation of a process to new levels. The theme of fragmentation is central: death, dying, and mourning cease to be integrated into everyday life; death first becomes moved into a segregated area, as a sub-section of medical institutions, and then into its own specialised institutions – hospices. Mourning 'floats' in a disorganised way for much of this century, established social rules for mourning losing their effectiveness, followed by the slow emergence of professional 'expert systems' to guide comparatively isolated individuals. In fact the harbingers were there in the 1960s. Bowlby's papers (1960, 1961) on mourning were published then and many later psychoanalytic writers on mourning draw from his theories; Gorer's book *Death, Grief and Mourning in Contemporary Britain* was published in 1965 and Hinton's *Dying* in 1967; the first edition of Colin Murray Parkes's in many ways admirable *Bereavement* was published in 1972.

The development of theories of mourning shows distinct shifts in emphasis. Our conception of the mourning process is being channelled in a direction that tends to underemphasise the straightforward strength of the pain that is involved, and it glosses over the depth of guilt, and our inherent ambivalence. What I mean is summed up by the reception of Parkes's book in *Social Work Today*, quoted on the back cover: 'he has helped us all to accept our share in the creative use of suffering'. I suppose that if we look for the silver lining we will not see the thunderclouds. The quotation cuts across the complexity of grief and mourning. Creation *can* come out of suffering, but it is also a loss, in the case of a death an absolute and irreparable loss in the real world. And in the development of the literature we can find a more or less subtle change in the way grief and mourning are thought of – from a part of normal life to an illness.

Something of what I am trying to say can be seen in the result of death itself becoming the object of an 'expert system'. Anna Witham (1985), following the American Robert Kastenbaum (1982), has pointed to recent ideas of a 'good death' – a dying that is comparatively peaceful, in which friends and relatives are involved, goodbyes are said, 'business' is finished (the marketplace metaphor perhaps being instructive), conflicts resolved, and the dying person is prepared and ready to go. She argues that these ideas are one side of a splitting process in which the other side – the real horror, pain and mess of death – is denied. Students who are taught these ideas can have real difficulties when they come up against an actual death.

I have no doubt that some deaths might approximate a 'good

death', but I cannot imagine a death which is not also approached with fear, perhaps terror at what is totally unimaginable. We have no symbols for death apart from those appropriate to life, and therefore entirely inappropriate. Nor can I imagine a life which, if honestly experienced, does not involve regrets, unfinished business, unresolved conflicts, loose ends, hatred and bitterness. It seems to me that all these feelings will be involved to varying degrees and in highly personal combinations. Death is likely to be extremely painful, extremely messy and full of conflict. Dignity is lost, while life remains. And I am only talking about deaths which are expected. The last dying person I saw had choked on her supper, and when I visited her in hospital, the functions of the primitive brain stem were the only ones working.

For those left behind, there will always be unresolved conflicts, unfinished business, and a reminder of his or her own mortality. There is also a conception of a good mourner. Such a person will talk about their loss and work through a series of emotions set out in textbooks. On one level this is quite reasonable. It is good to talk about these things, it is wrong to avoid the bereaved as if they were plague-bearers. But it seems to me that we often expect the bereaved to go through a series of emotions with which we – as carers in the helping profession – are comfortable. The fearful avoidance of death is perhaps as authentic a human reaction as it is possible to find. The fear with which we avoid death reminds us how awful death is – the final, unrepenting and incurable disappointment that we want to avoid.

THEORIES OF MOURNING

The earlier psychoanalytic theories of mourning, of Freud (1984b), Karl Abraham (1927) and Melanie Klein (1986a) all contain a distinction between normal and abnormal mourning and emphasise the importance of the structure of the inner world, of what goes in the psyche. In Freud's case, I am sometimes struck by a sense of gentle but firm paternalism – a voice which says, perhaps later rather than sooner, 'It's time to get on with life.' For Freud, mourning involves a withdrawal from the outside world, and a concentration on the one who has been lost; this is accompanied by painful feelings of dejection and an inability to find a new love object. We work through mourning, with great expense of energy, by repeated reality testing and finding that the loved one really *has* gone. We withdraw – decathect – our feelings from the lost one until we are ready to find a new love object. As with many of Freud's theories when he first formulated them, the basic model is a hydraulic, energy-flow system: energy is invested in the loved one, who dies or vanishes; the energy is then withdrawn into the mourner where it stays for a shorter or longer period, until the loss is accepted, when it is reinvested in a new love object.

Freud argues that because we are familiar with this experience we know that it will pass and we regard it as normal. The length of time it takes depends upon our willingness or ability to acknowledge that the loved one has really gone. However, he also identified an abnormal or pathological mourning that he called melancholia, which involves damning self-criticism and a fear of punishment and has its roots in the melancholic's identification with the lost loved one; the criticisms that the melancholic directs towards himself or herself are really those directed towards the lost loved one. Melancholia, then, is a state in which we have taken the lost loved one inside and keep him or her there, attacking ourselves rather than the person who is lost. Here there is a clear distinction between normal and pathological mourning, and the recognition of the former as part of life, and this is what has changed since Freud. With that change there has been an increasing interest in the aetiology of mourning.

Karl Abraham made an important link between normal and pathological mourning when he argued that the process of internalisation of the lost one goes on anyway, the difference being that the normal mourner is able to internalise the lost love object as a 'good' internal object, and restore the loved one *inside* himself or herself in a loving way. The melancholic is unable to do this because the degree of hostility to the lost loved one was so great. This way of approaching it draws attention to what goes on in the internal world, and it was this area that Klein explored in much greater detail than either of her two forebears.

For Klein, the loss of a loved one threatened the whole of the internal world; most basically it threatened the good internal objects that we had been able to make of our parents, a process that marks the negotiation of the infantile depressive position. I will return to this aspect of her argument later. For the moment I am going to take her example of bereavement (a Mrs A after the sudden death of her son) and examine in particular her first reactions.

Mrs A began by sorting out letters, keeping her son's and throwing others away – disposing of the indifferent and hostile, the bad feelings. This was seen as an attempt at restoration of the son, to keep him safe inside her, an obsessional mechanism used as a defence against the depressive position. The obsessive action wards off the bad feelings. For the first week there was an (incomplete) withdrawal, a numbness and an absence of dreaming – Mrs A usually dreamt every night. The first dream brought associations with an occasion when she had recognised that her brother was not as wonderful as she had thought, an event which was experienced as an 'irreparable misfortune'; but the event was also associated with guilt, as if it were the result of her own harmful wishes against her brother. Behind these harmful wishes, and 'very deeply repressed', was a desire to punish her mother through causing her to lose her son; she was jealous of her mother for possessing such a son. This led to the death wish against her brother; one of the deeper dream wishes was 'My mother's son has died and not my own.'

This was followed by sympathy for her mother and sorrow for herself; her brother had, in fact, died, and beside her earlier sorrow at this event she had, unconsciously, experienced a sense of triumph. Klein argues that some degree of Mrs A's ambivalence to her brother, 'though modified by her strong motherly feelings', had been transferred on to her son, and entered into the present grief.

The first defences, then, were the 'manic' defences against grief: denial and triumph. In her internal world, the grief was transferred to her mother, with the denial that they were one and the same person. Klein goes on to describe the process of movement into sorrow, and reconnection with the world, then the retreat into manic triumphalism and denial. The whole process is seen as involving the re-establishment of the good internal objects with which the mourner can identify, through a movement between the manic defences and the depressive position.

I have set out the example at some length because it shows the complexity of the internal, *psychological* processes of mourning, involving feelings that might not be readily associated with it: jealousy, triumphalism, a desire to punish. It shows the way in which a long personal history is brought into play, reactivated and relived. In this framework, pathological mourning is a sign of a deeper-rooted pathology dating back to the earliest stages of life.

The origin of the deeper-rooted pathology is not 'known in advance': it may stem from infantile or childhood trauma or it might be in some sense constitutional. As Isca Salzberger-Wittenberg (1988) puts it, the good parenting must be there and so must the ability to use it. In any case, these early theories, although the attempt to define pathological mourning is there, do not make clear distinctions between normal and pathological, and seem instead to point to the depth and complexity of our reactions and the way in which they reactivate conflicts from earlier stages of our history.

The most important stimulus to later developments in the theory of mourning has been the work of John Bowlby (1960, 1961) on early separation, most clearly developed in the work of Colin Murray Parkes. Earlier, I called his *Bereavement* (1987) an admirable book, and so it is, full of gentle and clear common sense. But it also marks a shift from the earlier theories that both extends and limits our understanding of what is going on. It focuses attention on the 'environmental failure' side of the equation and takes attention away from the 'constitutional' side and the central importance of symbolisation.

Parkes wants to claim that grief itself can be regarded as a mental illness, that all mourning is pathological. He puts forward a number of arguments for his position – or rather he deals with a number of arguments against it. The first is the 'labelling' argument: the 'mental illness' label stigmatises those to whom it is attached. Parkes's argument is that by declining to regard the bereaved as mentally ill for this reason, we are reinforcing the stigmatising connotations of the term. This is fair enough if one accepts the mental illness label in the first place as usefully applied to a range of people with certain symptoms. Much more depends on his second argument.

Grief is normal, it is often claimed, and therefore cannot be regarded as an illness; but so, argues Parkes, is measles, yet we would not hesitate to classify measles as an illness. Just as with physical illnesses, people may or may not seek help for grief from a doctor; grief, like physical illnesses, brings discomfort and disturbance of function:

On the whole, grief resembles a physical injury more closely than any other type of illness. The loss may be spoken of as a 'blow'. As in the case of physical injury, the 'wound' gradually heals; at least it usually does. But occasionally complications set in, healing is delayed, or a further injury reopens a healing wound. In such cases, abnormal forms arise, which may even be complicated by the onset of other types of illness. Sometimes it seems that the outcome may be fatal . . . I know of only one functional psychiatric disorder whose cause is known, whose features are distinctive, and whose course is usually predictable, and that is grief, the reaction to loss. Yet this condition has been so neglected by psychiatrists that until recently it was not even mentioned in the indexes of most of the best-known general textbooks of psychiatry.

(Parkes 1987: 25–6)

In trying to define grief in terms of presenting symptoms, Parkes settles for the pining or yearning that he immediately relates to separation anxiety and Bowlby's theory of attachment needs. One of the difficulties is that grief goes through stages, and at any one stage, a person may present with different symptoms. Parkes identifies three stages – initially a numbness, and then a pining, and then disorganisation and despair, recovery only beginning after this last experience.

Now what is going on here? On the face of it, Parkes's argument is plausible and humane. However, it is more than that. One way of looking at it in Foucault's terms is as an attempt at systematic classification by means of which Parkes brings grief within the orbit of professional medicine by classifying it as an illness. In other words it is an extension of the scope of the power of a particular profession. Part of the ambiguity of what I am trying to argue is apparent in that this is clearly not Parkes's motivation: that is the quite genuine concern of easing suffering, and indeed the work he has engaged in, particularly in relation to the development of hospices, *has*, without any shadow of a doubt, eased suffering. I am trying to portray a situation which has both a 'dark' and a 'light' side, and these can only be brought together if the whole is looked at from two very different angles. The interesting question, for me, is that grief has always been there, as have its similarities to physical injury, so why at this particular stage of history are these similarities pointed out; why do they become important in *this* way, *now*?

Here the answer, I suspect, lies less in the development of knowledge than in the development of professional boundaries and the need for professions to carve out areas of expertise for themselves. As medicine extends its effectiveness over already recognised pathologies, it moves on to 'pathologising' new areas that were not generally recognised as problematic. Another interesting question is where we draw the line – do all losses involve mental illness? Parkes is aware of this problem, but does not answer the question directly:

> Losses are, of course, common in all our lives. And insofar as grief is the reaction to loss, grief must be common too. But the term grief is not normally used for the reaction to the loss of an old umbrella. It is more usually reserved for the loss of a person, and a loved person at that. It is this type of grief that is the subject of this book, and this type of loss is not a common event in the lives of most of us.
>
> (Parkes 1987: 27)

Grief from the death of a loved one is, I suspect, more easily embraced by medicine because of its association with death, which is already a medical issue – in common-sense terms we expect grief at the loss of a husband or wife, say, to be greater than that at the loss of an old umbrella, but this in itself does not make grief a medical issue – no powerful emotion by itself is a clear medical problem. Powerful feelings, the powerful feelings of grief, can come from other losses – divorce or separation, loss of a job, for example, and most of what Parkes says about grief at the death of a loved one applies equally, including visits to the doctor to request help. But even now it would, I think, be difficult to claim that what we feel in a divorce is a mental illness. In fact Parkes's problem has been solved by the growth of psychotherapy as a profession in competition with medicine – therapy can get rid of all the problems of the label 'mental illness' simply by regarding all forms of grief as a special distress that can require specialist attention.

Certain things happen in Parkes's account to the concept of mourning itself. First, it is seen as less of an internal psychological process and the emphasis is more on emotions – what is felt at the expense of what might be going on in the psyche in terms of conflicts and reorganisations of the inner world. This is emphasised by framing the approach in terms of Bowlby's attachment theory, which can in certain contexts acquire a behaviourist connotation. The external behaviour becomes important rather than an understanding of pre- and unconscious psychological processes. The concept of grief, and of the grieving individual, becomes more shallow – not *wrong*, note, but more partial, less complete in this way, and in another way too. Whereas Klein saw pathological mourning in terms of a deep-rooted personality difficulty, if all grief is an illness, the deeper roots are lost sight of. This is not quite true: clearly one of the causes of difficulty in grieving is, from this point of view, early traumatising separations, but the relation tends to be seen in terms of cause and effect rather than an internal processing of experience.

THE DILEMMA OF PROFESSIONAL INTERVENTION

In contemporary work on grief and mourning, two tendencies sit uneasily side by side. On the one side there is an implicit or even explicit recognition of the implacability of death, the normality of grief and the never-endingness of mourning. On the other hand there is the desire of the helping professional to deal with unhappiness (which itself sometimes seems to be regarded as pathological), to justify their intervention and to produce their own type of gingerbread people. The disappointment of death can't quite be avoided, but as good helpers we must try to cover it up as far as possible.

A set of three papers in a recent issue of *Group Analysis* contains accounts of work by a group of therapists from a hospital in Edmonton, Canada, who have developed a programme of short-term group psychotherapy for loss (Lakoff and Azim 1991; Piper and McCallum 1991; McCallum *et al.* 1991), The first paper makes many of the points about modern society's attitudes to death that I have already touched upon, emphasising the absence of an adequate social recognition of the place for and nature of mourning, and relating that to the social denial of death. It also, interestingly, points to the complications of understanding what might be meant by successful or unsuccessful, normal or pathological mourning. Quoting a study by Osterweis *et al.* (1987), they point out that length of time is no indicator of pathological mourning, but rather the quality and quantity of reactions over time are so; and that a change that seems to indicate a 'healthy' recovery in one person may be the opposite for another: for one person, throwing himself or herself into work may be an avoiding strategy, for another it might indicate a new flow of creativity.

The second paper (Piper and McCallum 1991) is a survey of studies of group interventions in the process of mourning, beginning by lamenting the lack of involvement of traditional mental health professionals in the provision of group services for the bereaved. In a classificatory scheme, the authors suggest two independent dimensions, initial and transitional, and two types, normal and pathological; typically help is sought in the transitional stage, and if the mourning process is normal, it is a matter of support and practical intervention. Pathological mourning may occur at either stage, and may take the form of too little or too much grief, either in terms of intensity or in terms of duration. Some qualifications are then added:

> Utilising the 'type of mourning' dimension is complicated by the ambiguous and often arbitrary distinction between normal and pathological mourning ... the expected duration of normal mourning varies considerably among different cultural groups. The norm can be between six months and two years, while some contend that a loss is never completely resolved. In addition, individual differences such as personality type, age and religion may influence the progression through each task of mourning. This complication may be partially resolved by considering the debilitating impact of the loss in terms of symptomatology and impaired functioning when determining the type of mourning process occurring.
>
> (Piper and McCallum 1991: 365)

The third paper is an account of a study of the effectiveness of twelve-week groups for those caught in pathological mourning according to a standard diagnosis: 'Most patients received a DSM–111 Axis 1 diagnosis (usually affective, adjustment or anxiety disorder), and about one quarter received an Axis 11 diagnosis (usually dependent personality)' (McCallum et al. 1991: 377), and the groups were tightly controlled:

> Two experienced therapists each led four of the eight groups. They followed a technical manual and attended a weekly seminar where conceptual and technical issues were discussed and audiotapes of sessions were played. The theoretical orientation of the twelve-week, time-limited groups was psychoanalytic, and this was checked by conducting a process analysis of seven sessions from each group using the

Psychodynamic Work and Object Rating System (McCallum *et al.*, 1991) which confirmed that the therapists were active, interpretive and group-focused, as intended.

(Ibid.)

In the accounts of group sessions, it is clear that the therapists do not allow the group to engage in lengthy defensive manoeuvres. The interpretations point to anger with the group process and the therapist for bringing up painful feelings, difficulty in trusting when previous experiences of trusting have been met by disappointment and loss, fears of the therapist's death, difficulties in being angry with somebody who might die, and feelings of responsibility for the other's death. The central aim seems to be to enable members to express negative feelings which are re-experienced in the transference onto the therapist.

In these papers, we seem to have reached the point where the 'rightness' of professional involvement in the mourning process is taken for granted – it no longer needs to be justified by claiming the grief is a mental illness – and what is remarkable is the absence of professional participation. A standard diagnostic tool is used to distinguish pathological grief; there are manuals by which to guide a closely regulated therapeutic process, and it is clear from the account that whilst the therapist is listening closely to the group, he or she knows in advance what sort of interpretation he or she will make: it is mapped out according to a view of the appropriate emotions and their expression rather than on a conception of internal psychic structures.

On the other hand there are all sorts of reservations which imply that perhaps this is not the best way of looking at it. Pathological mourning seems to be a quantitative distinction with no clear borderline complete resolution is an illusion (at least so some people say), and symptoms can have individual and contradictory meanings. The suggestion that the problem in defining pathological mourning may be partly resolved by looking at symptomatology does not take into account the possible different and individual meanings of symptoms, and 'impaired functioning' seems equally problematic.

Generally these arguments can be seen as a continuation and hardening of the processes noted in Parkes's work. There are 'hard' criteria for identifying pathological mourning and there seems to be a selection of approved emotions: anger is OK, but hatred is not; guilt is OK, but a feeling of triumph receives no mention. There is, if you like, a taming of grief. The therapy is undertaken with a very clear idea of what grieving involves and what the patient *should* be doing. It is in ways such as this that psychoanalytic therapy becomes absorbed into therapy as an 'abstract system', which sets out to form the sort of person who, supposedly, can deal with the recurrent and often powerful losses of living in late modernity. The standards for identifying pathological mourning are external, not a perception of the individual mourner, and to move towards 'functional impairment' as a criterion gives everything over to the rapidly changing society that creates the intensified problem of grief in the first place – where there is no socially recognised period of 'functional impairment', a period of retreat from normal social and work activities, where there are no lasting public signs of mourning, and where, compared say with customs in other societies, the expression of powerful emotion is inhibited.

This way lies the path to the control and limitation of mourning – something summed up in a fairly recent book as the aims of a therapeutic assessment of bereavement:

1 To facilitate and consolidate a satisfactorily resolving bereavement.
2 To provide a framework for specific preventive intervention with bereaved who are at high risk of malresolution.
3 To provide a framework for specific intervention with pathological bereavements so that these may possibly be diverted to a more adaptive course.

(Raphael 1984: 347)

The technological job is to get the machine back on the road.

THE DISAPPOINTING NORMALITY OF LOSS AND GRIEF

What if bereavement can never be resolved? What if pathological mourning is always in the eye of the beholder? I suspect that grief and mourning are best seen, in Kleinian terms, as a continual movement between the manic defences (and it is often possible to *believe* that we have overcome this grief through discovering new levels of creativity) and the depressive position (where, for a while, we might believe that we are irretrievably caught up in the grief); we might swing at variable rates, but if we are going to maintain a conception of the pathological, perhaps it should be the absence of a swing – the existence of a limited emotional range, rather than the absence of certain specified emotions – that is the important criterion. This escapes pathologising all grief and employs a conception of the inner world, as opposed to identifying simply the existence or absence of feelings. The important question from this point of view, perhaps, is whether the absence of movement (or the degree of movement) is such that the bereaved might want to explore the possibility of deep-rooted change.

For Klein and other psychoanalysts loss is at the centre of the infant's development, at the centre of symbol formation and the ability to speak. To be able to recognise my mother and call her 'mother' I have at some level to have recognised that she is not part of me, I have to have recognised the loss. But that is not to have resolved it; I can move between treating the symbol itself as if it were the real person (hence the power that the term 'motherfucker' has or had), or experiencing the internal object 'mother' to which the symbol is attached as if it were a separate part of me (as in Klein's example) ; I can try to be as much like or as much unlike my mother as possible; I can remain close to her or set up a massive barrier between us; and I can go on doing all these things until well after she is dead, until my own death. At times the way I deal with her will be 'pathological', at times it will be 'mature', and again perhaps the danger point is the absence of movement. In the light of this, it is possible to question Klein's original distinction between normal and pathological. The original losses which contribute towards movement into the depressive position are obscure, prelinguistic losses – the losses that in fact push us forwards into language. Now one of the distinctions that Freud made between the normal and the pathological, the melancholic, was that for the latter the loss has been obscured, that it is difficult to know what has been lost. For somebody grieving, the loss is only too evident. One way of reading Freud's paper is not as a discussion of mourning in the modern sense, where it is isolated from the rest of life and becomes a specialism, but as a discussion of the personality as a whole. Klein's work is much nearer the modern specialised approach, but when she does talk about pathological mourning she too is saying something about the whole personality.

The first losses are much closer to what Freud discusses in terms of melancholia – obscure and distant losses. The French psychoanalyst, Julia Kristeva, writes: 'The speech of the depressed is to them like an alien skin; melancholy persons are foreigners in their maternal tongue. They have lost the meaning – the value – of their mother-tongue for want of losing the mother' (Kristeva 1989: 53), Some version of the experience of depression (not the depressive position) as Kristeva describes it seems to me not uncommon – the feeling that, mildly or dramatically, the words we use have lost their meaning, that they are *just* words: 'What's the point of talking?'. This is, if Kristeva is right, about loss, about the loss of something we cannot bear to lose and something that we cannot remember except perhaps as some vague and central space in our being.

Another and clearer way of putting all of this is in terms of an existential dilemma; Sartre (1957) described human consciousness as a 'nothingness', as always separated from its object; we have always already lost what we try to possess. It is, I believe, not just our very powerful fear of our own eventual death which gives us trouble, but the way in which the loss of a loved one reminds us not just of every other loss, but of the inevitability of losing, of having already lost whatever we might want before we get it. We can see the development of mourning and bereavement as specialisms within therapy as part and parcel of the development of late modernity, but a particularly powerful development, which has something to do with the readiness of experiential groups to employ death as a metaphor for their own ending, the readiness of students to write essays about death and mourning, reproducing the received wisdom of therapy. And indeed the orthodoxy of bereavement therapy is extremely powerful. I was first made aware of this during my own training. In an experiential group comprising the full cohort of trainees, conversation turned to a recently bereaved therapist who was continuing to work: there was an immediate and for a while unquestioned distress, puzzlement and then condemnation of this person. How was it possible to continue to work after the loss of a spouse? How could one continue to work well, especially as a therapist, in such a situation? Undoubtedly, this person would be so full of personal woes that no help could possibly be given to others in difficulty. We all knew that grief required time, a proper observance, crying, talking and the rest of it, and this could not happen if the person concerned carried on as before.

This was a very powerful reaction, broken only by the group

leader's comment that he would not wish to be one of our patients, having to face our moral condemnation. This was a powerful remark, at least for me – drawing me back to my own in- adequacies, making me aware yet again that I could not be the ideal that I might want to be. And, of course, it was a frightening comment – if grieving by the book did not deal with the problem of loss, then nothing could, and however hard we might try, in the end nothing can. The loss is always there. Sometimes this is frightening. I once listened to the story of a young teenage boy, whose father was in the final stages of a terminal illness. The boy was continuing with his life as normally as he could, declining offers to talk about the situation. While listening to the story I found that I was feeling what I could only describe as mad – the juxtaposition of tragedy and normality felt almost too much and the panic began to rise. It is, I suspect, the power of *this* feeling, and its unbearability, that lead us to think that we have somehow got bereavement taped.

In the face of something so powerful, it is in the end up to each of us to find our own metaphors and places for grief – to try to push somebody in the expression of emotions in a particular way, the expression of particular emotions, is simply unrealistic. But it can guard for a while against the full terror of disappointment.

In C.S. Lewis's *A Grief Observed*, written after the death of his much-loved wife, he writes:

> In so far as this record was a defence against total collapse, a safety-valve, it has done some good. The other end I had in view turns out to have been a misunderstanding. I thought I could describe a *state*; make a map of sorrow. Sorrow however turns out to be not a state but a process. It needs not a map but a history, and if I don't stop writing that history at some quite arbitrary point, there's no reason why I should ever stop. There is something new to be chronicled every day. Grief is like a long valley, a winding valley where any bend may reveal a totally new landscape. As I've already noted, not every bend does. Sometimes the surprise is the opposite one; you are presented with exactly the same sort of country you thought you had left behind miles ago. That is when you wonder whether the valley isn't a circular trench. But it isn't. There are partial recurrences but the sequence doesn't repeat.

(Lewis 1961: 50–1)

What makes this account as a whole special to me is that it belongs to C.S. Lewis; bereavement therapists often write as if they have a map of grief, not a history. Each *history* of grief will be different from all others, just as each biography is different from all others. Presented with a map, I look for my place and the right road; presented with a history, a *story*, I can look for what might be common and what might be different, I can take and adapt and reject; I can recognise and admire a personality different from my own. I like this quotation in particular because it contains the awareness that a history is never-ending, and the points at which we might begin and end are arbitrary. The way I will grieve is already there in my previous history, before the loss, and I hope I will be able to take up that previous history and develop it along *my* way, not Lewis's. I like it as well because he catches – albeit by reverting to a map analogy – the returns, the spiral experience of any live process; the same point is always subtly different each time we come back to it.

And of course Lewis's way of reacting to his grief, of producing a journal, is *his*; I do not want to appear like therapists I will discuss later, advocating keeping a journal as a way of dealing with grief. What I think is apparent, even from the short quotation above, is that the journal does not *deal* with grief; it records a grief and it prevents a total collapse. Others might prevent such a collapse by continuing to work, staying away from work, talking or keeping silent; writing their stories in their own heads or in an indifferent ear, or together with a fellow griever; by smashing things, by screaming, by getting drunk; by leaving their wife or husband for their lover; by wearing the dead person's clothes or burning them. I don't think I have come across anything so intensely personal as grieving, and it often seems to me that the only attitude to adopt towards it is one of respect.

Perhaps respect, rather than diagnosis, should also be offered to those who elect to pine away after the death of a loved one, and who describe themselves as crippled or their lives as ruined after the death of a child. Other people recover – comparatively – after such events, so clearly the individual psyche is important in determining what goes on, but perhaps we should ask whether we are dealing with a pathology or a different soul. Perhaps at some level such people have taken a decision that should be respected? I am reminded of Rickman's comment that 'Madness is not being able to find anyone who can stand you'; in terms of grief, this might be 'Pathological mourning is not be being able to find anyone who can bear the pain of death' – in other words it is in the eye of the beholder, and the beholders (even the professionals, or perhaps even especially the professionals) will often be running as fast as possible.

BEREAVEMENT AND THE MARKET

The development of a programmed treatment for bereavement is a product of modernity on two levels: through the process of fragmentation, an area of life is isolated and becomes the focus of a specialisation; and in a period of increasingly rapid change, such a programme becomes, paradoxically, a programme for life itself, emphasising the 'creative' possibilities of loss. This in turn is reinforced by two forms of competition. The first is the competition between professionals for 'territory' – the range of activities over which a particular profession holds sway: Parkes's attempt to extend the sway of psychiatry, the Canadian team's concern with the sway of health professionals. Much of the criticism of established professionals – doctors and medical models of mental illness – comes less from the laity than from rival new and nascent professions, the therapy professions in particular.

The second is the more or less direct effect of the market. One of the major political debates in Britain over the last decade has been to what extent the principles of the free market should be employed to govern the provision of health care. The influence of the market is there whatever the results of the debate; the way in which we think about the world is – in this world – inevitably coloured by the notion that we are selling a product which, in one sense or another, we have to justify in competitive terms: it works and it works better than the other alternatives on offer. In this context, I am not interested so much in the economics of the argument as in the personal 'front' that it seems to necessitate. Working in a market involves being a particular type of person, one who does not acknowledge what might be thought to be 'defects' in the product.

The danger here is that psychotherapy becomes an encounter not between a therapist and a patient in a joint search for meaning, but between two 'false selves'; the search for meaning, the individuality, the specificity of grief and mourning, its open-ended and often very peculiar nature fall from sight. If mourning is the discovery of the meaning of what has been lost, in all its ambiguity, ambivalence and complexity, then this discovery is prejudged and fenced in if we set out already knowing what should be happening. On the patient's side there is a self which is, or is potentially, inadequate to the conditions of late modernity, to the process of rapid change and concomitant loss that affects more and more among us. That original patient self might already be in some way a false self, but his or her inadequacy may be quite authentic and not at all false – but there is no room in such therapy for the authentically inadequate. In any case, the patient is not there to be understood, but to be socialised into a way of mourning about which the *cognoscenti* already know. On the therapist's side there is the false self which must offer a therapy which works, ideally in a measurable way, which must maintain a front in relation to colleagues who may differ from him or her, which must find ways of managing the demands of management and so on.

I will take an example of a bereavement from my own practice; a patient who was referred for therapy because he was suffering from depression, which, at the time of referral, coincided with the terminal illness of a much-loved parent. It took this patient some eighteen months even to hint at going beyond a powerful internal act of rage and denial, a period when the rage was occasionally and violently directed outwards, but largely turned inwards in self-destructive guilt. The reactions to the bereavement had been caught up and taken into a pre-existing and profound depression. What was clear from the beginning was that the strength of his reactions were barely containable and were, to the patient, a mystery. They were a mystery the very strength of which prevented their own understanding – any attempt even at an informative interpretation would be rejected angrily, for it cut across whatever emotion was in control at that moment and was therefore experienced as an attack, at the very least in the form of a refusal of the love which was so urgently needed. Anyone who tried to help in a positive way was immediately attacked.

Now this patient was clearly not a 'good' client for bereavement counselling in a hospice and would anyway be likely to reject help. He was immediately aware of a false 'helping' self, much more aware than the helpers were of presenting such selves, and he experienced the falsity as hypocrisy. This patient could not be encouraged, or directed through whatever I might regard as a normal mourning process; if I had been in a situation where my work was being judged by comparatively short-term results, I would have been anxious to push in one direction or another, and this would have been disastrous as far as providing any help was concerned. And if I had seen myself as doing good, and *in that sense* believed in what I was doing, the determined and potentially violent rejection of help would have left me angry about lack of gratitude. All that it was possible to do was to listen and try to tolerate my fear and anxiety and lack of adequacy, and interestingly, as I became more able to do this, so the patient became more able to tolerate such feelings and begin a process of understanding. But he could only begin it: after three years of hard work, he dropped out of therapy. I suspect this sort of disappointment is found much more frequently in reality than it is in the literature.

There is something interesting and difficult here about believing in what I am doing, for of course to sit there with this particular patient and learn to tolerate my own anxiety and fear I had to have some belief in what I was doing. But it had to be a provisional belief: if I hold on to this long enough, then something might happen. It was not a belief I could sell, nor was it an activity upon which I could place any time limits, and I am not sure how the beginnings of an understanding of suffering, which is itself still a suffering, could be measured in an outcome study.

CONCLUSION

I chose bereavement as the topic here because in a number of ways it is at the centre of what I am talking about in the book as a whole. It is at the centre of the process of rapid change in late modernity as the more traditional and socially sanctioned forms of mourning fade, and are replaced by a therapeutic conception which sees the process in terms of resolution and emotion, and aims to socialise individuals into a particular way of coping with loss. Loss, bereavement, is also at the centre of the personality, from the moment of the original loss, and, I will argue, raises all sorts of difficult questions about the inherently divided, unsatisfied and necessarily *disappointed* nature of the self. The demands placed on the individual through working with maps of bereavement become like the gestures of the anxious mother, drawing forth a compliance from her child, a false self. Just as the other forms of therapy draw forth the possibility of a false self – a self which on the surface is able to feel real and whole and not fragmented, can maintain that phantasy, can cope with loss and turn it into positive growth, a self which can hide and deny the destructive processes inherent in the dynamics of late modernity and therefore reinforce those very processes – so psychoanalytic theory can lend itself to all this or stand back from it. I will turn now to the contradictory themes of psychoanalysis, before going into a more detailed analysis of the type of society which encourages such phantasies.

Chapter 3

Psychoanalysis as the theory of disappointment

Popular reactions to Freud during the first half of this century often focused on what he had to say about sexuality and he was often assumed to be advocating uninhibited sexual expression. This was welcomed by radicals and condemned by conservatives. Teaching psychoanalytic ideas to undergraduates now, I find Freud most frequently condemned as a conservative: he is not sympathetic to homosexuality; he does not understand, and disapproves of, female sexuality; he overemphasises the body and the way it limits us.

I'm less interested in which view is right than in the apparent change in climate: what for a previous generation was dangerously radical is for the current generation dangerously conservative. As ideas enter the culture they are transformed and given new meaning; as proponents of these ideas we can be pleased and flattered that they are being taken up, only to discover that they are being taken much further than we realised. I suspect that if I were writing at the beginning of this century, I would be happy with a radical interpretation of Freud. Now I am happier with a conservative interpretation: I think that what is valuable in Freud, and the psychoanalytic theorists who followed him, is the always implicit, sometimes explicit, message that we can never quite be what we want to be.

THE NECESSITY OF MISERY AND THE 'MULTIPLE PSYCHE'

One of the things that Freud had to say about sexuality was that some repression is necessary if we are to maintain any sort of civilised life. He points out that, for example, the erotic tie between two people separates them off from the rest of society. This will, I suspect, be recognised by anyone who has fallen in love. The implication is that to ensure social cohesion, to ensure that our society is a going concern, we need to limit the erotic ties that people can form; some part of our sexual desire must be sublimated, to form close and co-operative relationships with others. This always requires some sacrifice, a surrender of pleasure, and although there are compensations, they are brought at the price of some misery. Most of Freud's writing (see especially Freud 1985a) about society, especially as he got older and lived through the experience of the First World War and the rise of Hitler, emphasises that the greater the level of civilisation we achieve, the more we have to pay for it in misery. He thought that large-scale war was one of the ways in which we try to relieve the tension.

Some evidence for all this comes from psychoanalytic work with groups. The simple fact of being in a group, of sharing a situation with other people, raises often acute anxieties. This will be recognised by anyone who has gone to a party where the majority of others were strangers, or joined a course, or who remembers their first day at school. Every other person is a potential threat, and whatever is good about the situation has to be shared; in a group it is clearly impossible to get everything we want. A number of strategies are available for dealing with this, but generally it seems the larger the group the greater the anxiety and pressure.

Group analysts working with groups of thirty or so people (De Mare *et al.* 1991), sitting in a circle with no agenda, but simply the brief of talking about what they feel about being there, argue that if the anxiety can be borne, the next dominant reaction is hatred of those others in the group who, it seems, stop one getting all one wants. To move beyond hatred requires a lot of painful work, which includes accepting that one has to share and that some reasonable way of living with other people has to be found if the enterprise is to continue. One particularly interesting feature in such groups seems to be, as the development continues, a very strict and disapproving attitude towards out-of-group friendships between members, and especially to any sexual relationships that might occur.

So, Freud was not arguing for some sort of *laissez-faire* sexual freedom; at its extreme, that would be a threat to organised social life. More mundanely, it is likely to be a threat to individual

stability, either our own or that of others. Sexual infidelity *can* lead
to breakdown or murder. At the same time, Freud was arguing for
a greater liberalism in sexual expression, particularly amongst
children. Too much sexual expression can cause one form of pain
and chaos; too little can cause a different pain and chaos, that of
neurosis. And even if we find a balance, we do not necessarily
avoid pain and chaos – although it might seem as if we do when
we are laying down rules for other people to follow. If we think
about our own experience from the inside, the position is more
complex and difficult. Neither self-restraint nor self-expression is
achieved without cost.

One of the more sobering by-products of group psychotherapy, for the therapist as well as the patients, is the presence of
other people who, on the face of it, seem to have got where the
grass is greener, to have found the way of life that, from the
outside, appears preferable, but who are now looking back
longingly over the hedge. Those who have held relationships
together over a number of years, who perhaps have adult children, are often aware, and certainly become aware, that the
relationship has been a compromise in which they have gained
and lost. Sometimes much heart-searching goes into the balance:
is the sacrifice too great, are the advantages worth it? Sometimes,
for those who have difficulty in forming and keeping any
relationship, this is heard with some amazement: the position they
want to get to seems to bring as many problems as the position
they're in. And sometimes, those in established relationships
listen, at first with disbelief, as those without such relationships
talk of the emptiness of their lives. Those who refrain from affairs
are surprised by the pain caused by those who have affairs; those
who have affairs are surprised by the comforts gained by those
who don't.

In the earlier stages of therapy, these discussions often have the
tone, and sometimes the content, of self-justification. It is as if each
person expects his or her position to be attacked or criticised by
others. Sometimes this happens, often it doesn't. When we talk
about ourselves, we protect ourselves against criticisms that we
imagine might come from others. What is actually happening is
that we are putting our own self-criticisms into the mouths of
others, often before their mouths are opened. When they are
opened, we might hear criticism whatever they say. In one group,
a new member, a fairly successful, single professional woman in

her thirties, sat listening to another woman of the same age talking about her relationship with her husband. She was, at that time, not working, and her husband finished work early, and she was talking about how, for both, the day did not really begin until her husband arrived home. It seemed to me that she was clearly defensive about this, interjecting comments such as 'We both enjoy it, so why should we think it is wrong?', when, in fact, nobody had suggested it was wrong. The new member responded immediately by talking equally defensively about her need to be alone a lot of the time, and how she could not imagine sharing a house with somebody, and she wondered whether she was wrong about that – whether it meant she could not form close relationships. This was a defensive exchange with both expressing self-doubt. In other situations, I have heard similar differences being used as a basis for attack: it is wrong to be so dependent, wrong not to be able to form a close relationship which involves living together.

This brings me back to Freud's theory on a much more mundane level. The point of all this, something that Freud saw very clearly and stated in a very powerful way, is that we are actually divided within ourselves. I have heard it described as having a committee meeting going on in the head. It need not be as intense as this, but I suspect the number of times we actually feel 'together' in what we are doing in any area of our lives is limited and there is a permanent possibility of disruption. Every time we make a decision, or find that we have to choose, there is an internal debate going on.

In Freud's model of the psyche this was seen in terms of three levels of organisation: the 'id', the drives that push us forward to seek satisfaction, the 'ego', the 'I' which is the 'centre' of the psyche, and the 'super-ego', the authority that we internalise from our parents and the wider society. The work of the ego is, amongst other things, to mediate between the demands of the other two: the internal forces that sometimes seem to push us towards doing things in spite of ourselves and the demands of our relationships to others, our work and our knowledge of the world. These conflicts can sometimes be torturous I have heard a man describe his conflict over whether or not to leave his wife and children as one which produced physical pain. Sometimes they occur with less discomfort, but the important thing is that they are always there. Freud's importance in the history of ideas is that his work marks the point where it is no longer possible to think of the individual as a unity, an entity that does things, makes decisions and acts in any simple way. Each of us is, in one sense, a number of entities, often pulling in different directions.

The conflict around sexual repression applies in other areas: there is always the same dilemma of whether to follow my own needs or curb them to reconcile them with the needs of others. This might apply to sexual relationships, the direct expression of feelings, or whether to finish the trifle when other people might want some. The fiercer the internal conflict the more likely we are to deal with it by setting up patterns of relationships that hide the conflict from us. Psychoanalysts talk about the defence mechanisms of 'projection' and 'splitting'. In the example of the two women that I used earlier, each is seeing and hearing some part of her internal conflict in what the other is saying. Each is trying to establish a world in which she is a certain type of OK person, either one who enjoys the dependent intimacy of her relationship or one who is happy keeping her relationships at arm's length for most of the time. Each is projecting onto the other her doubts and misgivings about what she is doing.

The message of all this is inherently disappointing. It is often the case that people come into therapy or counselling seeking an end to internal conflicts, and looking for permission to do what they are doing, and, of course, this cannot be achieved or given. Indeed an important part of therapy might involve becoming *more* aware of internal conflicts and the pain that they involve and realising that there is no one apart from themselves to give themselves permission for what they do. I tend to think about this in terms of a redefinition of what we mean by personal integrity. The dictionary definition suggests wholeness, integration (a common term in psychoanalysis) and adds an adherence to an inviolate moral code – it is usual, in fact, to refer to a loss of integrity when somebody is revealed to have broken a moral code that they supposedly uphold.

The notion of integrity that it seems to me should replace this carries a connotation of wholeness, but not of the absence of conflict. We are integrated and we maintain our integrity when we are aware of our internal conflicts and we can experience them without resorting too much to projection or to any of the other defence mechanisms that psychoanalysis talks about – denial, rationalisation, splitting, etc. The point is less resolution of conflicts

– the existence of conflict, internal and external, marks us off as human – than the way we live with conflicts, the honesty with which we recognise them *in and to ourselves*. Such integrity also involves the recognition that we need our defences, and a complete internal honesty cannot be achieved; and that a complete honesty with others is not always desirable – an idea which, I shall argue later, is also disappointing in that it runs against a popular cultural ideal.

The complexity and disappointment of life can be denied by taking one half of what Freud was saying, and seeing psychotherapy as being only about resolving internal conflict, gaining self-knowledge, learning how to satisfy one's needs, and so on. Psychoanalysis carries some idea of a cure (even though many practising analysts might dispute this) and of the 'perfectly analysed' person, someone who has really got it together, remains in control of himself or herself, and is in some sense always right. This is a powerful image, and it is arguable that it is part of our basic psychic make-up that we all carry around with us; people come into therapy sometimes with a conscious expectation that they can get themselves 'sorted out' and I am sure that many people undertake training as psychotherapists in the unconscious hope that they will end up such a person.

It is, then, difficult to accept the internal conflict that Freud thought was a normal part of human life: we find various ways to 'get rid of' the parts we don't like. Nevertheless, our internal life consists for much of the time of internal conflicts, internal compromises, choices between pursuing our own interests and those of others, of choosing, consciously or unconsciously, what will be expressed, what we will repress or suppress. The message of Freud on this level is not about liberation, sexual or otherwise, nor about conservatism; it is about the necessity of conflict, and the necessity of both liberation and repression, the result being summed up in his classic phrase 'normal human misery'.

THE BODY AND LANGUAGE: THE AWKWARD CONTRADICTION

When my students object to what they see as Freud's biological determinism, his emphasis on the importance of the body, and particularly sexual characteristics, they are in part, I think, manifesting a strand of modern culture which has difficulty in acknowledging that we are really physical beings, that we have bodies which affect what we can and cannot do. A number of phenomena over the past forty years illustrate this. One is the growth of sociology itself as a major discipline in the social sciences, and within sociology, what seems to be the increasing dominance of what are known as 'social constructionist' theories. The emphasis in sociology itself has always been on social causation: that a range of phenomena, from suicide rates to types of medical problems, has a social origin; they are a product of the way our society is organised. Thus in Britain, for example, it seems to be the case that more women than men suffer from depression, that more men than women suffer from schizophrenic disorders, and that both types of illness are more likely to occur in one social class than another.

Now this sort of explanation has a lot going for it. It is not, however, a total explanation – not every woman becomes depressed or every man schizophrenic – and for a full explanation we need to take into account other factors. Sociology, however, has always tended to overemphasise the social causes, and as it has developed, and become more caught up with modern developments in philosophy, so it has tended to favour only social explanations. We find arguments not only that what it means to be a man or a woman is different in different types of society (which of course it is) but that what it means to be a man or a woman is entirely a social matter, a matter of the way in which a particular society defines masculinity or femininity. It seems to me that this is plainly not the case: however hard we try, for example, we cannot find a society in which men bear babies or women have penises.

My point is that we have rather difficult and complex relationships to our bodies, and part of that relationship involves us being limited by our bodies. The cultural strand I am trying to identify tends to deny that limitation, and Freud is rejected because he draws our attention to it. Now there are times, to be sure, when he draws our attention to it in a crass and unhelpful way, or in a way that is simply wrong. There are times when he seems to be suggesting that, in the famous phrase, 'anatomy is destiny', or that women are somehow inferior persons because they don't have penises. At other times, he is, more honestly, openly baffled. If we look closely at his work, however, there are a number of interesting and difficult ideas about gender and human sexuality which have been developed by psychoanalysts and others over the past century. (See especially Chasseguet-Smirgel 1985; Chodorow 1978; Mitchell 1975; Samuels 1993),

In his *The Denial of Death* (1973) Ernest Becker makes a fundamental point: that human beings are painfully divided between our finite animal existence and our apparently infinite symbolic existence. We are beings with bodies that not only prevent us from doing things (flying by ourselves, for example) but that we know are not going to be there for ever – they grow, decay and die. In our heads, however, we can think ideas that can last for ever; there is nothing about our language, the things that we can say, which means that they will disappear. We are born into a world which is full of the words, the cultural symbols and artefacts of past generations, and there is always the possibility that we too can contribute to this apparently immortal world. For Becker, the awful and unbearable thing about this duality is that, as far as we know, unlike other animals, we are aware that we will die a long time before it happens. He thinks that not only is this knowledge unbearable, but that practically everything that we do with our lives is a way of avoiding it.

What I want to take from this is the idea of duality, that we are two different things, animals and language users. For many psychoanalysts, the development of the ability to use language has been a crucial concern, and since the earliest days psychoanalysis has been known as the 'talking cure'. An important area of attention has been on what is often referred to as the process of 'symbolisation', the way we 'enter into language', learn to speak, and become able to 'translate' feelings into words. There are a number of aspects to this work.

The first I want to deal with is that connections are regularly made between symbolisation and loss, or a lack of some sort (see especially Klein 1975; Segal 1991; Lacan 1977), What does this mean? When we symbolise something we take into our heads a word that, in one way or another, symbolises that thing – whether the 'thing' be a person or the object of a feeling or a relationship. For Melanie Klein, who I will be considering in more detail later, there is a close connection between this process and handling our destructive feelings. For the moment, however, I want to concentrate on what is lost and the process of dealing with the loss. A normal part of growing up, or more appropriately growing through our earliest years, is the loss of the security of the womb and the loss of the comfort of the breast. Although these will, if we are reasonably lucky, be replaced with other comforts, they are, in the life of the infant, major losses. The focus of Klein's theory is on the loss of the breast, a loss which, before it occurs, is experienced as the potential loss of the source of life itself. In Kleinian theory the use of symbols, the entry into language, is motivated by this potential loss.

It is as if, faced by the feared or phantasied loss of the most important thing, the infant must create a mental replacement, an 'idea' which acts as a substitute for the lost object. This is already happening when the infant gains comfort from sucking its thumb, and as he or she gets older, the physical imitation can be replaced by an internal representation. In so far as the internal representation involves words, then the words are involved in making up for the loss and drawing attention to it. They are like the memories of a lost loved one, comforting and distressing at the same time. What is lost is a physical wholeness, an at-oneness with the mother, and an ideal of being at one with oneself. Whether this at-oneness actually exists, or whether it is a primitive, phantasied ideal, is a matter of debate; the important thing is that it, or its possibility, has been lost. It is a phantasy, however, which recurs during our lives, most evidently when we fall in love. For a while with the loved one it can feel as if words are not needed, or the only words we need to speak are the declarations which bring us closer to the loved one. Part of the disappointment of love is that when words are spoken seriously, to convey the different experiences and perceptions of two different people, the ideal is lost once again. It is easy to see why people can fall in love with love.

Of course, the whole business is more complicated than this. Our body itself prevents us from achieving the identity we might desire. The physical connection of sexual intercourse involves some mutual joining and physical closeness, but the identity with the other that we find in sexual ecstasy is phantasied: we are not really, physically the same person as the other. We are isolated in a body and we use phantasy to escape that isolation. And we use words, the words of love, to maintain the phantasy. And the phantasy itself can also frighten: identity with another person is also a loss of oneself. Just as some people become addicted to being in love, so some avoid falling in love as if it were the plague; and of course one of the ways in which we avoid love is through words.

We emphasise the difference between ourselves and other people, we affirm our freedom and our separateness.

Now when my students object to what is basically Freud's reminder that we are animals, that our bodies are there and that, in one way or another, they are important for us, they are certainly objecting, quite rightly, to the sexism of his time and the way it appears in his work. It goes beyond that, however: a reminder of our bodily existence is at the same time a reminder of our limitations, our separation from others and the impossibility of merging with others; and when the body is coupled with child-bearing, the reminder is of our infantile helplessness, the fact that each of us was once merged physically with another person.

There are other difficulties as well, most clearly connected with sexuality, where, paradoxically, the body is both a vehicle and a hindrance. One feature of human life that distinguishes us from other animals, which Freud saw quite clearly, is that our sexual drives are not genetically determined and directed towards genital intercourse with a member of the opposite sex. Human beings are born too early – by comparison with other animals we are all premature; as a consequence, the drives become attached to mental representations, there is a sense in which our sexual objects are first mental objects, and the range of sexual stimuli for humans is immense, well beyond the range of stimuli that affect other animals. We do not find other animals who are turned on by suspender belts, high heels, cream cakes or wet fish (except perhaps other wet fish), the thought or reality of being tied up, spanked or whatever. There is little evidence that other animals are systematically attracted to members of the same sex. Ideas, fantasies, play an essential role in human sexual arousal; in fact arousal without fantasy is very difficult. In other words, human sexuality, the practice of human sexuality, even 'normal' human sexuality, is inescapably bound up with symbolisation; it is first sex in the head.

This of course gives us an immense range of possibilities; there are likely to be as many forms of sexual stimuli as there are human beings to be stimulated. Yet, for all this, we only have one body, and most of us only have one set of genitalia that confine us to one sex. In our physical reality we can only be the sex that we are, with a limited number of orifices and protuberances, and – this, I suspect, is the crux of the matter – only one half of the equipment necessary for reproduction. In our heads we can engage in any and every sort of sexual activity but our bodies are limited, and, if the species is to reproduce itself, our limited body has to be used in a limited way for at least part of the time. Freud's description of the sexual development of the child, his psychosexual stages, and his controversial analysis of the Oedipal conflict, were, at their most general, an analysis of the way our symbolisations of the sexual drive are limited to fit, in one way or another, the body we possess, and were directed towards the activity that would result in reproduction.

To point out that this happens, that we are caught between our unlimited mental potentialities for sexual expression, and the much more limited potentiality of our bodies, is to underline, yet again, disappointment. It is not just pointing out our limitations, but pointing out all the restrictions, social and natural, which mean that we cannot do everything we want to do. Freud talked of polymorphous perversity in the infant, meaning that at the earliest stages, the sexual instinct is comparatively undirected, at least potentially capable of finding a vast range of objects; he also talked about the unavoidable nature of at least psychological bisexuality. The difficult dilemma is that psychologically we may retain bisexuality, or perhaps even polymorphous perversity, in a number of ways, in phantasy, in sublimated form or whatever; physically, however, we have only the one body, and socially the impetus is always towards using it in a limited way. We can never be physically what we perhaps always are psychologically, let alone what we might want to be.

DEVELOPMENTS OF FREUD

Disappointment comes not only from having to restrict ourselves, from having to share with other people and from having to make choices in our lives; it also comes from the recognition of what we are, and it is not a world-shattering announcement that we are not always what we might like to think we are. We can be reminded of this on an everyday basis. I can think of a dramatic (for me) recent occasion from my own life: two of my colleagues and a friend in another department achieved promotion, a promotion which I had quite consciously decided not to pursue. I congratulated my colleagues with a degree of sincerely felt pleasure, told them how pleased I was, and then I heard myself say with a very firm emphasis that I was *really* pleased about my friend's promotion; as I said it, I realised that this was a slight on their achievement.

I will return to this later.

During the later part of his work, Freud developed a conception of a 'death instinct'; it was based less on his clinical work than on his experience of the First World War, and it was closely bound up with the analysis of civilisation I discussed earlier, the intimate connection between increasing levels of civilisation and the misery resulting from increased levels of instinctual renunciation.

Freud's (1984a) development of this notion has always been controversial. It encapsulates, almost exquisitely, what is sometimes seen as his 'pessimism', or 'conservatism', a view of human beings which emphasises metaphorically the physical reality of their origin, 'born between piss and shit'. Some commentators suggest that the idea represents some aspect of Freud's own personality that he was turning into a part of his theory. This is certainly possible: the experience of the war was interpreted by others as the salvation of civilisation and it might be that it was a matter of personality which decided how the same evidence should be seen. But there are other, more important and interesting theoretical reasons behind the development of the notion.

The crux of the matter is internal conflict. If we were purely 'instinctual' beings, or, more accurately, if we possessed only one instinct, the sexual instinct or libido, there would be no reason for internal conflict, yet such conflict seems to be a universal experience. In the earlier part of his work, Freud saw the conflict as arising between libido and another set of instincts which aimed at self-preservation – a conflict, as he sometimes put it, between love and hunger. This refers us back to the familiar idea that whilst we might want immediate satisfaction, in a world of scarcity we cannot get it, and to seek it is a dangerous enterprise. However, as his ideas developed, the concept of 'narcissism' came to the fore, throwing doubt on the division between love and hunger.

Narcissism will feature quite a lot in what follows. In everyday terms, we tend to think of it as simply self-love, absorption in one's self. In psychoanalytic theory it has a more complex meaning, and includes as well self-hatred. For the moment I want to look at what is known as 'primary narcissism', the idea that, at a very early stage, the infant takes itself as a love object. Paradoxically, it is precisely this that makes it possible, in Freud's theory, for the infant to enter into social relationships. It does so through a process of identifying itself with its caretaker, usually the mother, and the self-love becomes love of the mother. Here we find an origin of something which can sometimes be remarked on as a form of everyday wisdom, and sometimes paraded as a psychological truism, that one cannot love another person until one can love oneself.

Before continuing, it is worth pointing out one very important implication of this view, particularly in the light of the arguments that will follow. It is common now, and not just amongst sociologists, to think of humans as the result of a process of socialisation: that what we are depends basically on how we were brought up. The alternative to such a view is usually posed in terms of genetics: we are what we are because of what we inherited from our parents. This sort of debate is often encountered in psychology courses, and usually the reasonable solution is offered that we are what we are through a combination of both. Freud's theory of narcissism adds what we might call an intervening variable in between our genetic inheritance and what we are made by our upbringing: an internal, *psychological* process by means of which, on the one hand, we make ourselves able to 'take in' what is on offer from the outside, and, on the other, make ourselves ready to acquire the capacity to symbolise that can translate genetic inheritance into some of the huge range of human possibilities open to us. Later developments of psychoanalysis have in some respects tended to underemphasise the role of this intervening variable.

Anyway, returning to the death instinct, the problem with the theory of narcissism is that it seems to leave us with only libido. Libido takes as its first object, if you like, the self, the nascent ego of the infant, and the self-preservation instincts thus emerge out of the libido. There becomes no apparent basis for internal conflict. Hence Freud introduced the notion of two directly opposed instincts, the life instincts and the death instincts. These both have the same aim, the release of energy and a return to stasis, but they seek it in different ways. The life instinct seeks to produce further life as a means of achieving its end, the death instinct aims at the destruction of human life.

Freud, like many later psychoanalysts, was concerned to base his theory in biology. At first sight, it might seem impossible to find a biological basis for a death instinct. An instinct to destroy life seems to have no evolutionary function; it would lead to the destruction of the species itself. Freud's way of overcoming this was to see it as related to the inevitable and natural death of the individual. It was as if, for each of us, the end point, the aim, of our life was the 'peace' of death; each of us 'owes nature a death'. The death of an individual does not threaten the species. It is our biological 'growth' towards death which emerges in human destructiveness, whether that is directed outwards towards external enemies, or nature itself, or inwards.

Now all this is still fairly abstract and can be discussed abstractly. However, when the idea is translated into everyday terms, or into terms of what happens in the consulting room, it becomes much more problematic. The psychoanalytic theorist who has succeeded in doing this most clearly is Melanie Klein (1957), for whom the death instinct is an everyday reality, in the form of envy. In common-sense language, there is usually some confusion between envy and jealousy, and Klein distinguishes clearly between them, and between these two and greed. The crucial distinction lies in the desire to destroy something that is good, precisely because it is good. If I am greedy, then there is a sense in which I destroy something, I prevent other people getting it, but that is a by-product of my action, not its intention. If I persuade my son to leave some of his chocolate for tomorrow, and then struggle with myself over whether to eat it after he has gone to bed, then I am recognising that the chocolate is good, and I do not want to deprive him of it, but I do want this good thing for myself. Similarly, jealousy recognises that something is good; if he sits there in front of me eating it, my jealousy takes the form of wanting it for myself. Equally, sexual jealousy recognises that there is something, a person, who is good and desirable; the feeling is, amongst other things, that I, not somebody else, should have this person.

With both greed and jealousy, we are already in the realm of disappointment. They are not pleasant feelings to acknowledge in oneself, and jealousy can be extremely painful – 'ordinary' jealousy, not only obsessive or pathological jealousy. This is made worse if one believes that jealousy shouldn't be felt. There is certainly a contemporary view that to expect faithfulness is wrong, that people do not own each other and if a partner prefers

somebody else then nothing should be done about it. I have a
certain sympathy with this idea, at least in so far as it is a preferable
alternative to the transformation of a marriage into a prison. But
a moral view about how to handle a situation is easily transformed
into a sense that certain feelings should not be experienced. I have
heard people – men and women – whose partners are having
affairs say that they should not feel jealous, that the feeling itself is
wrong. And I have heard people who have embarked on affairs
express horror and indignation at the jealousy of their partners,
as if such a reaction were not entirely predictable. If we value
something and it seems that some other person might have access
to that something, and might possibly take it away, then we are
bound to feel all those reactions – a fear of loss, a sense of betrayal,
anger and resentment and more – that go to make up what we call
jealousy. Jealousy is a sign that something is valued and desired,
on the whole, I think, a positive – if unpleasant – emotion. Why
people should now think the opposite is something I will go into
later.

In any case, if both greed and jealousy recognise that there is
something good and desirable, envy tries, sometimes blatantly,
sometimes subtly, to deny that something is desirable. It is the
sour grapes reaction: the fox can't reach the grapes on the vine,
and walks away commenting that they were sour anyway. The
feeling of envy seems to be saying something like: there is
something that I want which is very good indeed, perhaps perfect;
it is so good that I can never have it and I cannot bear the thought
of never having it – that emphasises my own inadequacy, my
poverty, my lack. I have to find some way of easing these feelings,
and that can be done by finding some reason why this thing is not
so good at all. Thus I undermine it in some way. We need to avoid
bad feelings about ourselves, and envy can be attached, in my
experience, to any difference between people that can exist; if
somebody else has something that I do not have, I can always find
reasons why I do not want it, and reasons to belittle it. Sometimes
this can happen with great subtlety.

In the example above it was my hitherto unconscious envy of
my colleagues' promotion that emerged and embarrassed me.
The implication was that I was not *really* pleased about their
promotion, which brought into question my decision not to seek
it and raised the issue of whether I would have got it if I had
applied – and the possibility that my decision not to apply was

through a fear of failure rather than a rational decision that I did not want a particular post. In other words, my original decision involved an envious devaluing of the promotion.

My internal reaction to this was one of embarrassment and acute shame in my own eyes (I am not sure that my colleagues consciously picked up the slight) as well as the creeping feelings of inadequacy that I had been perhaps trying to hide by not applying in the first place. This is what makes envy – in a clinical or an everyday situation – so difficult to acknowledge and accept: it is an attempt to get away from very painful feelings. If the envy is consciously realised, then not only do the original painful feelings emerge, but there is an extra increment in recognition of the destructive or spoiling way in which they have been dealt with. That makes the recognition of envy as part of oneself a very different matter from the recognition of the death instinct as an abstract idea. In fact I suspect we can only really discuss it if we distance ourselves from it – as I have done here – with some degree of sophistication.

The problem with envy is that it is just there, in all of us. We can do nothing, in the end, but feel bad about it. If we are, for whatever reason, endowed with too much, then it can inhibit and restrict our lives – and by its nature, the more we feel inhibited and restricted the more envious we are likely to become. On the other hand, the more we allow ourselves to acknowledge envy, the more we have to take account of other painful feelings. For Klein, the death instinct was an instinct. We all possess it by virtue of being human, and if some have more than others, then it is simply a matter of constitution. I don't think that there is, actually, any biological basis for talking about a death instinct, but if we take seriously the arguments I discussed earlier, that part of being human is to be divided between the symbolic and the physical (mortal) sides of existence, then we can see the 'death instinct' as a metaphor for something built into being human. We know of the inevitability of death, and we affirm it even as we try constantly to avoid it. We can, if we are open to them, find intimations everywhere: 'And the crack in the tea-cup opens / A lane to the land of the dead' (Auden), In our knowledge of its inevitability, death holds a fascination for us. Part of our reaction must be – to a greater or lesser extent – that if we are going to die anyway, then nothing is worth doing, and we have to establish that nothing is worth doing, the envious reaction *par excellence*.

Now this is a sort of speculative rationalisation – what I am trying to do is acknowledge that perhaps we cannot talk about a death instinct as a biological *instinct* but at the same time suggest reasons why the envious attack, the devaluing of the desirable, is there in everybody. Psychoanalysts are often reluctant to accept the idea, preferring to emphasise the environment in which we mature. I will argue later that it is the emphasis on the environment that contributes to unrealistic expectations being placed on the helping professions generally.

Klein's argument, like Freud's, entails a countervailing force, a life instinct, but for the moment I want to stick with envy, and look at what might be the positive side of 'pure' envy. One of the points that Klein (1937) makes is that envy can become the basis of something socially useful, and the most obvious example of this is in political life. It is often argued by the right that left-wing politics are the product of envy, whilst those who wish to maintain some sort of balance point out that right-wing politics are the politics of greed. I think both sides are right, but the envy of the left is not necessarily a bad thing. Social differences and in particular differences in wealth, like any other differences, attract envious attacks, yet such attacks generate a positive notion of a 'just' society, which does not allow large inequalities and tries to guarantee some sort of 'level playing field' on which members of a society can compete on an equal basis. Perhaps the crucial difference between a negative and a positive envy in this respect is whether the political emphasis is on lowering those at the top or improving the lot of those at the bottom, although reality – the fact that we do not have unlimited resources – means that both must occur.

Yet it is important to be aware of the dimensions of envy in this sort of argument since an action, personal or political, which is based almost entirely and unconsciously on envy will only be successful if it is destructive. The righteous indignation that those of us on the left tend to feel at the accusation of envy is a protection against the acknowledgement of our envy. Such indignation is a common reaction when envy is pointed out and perhaps protects against shame. In my earlier example, I suspect that, paradoxically, it was easier for me to experience shame because my envious attack wasn't publicly pointed out. If it had been pointed out, then my first reaction would have been angry denial, or to explain my comment away, probably in a fashion that would have emphasised the slight. The public exposure of envy is extremely upsetting; since we *are* envious, its public exposure cannot be avoided.

FROM ENVY TO DEPRESSION

For some time, a matter of more than a year, I worked with a group that was more or less evenly divided between people who were unhappy and concerned to learn about themselves and change, but who were living reasonably normally in the world and holding down and even doing well at jobs; and others who were for the time being disabled – unable to work, but living at home with their families – by what had, in each case, been diagnosed as depression, but in each of whose cases there was an underlying psychosis – one person would resort to self-inflicted injury, another would become gripped by paranoid ideas, and so on. The group regularly divided itself into those who saw themselves as more 'sick', or suffering from an 'illness', launching an implicit or explicit attack on those whom they did not see as sick – always along the 'It's all right for you . . .' lines, and sometimes denying that they had anything in common at all with the members of the other group.

Watching the group at work, however, two things were apparent: the 'non-sick' group were at times afraid of the disturbances claimed or manifested by the others, but at times were able to talk about their own variations of these same disturbances; and for all their claims to disability, the 'sick' group were able to be competently helpful to each other and the 'non-sick' group. In other words, some real processes of identification and co-operation were at work. What was difficult was for either side to acknowledge their common humanity with the others. What were they afraid of? On the one hand it was fear of finding one's own 'crippled', 'sick', or whatever, dimension – of finding what one had in common with people who were so apparently disabled. At those moments when the envious attack emerged from the latter, the former's distance from all this was confirmed. I think what was going on in the 'sick' group was somewhat more complicated. There was a tendency to regard their problems as an illness on a medical model, and to fall back on an implicit or explicit demand that I should cure them.

In this way, for a period at least, there was the relief of

experiencing their difficulties in an external way, as something which happened to them from the outside; beyond this, it provided a basis to demand the attention, the love that we might surmise had originally been absent from their lives – it was, in one sense, a regression to a stage where no responsibility could be borne for what was happening to them. There is a complex and subtle psychoanalytic literature around the idea of regression that I do not want to go into here – I am interested in painting a larger picture with broader strokes. What I mean by responsibility in this sense is not a moral responsibility – morality might very well enter into these things, but that is not what I am getting at – but rather some sort of acknowledgement that the illness is part of themselves, if you like an authentic experience, as authentic as what were seen to be earlier experiences of competence, success or even happiness. There is a sense in which everybody in the group, both sub-groups, were struggling not to enter what Klein (1986a, 1986b) calls the 'depressive position'.

Klein was especially concerned with the early experience of the infant, and it is important to remember that she saw the death instinct, envy, as a constitutional feature of human life – the central question was not whether it was there but how much of it was there. The baby has to deal with two types of experience: those that are satisfying, literally full-filling in the case of feeding, experiences which bring comfort, the release of tension, the satisfaction of needs; and those which bring discomfort, dis-satisfaction, unpleasant and threatening feelings. The latter may be internal – colic, for example, or hunger pains – or external, and it is unlikely that the baby at this very early stage can be aware of the difference. Klein suggested that the way in which the baby deals with these experiences, using fairly primitive psychological mechanisms, is to divide the world into good and bad ('splitting') and to experience all the bad as external ('projection') and the good as internal. Thus when it feels bad, it feels itself to be under attack. The splitting and projection is necessary to protect a primitive and still very weak ego – others might talk in terms of protecting a very elementary and still shaky sense of self.

She referred to this developmental point as the 'paranoid-schizoid position'. The splitting accounts for the 'schizoid' part of the label, and the projected bad experiences are then felt to be attacking – the 'paranoid' element. The term 'position' is important as well: it is not a stage that we pass through and leave

behind, although it certainly becomes modified as we grow older
– if we are lucky. It can be seen as a way of being in the world that
we all adopt to some degree. The 'sick' members of my group
sometimes lived in a world which was full of healthy, competent
people who regarded them with disdain, whilst the 'healthy' ones
lived in a world where they were persecuted by people who were
worse off than themselves, who would not allow their difficulties
to be taken seriously. In both cases what was being projected was
some feeling or experience which they were, at least for periods,
unable to contemplate: it felt too destructive, too much of a threat
to the selves that they were trying to maintain.

The decisive move for the infant, as it becomes more physically
able, more confident in itself, if it is cared for in a reasonable and
considerate way, not allowed to go hungry, cold, unfed, not
treated brutally or with indifference, is to move from the
paranoid-schizoid position to the depressive position. This
involves two significant points for my present discussion. First, it
involves something like a more realistic perception of the outside
world and of the self. On the one hand, we come to realise that the
world is not necessarily persecutory – it might be at times, but
never totally so – on the other hand, we come to realise that we are
not quite as perfect, not as much at the centre of the world as we
imagined or desired. We begin to experience things in shades of
grey. Second, and as part of our growing self-awareness, we take
back into ourselves some part of the capacity to persecute, to
destroy, that we had put into the outside world. The depressive
position can be associated with feelings of anxiety (about the
damage one can or might cause), of guilt, of shame, of
self-directed hatred and, most importantly, of the loss of an ideal
– whether it be the ideal carer, who will always give one what one
needs, or an ideal self that can do everything one wants, achieve
every satisfaction. A common adult defence against envy is an
idealisation: one wants something so much, regards a particular
quality or ability as desirable, and rather than destroy the
possibility of getting it by devaluing it, one sets about refusing to
recognise that it has any limitations or undesirable aspects at all.
That loss of an ideal is something which, I suspect, most of us have
to come to terms with time and time again during our lives, and
we never quite succeed.

A lot of this, for Klein, goes on in our unconscious phantasy life,
and it is there that we discover the possibility of reparation, of

renewing, restoring, the things we value but feel we might destroy or have destroyed. I always think that this is described exceptionally well by D.W. Winnicott (1988), who, as we shall see later, was unable to accept the existence of the death instinct. Instead of the depressive position he preferred to talk of gaining the ability to care, of the baby 'gaining ruth' where before it had been ruth-less. He talks of a distinction between the 'id' mother, the mother on whom the infant satisfies its desires, and an 'environmental' mother, the real mother. It is the ability of the environmental mother to survive and continue to allow the baby to feed that enables the child to come to terms with the potential destructiveness of its own needs. Returning to Klein, it is with the internalised or introjected phantasy of the mother, the 'internal object', that we find the ability to restore what we fear we might have destroyed, make reparation for our destructive tendencies. If we are lucky we build up a store of good internal objects that comprise a central part of our personality, but we do so through a loss, here a loss of an ideal, and in a sense, an innocent state.

Returning to my group, we can see each of the respective sub-groups as engaged in a sort of dance, a movement to and from the depressive position. For the 'sick' group, the depressive position would mean recognising their own persecutory destructiveness which they had put into the others, and taking in and recognising their own failure to be what they want to be, the 'loss' of stretches of time and aspects of personality that they might have desired to use differently. This was very apparent in their talk about themselves. The benefits of entering into the depressive position – which would involve considerable pain – would be to bring them into a closer contact with external reality and the reality of themselves, enabling them to live less ambitious but more competent lives. For the 'less sick' group, it would involve also a recognition of their own destructive potentialities, their ability to cripple themselves as a response to the difficulties they face; in some respects it might also involve a recognition of their own persecutory tendencies in so far as they accepted the other group's projections, regarding the 'sick' as different from and less competent than themselves, as it were, 'by nature'.

I now want to distinguish between the clinical and wider aspects of these ideas, for my main interest is in how these ideas are taken into the wider culture. One way of expressing the clinical aim in the therapy group is in terms of establishing an environment where each member of the group can take in those parts of himself or herself that have been projected onto the others, and organise them into his or her personality. It is a matter of being able to hold – experience – difficult feelings without being driven into finding some way of getting rid of them, by projection, denial, action or whatever. Another way of putting this is in terms of 'containing' feelings. Indeed, Wilfrid Bion (1967), who developed many of Klein's ideas, talks about the psychoanalyst – and the mother – as a 'container', a person who can allow the experience of feelings and when appropriate deliver them back to the infant or patient in a more intelligible and manageable form.

Now when this process is going on in the consulting room, and when it is going on in everyday life, when the patient has left analysis and is struggling with the difficult and powerful and conflicting feelings that are likely to be part of his or her everyday life, there is no escaping the difficulty, the awareness of internal conflict, the hope that love will overcome hate and the despair that sometimes it will not. Life is not like this all of the time, but it is certainly like it some of the time.

The paradox is that outside the consulting room, the theory can sound trite, even smug. It comes across as an easy solution. I can remember, some thirty years ago, a record by an American comedian – Bob Newhart, I think – in the role of a psychoanalyst, listening to an unheard patient. The monologue went something like this:

> Oh, so you have something important to tell me, well that's what I'm here for . . . You've fallen in love; well that's good . . . With my wife? Well, I can understand that, she's a very attractive woman and it's quite normal to feel attracted to such a woman . . . Oh, she's in love with you and you're running away together; well, that's perfectly understandable, I'm a very busy man and I don't get to spend much time with her, and she's a healthy, active woman . . . You're angry with me; yes, well that's quite understandable and normal, jealousy and anger is quite acceptable . . . Oh, you've bought a gun; well, it's quite understandable that you should want to kill me . . .

I can't guarantee that my memory over thirty years is accurate, but I imagine the general idea is apparent. I have already mentioned the 'myth' of the perfectly analysed analyst. Such a figure is totally imaginary and he or she exists alongside a general recognition that analysts have their blind spots, their failings, and that sometimes they might actually help the patient by failing. Such a figure has worked through his or her conflicts, is aware of and in control of his or her various pecadilloes, and acts rationally and for the best in all situations. He or she is often used – in his or her absence as it were – to hit colleagues with whom one disagrees: 'You haven't been sufficiently analysed.' In a recent review, Sherry Turkle argues, rightly I think, that the difference between a mature and an immature psychoanalyst lies in an ability to acknowledge the existence of psychological vulnerability without claiming that it invalidates everything or anything the theorist might say. She quotes approvingly the French analyst, Jacques Lacan:

> In a conversation with an American analyst who claimed she had chosen her profession out of her sense of being the sort of strong person to whom others could turn for help, Lacan admitted that he had come to analysis 'in just the opposite way', drawn to Freud for the emphasis he had put not on man's strength but on his vulnerability. Lacan spoke of the analyst as someone deeply in touch with the sense of being at risk and deeply in touch with the knowledge that it is possible 'for each of us to go mad'.
>
> (Turkle 1990: 9)

My point is that even in thinking and writing about the possibility, the unavoidability of the experiences and feelings I have referred to under the general heading of disappointment, it is possible to deny them, to promise a solution at the end of one or several training analyses, or leave them to other people.

Chapter 4

Looking on the bright side

Whilst I have drawn out the aspects of classical psychoanalytic theory that see disappointment, in one form or another, as central to human life, much modern psychotherapy, including psycho-analytic therapy, presents itself as a liberating, enriching and growth-inspiring process. It is probably all these things, but in a limited and paradoxical way.

Paradox haunts psychoanalysis and it haunts this book. Many of the ideas that I will discuss critically in this chapter are taken from the development of the British independent school of psychoanalysis that emerged from the arguments between Freudians and Kleinians in the 1930s and 1940s (see Rayner 1991). Many of the ideas are subtle and stimulating, and in my work as a therapist they are a never-ending source of inspiration, thought and insight; outside of the consulting room, however, they become bound up with and carried away by ways of thinking and cultural trends which are, I think, contrary to the values of psychoanalysis. As a parallel paradox, the work of Lacan, which I have already quoted favourably, seems to me to be an important assertion of certain psychoanalytic values in the wider culture, but I find it of very little help clinically.

In teaching undergraduates and in my work with trainee counsellors, I am constantly meeting two radically opposed reactions to the core of these ideas which centre on early infancy and in particular the role of the mother, and were developed first in the work of Winnicott (1958, 1965, 1971) and Bowlby (1953, 1971, 1975, 1981, 1988), My undergraduate students will reject them angrily; the trainees will embrace them with an equally blind passion. My students ask how men can write about mothering. What they say cannot be taken seriously because they are men. It is all part of an ideology that aims to keep women in the home, part of an unrelenting system of patriarchy. Winnicott expects too much, and produces a feeling of guilt; everything that goes wrong with children is the responsibility of the mother. In experiential groups, on the other hand, trainees embrace these ideas, which seem to feed their anger with their own parents, and to lead them to recall what they perceive as past injustices. It is almost as if there is a wish to return to an imagined innocence of childhood, to an all-accepting and unproblematic environment which did not exist, and I suspect can never exist. The power of this reaction becomes clear if a group member threatens the collective phantasy.

There was an example of this in one of my trainee groups. What was going on was actually a form of scapegoating. A man in the group talked, very straightforwardly, about how, when he was working at home, which he had to do quite often, his young children could be a constant interruption, and a disruption if they tore up or drew on his papers. Therefore he kept them out of his study. This was immediately interpreted by others in the group as a damaging rejection of his children, and they tried in turn to analyse it, interpret it and finally condemn it. The feeling of condemnation was very strong indeed.

Now none of the writers I will be considering actually deserves either interpretation. Like the ideas of anybody who thinks seriously about these issues, their ideas are qualified, modified, room is left in each case for elaborations. Bowlby, for example, writes about the importance of caretakers other than the mother, Winnicott writes about how the mother also hates the baby – and the ways in which that might be useful. But at least in initial reactions, none of this seems to be heard or understood – I have had the experience of going out of my way to stress such points in lectures, and finding nobody, in a room of between thirty and fifty people, had heard me do this. I think that what happens on these occasions is that certain sensitive social and individual reactions are touched off, and the force of these swamps the more rational capacities of the hearers.

The misinterpretations, the mishearings, despite their apparently opposite content, for and against the writers I am talking about, are, I think, basically similar. What they do is draw the ideas into a battle between victims and victimisers. On the one side are those who are innocent and powerless – or at least comparatively powerless – and who are limited, treated unfairly, denied opportunities, have their experience distorted and denied by those on the other side who have power. Now of course there is a reality to all this: in a range of areas, men exercise power over women, parents over children; yet it seems to me that rarely is this power exercised in a context where we can see it as *simply and only* a case of victim and victimised, and in the case of parents and children the exercise of power is often beneficial; I would, for example, not be doing my son any favours if I let him experiment by sticking his fingers in electricity sockets. What is more often happening – most clearly between men and women, perhaps less clearly between parents and children – is a conflict over power, in which neither side is completely powerless and neither side has complete power. Yet it is attractive, and for some people, perhaps for all of us some of the time, apparently necessary to see the world in these terms.

I will be returning to these issues later, when my point will be that there is a range of sociological factors, to do with the sorts of social change that we have experienced over the last century, which encourages us to see the world in this way. From what went earlier, it can, I think, be seen that it involves processes of splitting and projection. What is happening is a process of cultural selection and emphasising of select strands of thought from modern psychoanalytic theory. These are the strands I will be looking at: my justification for picking them out is that the culture picks them out.

My criticisms will, in fact, go beyond saying that these ideas need to be taken in their proper context of everything else the authors say – although, of course, that is true. There is, I think, a sense in which these ideas give too much – or owe too much – to the society in which they are produced. Much psychoanalysis lacks reflexive ability, an ability to see itself as a product of a particular society at a particular time. This inability has always left it open to criticism. One hears, for example, the point that Freud's original conclusions might have been appropriate for middle-class Viennese but do not have much validity elsewhere. I don't think this is true, but one of the lessons of modernity is that we need to be aware of this possibility, just as, in our personal lives, we need to be aware that the world does not always look the same to everybody else.

THE IDEALISM OF THE ENVIRONMENT

In the background of psychoanalysis, and very much in the foreground of Bowlby's work, there is a form of what I can only call benign evolutionary theory. Freud (1985b), ever anxious to ground psychoanalysis as a science, placed his work firmly in an evolutionary context, arguing that there is a parallel between the evolution of the species, the evolution of society itself and the evolution of the individual; I don't think anybody would take this very seriously today, although the idea sometimes provides useful metaphors. In the work of Bowlby and others, the theory of evolution seems to run as follows: there is something like a 'natural' development of the individual, perhaps analogous to the development of the flower from a bud. If this development fails, or is distorted in some way, the problem is a result of 'environmental failure': the failure of the parent, in our society usually the mother, to provide the right conditions for the infant to grow, physically and psychologically. The crucial disagreement between the British independent school and the Kleinian school is on the importance of the early environment.

Now the difficulty of the ground on which I am treading is illustrated by the fact that although this is often identified as the crucial difference, nobody on either side will, as far as I know, take a firm and adamant position; and it seems to me that anyone who maintains a common-sense attitude will see (a) that it is indisputable that many of our problems are caused by what happens to us when we are babies, infants and children; and (b) that these events are not sufficient to explain the difficulties that we all might experience, the difficulties of being human *per se*. And indeed, whilst many people who come into psychoanalysis come from clearly damaging backgrounds, for others the origins of difficulties are by no means clear. Both groups can, perhaps, be seen as suffering from a particularly bad case of life.

The evolutionary view espoused by Bowlby is problematic. To begin with, it is teleological; by that I mean that it is presupposed that the end point is there at the beginning, that the rose is somehow present in the bud, the young shoot in the original seedlings. Whilst it is possible – perhaps – to talk like this about human beings, where we could say that when we decide to conceive, or try to conceive, we intend to produce a future competent adult, such an intention is not there for the seedling or the bud, or the sperm or the embryo. If we do not want to say that everything that happens is God's intention, then there seems to be no intention in nature. In fact the interesting thing about evolution is that it seems a matter of chance. As far as I can tell, this seems to be agreed by all modern evolutionary theorists, even those who believe that chance is limited by certain mathematically calculable possibilities. These ideas can be found clearly and delightfully explained in the work of the biologist Stephen Jay Gould (1989: Ch. 1), What this means is that in nature, there is no such thing as environmental failure. There are organisms and environments, and sometimes the environments enable organisms to survive or to change in unpredictable ways, and sometimes they don't.

This takes us to one of my main arguments. If we assume the simple form of evolutionism, for example, then we can be led to attempts to ensure 'environmental success', forms of social engineering and social control that undermine our freedom to choose how to live and how to be. This is the direction taken by the trainees I mentioned earlier: the force of moral disapproval that they can generate against anyone who disagrees is immense, even within a small group; interestingly, the students who take the opposite view generate an equally strong disapproval. Nikolas Rose, in a recent book powerfully entitled *Governing the Soul* (1990), points to the ways in which the work of Winnicott and Bowlby has been taken up to demonstrate how people *should* be, and I think it is the case that their work is open to such an interpretation. The comparison with Freud and Klein should be apparent; their work focuses on how people *are* – as messy and conflict-ridden and nasty as they are integrated, capable and nice. A programme of social engineering can be found in their work, but it remains ambiguous; in the work of Winnicott and Bowlby, it becomes much clearer.

But, as always, there is an opposite side. One of the ways in which human beings can be distinguished from other animals is that humans have a greater degree of control over their environment. I think it is easy to overestimate the degree of control that we do have, and perhaps to assume that our control is always beneficial – although both assumptions should be thrown into doubt by modern ecological crises. The control is, however, there, and it would be difficult to make a case that it should not be exercised. An illustration might be useful. Bowlby posits, on the basis of an immense amount of evidence from ethology and from human life, that there is an evolutionarily useful 'attachment need', that the young and as yet incompetent member of a species needs an older and more competent member – usually the mother. This is independent of the need for food and the sexual instinct, and involves a desire for proximity, the survival value of which is that it offers protection from predators. We could think of it, perhaps, as a clinging need – in everyday language we experience it as a need for the comfort of physical contact with another human being. As we grow older, the need remains, but if all goes well, we can move further away for longer periods before returning to the necessary 'secure base'.

If the attachment need is not provided for or if a separation from the major figure occurs during the early years, the result can be damaging. The human child is likely to grow up to show severe separation anxiety in situations where it is not necessarily appropriate, keeping himself or herself aloof from close relationships, and experiencing severe difficulty if a close relationship is formed. Much of Bowlby's evidence for this amongst humans came from studying the effects of the separation of mother and child during the hospitalisation of one or the other. At the time, during the 1950s and 1960s, it was customary to limit, or prohibit, parental visits to young children in hospital because they became so upset; one of the more dramatic results of Bowlby's work was to transform hospital practices, so that now long visits are possible, usually together with facilities for parents to stay overnight. This is an example of the way in which we can control our environment so that it doesn't 'fail' a child, and it seems to me reasonable to allow and to encourage a parent to spend as much time as possible with a hospitalised child.

But is it? I have no trouble with 'allow', but 'encourage' is a can of worms. What form should my encouragement take? I might disapprove of parents who do not want to stay, and I might encourage them in such a way that they feel persecuted, driven by a guilt that is almost certainly already there. Does it matter, if my persecution is successful? Rather than persecute, should I try to educate and therapise the parents into staying with their child? Is there any difference between this and persecution? And in doing either, am I implementing a form of social control that is necessary for a reasonably civilised and good society to come into being – perhaps not as basic as using force to prevent murder – or am I enforcing a social control to maintain a society that is undesirable? Does, indeed, the exercise of my 'encouragement' make such a society undesirable?

These are the sorts of question I want to approach. In the case of my students, one clear set of answers was being given; in the case of the trainees, another. I do not think there is any clear answer, but there are a number of contradictory answers, and above all we need to be aware of the questions, and, I suspect, we need to be confused about them. The question I want to ask at the moment is this: is there a possibility of success in encouraging parents to stay in hospital with their children? If hatred as well as love is a part of the human condition; if people possess self-concern as well as concern for others; then there will be parents who decline the offer, perhaps even welcome the release. But of course, that does not mean that we should not try. It affects, perhaps, the way we should try.

Returning to the discussion of evolution, it seems to me that we can accept the notion of an attachment instinct without too much difficulty; the evidence, not only in regard to humans, is very strong. But the interesting question is about what happens to instincts in humans. The two reactions I have spoken about so far are mirrored in reactions about the idea of instinct in human beings. Those who accept enthusiastically Bowlby's work accept the idea of an instinct without any problem; those who doubt it – especially sociology students – tend to reject any idea that instincts are important at all in human behaviour.

Bowlby (1971) sees instincts as behaviour systems of complex chains, networks and hierarchies of feedback arcs – a conception which I think biologists would recognise. As I understand it, he means that there is a reflex reaction to a potential danger – in this case loss of the protecting person – which involves a chain of interacting elements which produce a behaviour which might avoid the loss. In human beings, this can involve anger, yearning, etc. Bowlby seems to think that an instinct can be modified by learning, but it is the presence of the response in the absence of any opportunity for learning that establishes that it is an instinct.

Now Bowlby is truer to biology than Freud, or, more accurately, Freud's translators. When, in Freud's English work, we read the word 'instinct' it is usually a translation of the German word 'Triebe' that would be better translated as 'drive'. For Freud, the drive was the instinct attached to a 'psychic representation' – an idea or image, conscious or unconscious. The difference between Freud and Bowlby here seems to be that Bowlby somehow underestimates the importance of the human ability to symbolise – certainly a useful evolutionary trait. It is often commented both that Bowlby has a comparatively undeveloped conception of the inner world and that he tends to be pessimistic about the possibility of recovering from early damage – in fact much of the thrust of his work has been towards prevention.

We are back with the dilemma – perhaps on occasions the contradiction – between our animal, physical existence and our existence as users of language. It is this which I think must bring disappointment to both sides in the reaction to Bowlby's work. On the one hand, we are animals, with our instinctual inheritance – I think it is not possible to deny the behavioural reactions that Bowlby identifies as instinctual – and on the other hand, we are language users, which means that these instinctual reactions are always mediated by something that is non-instinctual. What this means in terms of the questions posed earlier is that if the parents do not visit or stay with the child in hospital, it is likely that some damage will be done; if the parents do visit or stay with the child, damage might still be done. This needs further elaboration, but I think the connection with my theme of disappointment is evident. We cannot get rid of our problems by controlling the environment, and if we try to do that, we run the danger of producing an unacceptable form of social organisation.

THE PROBLEM OF LANGUAGE

Turning now to the psychoanalyst whose work I find least useful in practice, Jacques Lacan (1968, 1977, 1979, 1988a, 1988b) we can find much rhetoric about going back to the original insights of Freud. There is one sense in which he does do this: in his insistence that human beings are in a crucial way divided against themselves. There might be times in our experience when we do feel at one with ourselves, but that feeling does not necessarily correspond to a reality.

Lacan builds up his version of this by giving priority in human development to the acquisition of language; it is with this acquisition that the unconscious itself is established. Perhaps the most important feature is the recognition that our language is *conventional* – there is no necessary connection between the word and the thing it describes. We do not have to call the thing on top of my body a head – we could call it a cauliflower and eat heads for dinner. Nothing would change in the world; we call heads heads simply because that is the language, the 'agreed' language. Thus when we take in the concept of something – whether it be an object external to us or an internal feeling – we are not taking in the object itself; there is the dimension of loss that I talked about earlier. Another way of putting this is that we are always struggling – sometimes very consciously – to express what we mean, and we never quite succeed. We are also, for Lacan, engaged in a constant struggle to attain an illusory identity with ourselves – he calls it the 'imaginary' – and we are always doomed to failure.

Lacan also offers the possibility of looking at psychosis in linguistic terms: it is what happens when the connections between words, organised around certain fixed points (particularly in relation to gender), break down and we slide from word to word in no apparent order. However, most important for my argument is our existence as symbol-using and symbol-producing animals, which though a clear evolutionary advantage, also exposes us to dangers, psychological dangers that Bowlby tends to see in terms of the environment alone. The object to which we physically attach ourselves is, psychologically, lost as soon as we become aware of it even at a primitive symbolic level. In a famous example, Freud pointed to an infant's game of 'losing' and 'finding' an object as a way of dealing with this, but most parents are aware that there are times, fairly early on in many infants' lives, when no separation seems bearable. It is not a matter of a hospital stay – it is a question of leaving the room to fetch something. The conventional way of describing this in psychoanalytic theory is that the infant has not yet achieved a sufficiently reliable 'internal' object that will enable him or her to bear limited separation from the parent. This implies that, without traumatic separation actually taking place, a representation of traumatic separation is already present. We can assume this because we are looking not at any young animal but at the sort of young animal that has a symbolic capacity which is intimately bound up with a very rapid learning process, and we are witnessing the early stages of symbolisation.

Now what follows from this is that the sense, the symbolic experience, of traumatic separation is there for all of us; we experience it and fear it whether or not it happens. It is an 'internal' reality which is perhaps emphasised and thus much more damaging if it becomes an external reality. But it is also clear that separation can be on a symbolic (emotional) level as well as an external physical reality. George Brown's (Brown and Harris 1978) work on the social origins of depression indicates that a depressed parent (usually the mother) has consequences similar to those of physical separation. To take it further, Wilfrid Bion attributes psychotic symptoms in one of his patients to the mother's inability to contain the infant's fear of death. Now returning to my example of the child in hospital, it seems the urgency of persuading the parents is less if it is realised that this sort of separation is only one of a range of possible damaging interruptions to attachment – and one of those interruptions is our own ability to imagine. In other words, environmental success is not a possibility; we cannot persuade people not to be depressed, or not to fear death, any more than we can persuade the infant not to imagine or phantasise. I suppose I am saying that however desirable parental presence might be, we should see it in proportion. Part of that proportion can be found in Bowlby's own work: it is possible to mitigate the effects of separation if there is a sensitive replacement figure.

If the self is always divided, if all relationships involve a degree of ambivalence, it also follows that attempts to therapise or bring moral pressure to bear are likely to be self-defeating. In my trainee group the feeling was that any sort of rejection or boundary would be damaging – even the fairly mild one of keeping children away from papers they might destroy. But I think that an impetus behind the group's reaction, and their attack, was their perception of the way in which this man – and all parents – experience their children as burdens. It often seems important for people to deny this reality, as much as others deny the reality of the effects of separation. There is a mutual disappointment necessary on both sides if progress is to be made. Winnicott (1986) recognised the burden side clearly, commenting to the effect that a baby is a burden that two people have decided to call a baby. We need to be aware of the times we might fail or even damage our children, with all the guilt and distress that involves: that is true for parents who don't want to stay overnight in hospital; but – if we start from the opposite side – we also need to be aware of our own resentment of our children (perhaps especi- ally if we have to stay overnight in hospital with them) and the way that

that might distress or damage them because they perceive it when we deny it.

TRUE SELVES AND FALSE SELVES

Language is important in other ways as well. Recently, a trainee counsellor in an experiential group was saying that what had brought her into therapy and then into training was a desire to discover what she felt and thought about herself and the world, not what her parents thought and not what society thought. Listening to her, the sentiment felt familiar, something I had experienced myself and something I had heard and seen in many different forms. A search for a 'real' self is perhaps a hallmark of modernity. By modernity I mean that period of several hundred years over which the sort of self required by social life has become more complex. It underlies – perhaps it is the origin – of the novel form, and the need that many people now seem to feel to write autobiographies, which up until the sixteenth or seventeenth centuries were all but unknown as a literary form. It is a feeling that can be accompanied by excitement, by a sense of something solid and reliable inside and a future of new possibilities opening out in front of one.

But I also had another reaction. I found myself wondering what, if we took away parents (and siblings, etc.) and society, would be left? Perhaps there would only be the animal self, inarticulate and instinct-driven, the precise opposite of what was hoped for. Perhaps the idea of a true self, a real self, my own self, is – or can become, if we don't recognise its limitations – an illusion, a chimera we chase after only to be regularly disappointed. This is precisely what Lacan means when he talks about the 'imaginary' – we have the fantasy of a person whole and undivided, fully self-possessed, and we try, at the cost of immense energy and equally immense disillusion, to become such a person. Yet the notion of a 'true self' and of a 'false self' is a potent one in British psychoanalysis. We find the idea in Winnicott (1971), who as ever is aware of all the complications. 'There is no such thing as a baby' he writes on one occasion, meaning that there is always the mother–baby (or caretaker–baby) unit; from the start there is a relationship and communication.

It is perhaps easier, to begin with, to see what Winnicott means by the false self. Referring briefly to one of Bion's cases, I talked about his speculation that the mother was unable to contain his patient's fear of death. This notion of containment is in some respects similar to what Winnicott means when he talks about holding. Certainly one aspect of that is the ability to accept the baby's feelings and to be able to 'carry' them until the infant is ready and able to receive them back, to experience them for itself. Part of this process is the ability to give meaning to the baby's gestures – something which I see as a process of 'inducting' the baby into the currency of relationship, of enabling it to begin to make sense of its world. A 'false self' is formed if this relationship is reversed: if for some reason the parent is so anxious that the infant is expected to reassure the parent – give meaning to the parent's gesture.

Now I suspect that both processes are present in any parent-child relationship, and as ever it is a matter of degree. We could not survive without a false self, without making some adjustment to the requirements and needs of others; but too strong a false self can involve a cutting off from one's internal sources of life and a severing of the ability to form intimate and genuine connections to others. The power of the statement that I quoted at the beginning of this section comes from this: from the false self that we all possess to some degree or another, and the way that that self can act like a hard shell between us and our – and others' – spontaneity. Much work in object relations theory focuses on this area, and if the environment is seen as 'failing', then this is where it fails most importantly; Masud Khan (1974), for example, talks about an impingement on the infant's self, a repetitive impingement having a cumulative traumatic effect. In Marion Milner's work on art and artistic creation (especially 1969) she seems to be talking about access to some physical 'true self' perhaps beyond words, the earliest physical sensations of which form a large part of the baby's side of the mother–baby unit.

It is important, however, to hold on to the idea that we are not simple 'true' selves, that a false self is necessary. Occasional 'impingement' is, I suspect, inevitable, and Winnicott talks about how as the infant develops it becomes necessary for the parent to fail it, just as in psychoanalysis itself, the analyst's failure is sometimes necessary. In British psychoanalysis, the 'true self' – or perhaps we should call it the 'true-self relationship' – is treated with immense delicacy and subtlety on both a clinical and a theoretical level. This, I believe, is quite right, but I was struck by a comment in a recent interview with the French psychoanalyst Cornelius Castoriadis, which reminds us of the other side of the very difficult process of growing up; I am quoting at length because I believe this is particularly important:

> (Interviewer) This takes me to the question of the socialisation of the individual, what you have described as the break up of the psychic monad. You describe this in terms which are quite violent . . . the mother destroying the psychic monad and the fact that she has to. And these are terms which are quite different from the picture we often get from within the British psychoanalytic tradition . . .
> (Castoriadis) Violent does not mean that the mother beats the child. The psychical monad tends to close itself upon itself and to find pleasure in its own representations [and this leads on to omnipotence of thought in which] . . . the psyche would never want to recognise that it is a limited something among other limited somethings in the world, that pleasure is not permanently due . . . So when I speak about the violence of the social fabrication of the individual, I mean that this radically closed psychical monad has to be somehow or other broken. Whether you do it by the gentlest means or the cruellest means . . . Unless you break it you just leave the baby to go over to psychosis.
>
> (Castoriadis 1991: 492–3)

There are cultural and historical as well as theoretical reasons why Winnicott and Castoriadis should talk about the same process in such apparently different ways, but I am primarily concerned with why it seems to be the ideas of the British school – Winnicott and Bowlby in particular – that have tended to permeate the wider culture; many in the helping professions will have heard of these names – compared, for example, to the modern Kleinians, Bion and Meltzer. And in the United States, it has been the work of Kohut (1971), with distinct affinities to that of Winnicott, that has been important.

For both Kohut and Winnicott, the way in which this early omnipotence is dealt with – is disappointed – is vital. The difference is that they seem to understate what Castoriadis emphasises as the violence of the disappointment – the *normal* violence of the disappointment. In Winnicott's work this is very much bound up with his gentle evolutionism. It is as if the human infant has a 'natural' growth towards the abilities and adjustments required for normal social living, and the parent's responsibility is to allow this to develop as appropriate. There is a contrast here with Freud's emphasis which assumes the premature birth of the human infant and the replacement of genetic programming by a social 'programming' – always more difficult and less secure than its genetic equivalent. The capacity for social life might be an integral part of the child's development, but realising the capacity is not a natural occurrence.

If this is allowed for, then Winnicott's description of how it all happens seems to me fair enough. The original omnipotence of the infant is important. Perhaps it is useful to compare what he says with what, until a generation or so ago, seemed to be common sense about babies – and perhaps in some areas of our society is still regarded as common sense. The newborn baby is not quite yet human and it is the parents' job to make it human; if it is not human it is closer, perhaps, to an animal, and our job is to train it to be human, perhaps much as we might train a puppy. We have to train it into a human that can control itself and not be dependent on others, and not give in to its desires. Thus, it was common to regulate feeding to four-hourly intervals, whatever the apparent needs of the baby, to potty train from birth, and to limit shows of physical affection perhaps to a kiss at an appropriate time.

In what has been described as one of the most remarkable changes in the discipline of psychology over the last two or three decades, our knowledge of the newborn infant has changed dramatically (Chamberlain 1987; Verney with Kelly 1982), There is evidence that the process of learning starts prior to birth and that from the moment of birth the infant is an active participant in relationships with those around it. Relationships – relatedness to others – are there from the beginning, and Winnicott (and, one might add, most mothers) was aware of this well before conventional psychology. In this context, the established child-rearing practices could be seen as a form of deprivation of relatedness, the parent being encouraged not to respond, to give meaning to the baby's gestures; or perhaps more accurately, to give the meaning that their gestures, their communications, have no importance, except in so far as they satisfy the demands of the parents. We can see it as a strict enforcement of a false self from the beginning.

Winnicott (1964) always talks about 'good-enough mothering', to emphasise the point that if mothers react spontaneously to their baby's needs, they will not do so badly, and he is consciously *not* trying to produce an idea of intimidating perfection; yet despite this, many people feel intimidated by his work. This is, I think, because he was not simply describing what happens in most cases – he was also prescribing, writing in a context where conventional or 'recommended' child-rearing methods were very different from 'good-enough mothering'. He was quite aware of his own 'expert' status and I suspect that one of the ways in which he dealt with his position as one expert disagreeing with others was to refer to what he claimed mothers did anyway. I do not think he was wrong; my guess is that the vast majority of mothers do react to their babies in the way Winnicott says they do – even if they feel guilty and resentful when they read his work. But he was also prescribing, in a world where it is now impossible not to prescribe around these matters, and the context – the expertise he disagreed with – led him perhaps to overemphasise the 'naturalness' of the development from omnipotence, through the sense of a true self, to the ability to act as part of a wider society.

This movement is facilitated by the mother, as he puts it, 'implementing' the baby's omnipotence, responding to its gestures and satisfying its needs. At this stage the 'worst' thing that can happen to the child is what it experiences as the disintegration of its nascent and fragile ego; the phantasy of the baby, however, is that it is at the centre of the world, and beyond this, that it creates the world, creates its own satisfactions. When it cries for food, it is not aware of the mother dragging herself out of bed in the early hours, or rushing off to the kitchen to prepare a bottle. It feels the pangs of hunger and cries, and food arrives – it is as if by its feelings, by its crying, it creates the food that satisfies it. For Winnicott, maintaining this sense of creativity is essential; as the infant becomes physically and mentally more able, then it can begin to experience and contain the frustration of not having its desires met – the parent can begin to 'fail', and the infant comes to be more aware of the constrictions of the outside world. Yet it maintains a sense of what we might call the 'transitional area' – an area which is not entirely 'me' and which is not entirely 'the world out there', and in which we can maintain our everyday creativeness. If the baby's omnipotence is not implemented, we might expect the child to carry through its life its anxieties of disintegration and an inability to respond spontaneously and creatively to what happens to it.

So far, I have used the term 'self' as if its meaning is obvious, but perhaps this should be questioned. It is not just my trainee counsellors but students and friends who talk about finding or revealing their 'real selves'. The word has a certain power for those of us who live in the 'advanced' Western societies, sometimes, perhaps, not all that far away from the value that our ancestors might have placed on the 'soul', with one crucial difference. We can think of our 'real' or 'true' self as the most important thing about us. It often seems, when we speak of it, to be associated with feelings of fragility and preciousness, as if it were an immensely beautiful and valuable vase that could be easily broken or destroyed. We are careful who we show it to, and we guard it jealously. Sometimes, it would not be going too far to suggest that perhaps we feel it as a link with God in an increasingly Godless world.

But there is another side to its use as well, a side not present in the way we might talk about the soul. 'Self, self, self, that's all I hear from you!' We can be selfish, absorbed and interested only in ourselves, drawing all that goes on around us and everybody we know into its orbit – as if we still imagine ourselves omnipotent. For many modern psychoanalysts, the 'self' seems closer to the soul than the source of selfishness. For Winnicott, it is the experiencing person, whether the experience be conscious or unconscious, and the notion is intimately bound up with evolution. It is an inherited potential which we can realise through the process of maturation – in a sense, the process of becoming what we are. Christopher Bollas (1987, 1989, 1992), working within the same tradition, takes this idea further. He talks about each person having his or her own potential 'idiom', a way of being in relation to the world, which is originally rooted in our bodies, and engaging in a dialectic with the environment. He distinguishes as well between 'destiny', which is the realisation of our 'true-self' potentials, and 'fate', the simple compliance with environmental demands.

Now I think there is enough truth in this to enable one to recognise it in one's own experience. It is central to what the trainee counsellor was saying: she wanted to discover her destiny and break away from fate. There are moments in our lives when we feel imprisoned by the world around us, internally restricted and stifled, and we try to do something about it. What intrigues me about this experience is how we distinguish between those occasions when it is a desperate cry for a more authentic way of being in the world, and those occasions when it is a desperate refusal to acknowledge the reality of the world, internal and external, and an insistence that *somebody* continue to implement our omnipotence. When is it a matter of personal growth and when is it a tantrum?

In the long development from Freud's work, I think the increasing popularity of the idea of the 'self' has entailed a loss, or de-emphasis, of the other, selfish, side. The self, even though it is built up through the incorporation of 'parts' as we come to understand our bodies and ourselves and the world around us, always seems to remain, implicitly, or perhaps ideally, a 'unitary' thing, against which we can juxtapose the environment. If we compare this to Freud's model of the id, ego and super-ego, or the Kleinian world of varied internal objects, we can see the complexity that is lost, and most important the complexity that comes from making the environment, including the society in which we live, an integral part of ourselves. So our lives are not only a matter of a developing true self and the various environmental impingements and facilitations – although that, I think is clearly there – they are *also* an internal world of necessarily conflicting elements, amongst the most important of which are parts of the environment which we make our own. In all psychoanalytic theory there are elements of both, but the emphases are different.

THE MODERN SELF

I mentioned earlier the American psychoanalyst Heinz Kohut, certainly the most notable figure of American psychoanalysis over recent decades and the founder of what has become known as 'self-psychology'. In his work, too, we find the conflicting themes, the conception of the self as made up of different parts, the possibility of conflicts between parts, and the implicit, sometimes explicit, notion that perhaps the way it should be is integrated, whole, undivided. What is at issue here is two different notions of integration. They both involve laying claim to the many different aspects of ourselves, but one implies that when we have done this, we will be more aware of internal conflicts as and when they occur, of conflicting impulses, and of the parts of ourselves that we don't want; the other carries some implication of being at home in the world, of being 'whole' in a harmonious sense. Now one of the interesting aspects of Kohut's work is that he attempts to explain why it is, what has been happening in society at large, that these changes of emphasis and ideas in psychoanalytic theory have occurred. These ideas have in turn been taken up as a basis for a far-reaching critique of American society in particular and Western society in general.

Kohut's starting point is the sorts of transference that occur during therapy – transference being, roughly, the feelings that the patient brings to and focuses on the analyst. Generally these are regarded as being feelings, phantasies, ideas about the analyst that are transferred from previous significant relationships, usually those with parents. Kohut talks about two kinds of transference: patients who exhibit what he calls a 'grandiose self', which they expect the analyst to reflect and approve; and those who idealise the analyst as omnipotent. His argument is that in the first case, the parent had failed (using Winnicott's terms) to implement the infant's omnipotence, and in the second case the parent had declined to allow idealisation. Either produces a 'narcissistic trauma', the infant's sense of self is injured – although development by this stage has gone far enough to allow further, albeit injured, development. Again, what *should* happen is that the parent reflects the growing infant's grandiosity and allows himself or herself to be idealised as an omnipotent figure; as the child develops, so disappointment occurs slowly and in a manageable way. The child's narcissism becomes modified into more mature ambitions and ideals.

When this fails to happen, these parts of the personality are split off and either are repressed, losing contact with conscious awareness, or, more commonly, remain as undeveloped parts of the personality, leaving the mature self depressed through lack of contact with the other parts. From this point of view, narcissism has its own independent development, whereas for Freud it was a precondition of and became absorbed in 'object-love' – love for another person as another person. Kohut makes the useful observation that it is wrong to assume that the narcissistic personality is incapable of relating to other people; rather it relates to other people as if these others were parts of itself. It is not incapable of loving others, but it is incapable of loving another as another person. I suspect this is a common experience in relation to those with whom we fall in love, or our children – the pain of letting go of our children is perhaps the most difficult part of being a parent, and sometimes, I suspect, harder than it would be to let go of some physical part of ourselves. My use of 'we' in this book is a sort of rhetorical narcissism, assuming that everybody who reads it shares an automatic identity with me.

Central to Kohut's work is that the 'self', the 'centre' of the self, the 'nuclear' self, is something that is originally acquired from the outside, from the parent's recognition of the grandiose self, which enables the development of 'self-assertive goals and purposes', and from the idealised parent, which enables the development of central values in the super-ego. We are back with environmental failure again and with the 'correction' of environmental failure through therapy. It seems to me that the danger lurking in Kohut's work, rather more than in that of Winnicott, who was always aware of the paradoxes and contradictions of it all, is that therapy gives permission to the narcissism without disappointing it. I was struck by a passage in a review of a previous book of mine. The reviewer, a psychoanalytic scholar, wrote: 'A sidebar to reading this book gave me a clue as what has been bothering me about self-psychology. It would seem that too many of the analysands were left in the grandiose self stage . . . In order to be a competent fine artist, one must first learn to draw' (Fine 1991), It is learning to draw that is the difficult, disappointing part.

Kohut also notes that in the course of treatment, the narcissistic patients would experience moments of fragmentation, the experience of falling apart. He also points to the fact that this is a common theme in modern culture; he describes this as a development from 'Guilty Man' – whom Freud was talking about – in conflict with desires and instincts, to 'Tragic Man', struggling with despair and fragmentation. He attributes the change to a change in family structure. Freud was writing in a context where the family was close knit, spending much time together, doing many things together. The danger of this proximity was the overstimulation of desire, particularly, one may assume, Oedipal desire. The family has changed, over the last century, to a situation where the danger is understimulation: too little contact with working parents and little chance to observe parents at work and to idealise their competence.

Now there is certainly a truth in this but, I think, a limited truth. Modern societies are much too complex to allow us to see simple causal relationships of this sort: family structure and processes are themselves as much a symptom as a cause of changes over the last century, and the work of Christopher Lasch (1977, 1980, 1984), who has extended these ideas, suggests that, for example, the 'grandiose self' is in some way an attempted solution to the difficulties posed by social change, even if it is problematic for the individual. And if self-psychology in practice leaves its patients at the stage of the grandiose self, if its emphasis on this type of personality structure leaves it, despite itself, unable to take its patients through the process of disappointment, then it is itself part of the problem that it identifies. In the following chapters I want to look at these social changes. For the moment, however, I want to make a connection between these ideas and what I was arguing about earlier in relation to the idea of environmental failure and its avoidability.

When I think about my own clinical work, with patients and trainees, I can identify the sort of personality that Kohut talks about without too much trouble. There is an interesting imbalance, however: while I have had a few patients who fit this model, there have been many trainees for whom it seems appropriate. I wonder if there is not an affinity between the world of psychotherapy and counselling and the narcissism that Kohut identifies. All the components are there. In the idea of the therapist we can find both the idealised parent figure and the grandiose self. 'The Therapist' as an internal image is someone who will provide an infinite love and care. He or she will heal all wounds and prove the font of wisdom. The thought and feeling of becoming such a person can draw on a powerful sense of internal warmth and expansive, beneficent power. I am The Therapist: I will take all your troubles, all your pains and ease them away. I wonder how many steps there are between this and the sentiments of Lacan's interlocuter: 'I am a strong person and I can help people.'

The way in which a group of such trainees works is interesting and, for me, sometimes frightening and sometimes enraging. I talked earlier about the tendency to project our own injuries into other people and try to 'cure' them there. This produces a reluctance to look at ourselves, to experience the scale of our own internal damage. A strong tendency in such groups is to turn one or several members into honorary patients and therapise their difficulties away. When this happens, I feel a strong and unspoken pressure on me to endorse what they are doing, and often, in fact, to praise – as if I were watching my children put on a play. If I join in the flow of therapising, then there is no problem; and if I remain silent, there is often no problem. Both of these courses of action enable the group to maintain a phantasy of myself and each other as part of themselves. They are trying to ease away moderate manifestations of their own pains in each other, and the experience of me will be that I am providing a benign recognition of what they are doing.

Two events may disrupt this process. If I make an interpretation of what is going on, perhaps in terms of describing the process, it is 'not heard'; often it seems as if I have not spoken at all, a rather eerie experience in a roomful of people, or I am attacked, often with immense rage and damnation. My experience of such an attack, and, to a lesser extent, of not being heard, is of being 'possessed' by the group, and of having no independent voice, no space in which to differentiate myself from what is going on. It is perhaps not so different a feeling to that of growing children in relation to their parents, but it is reversed. I am the parent figure – a much-needed parent figure – who cannot yet be allowed a separate existence. I am only an extension of the selves in the group, just as they are extensions of each other.

The second event is that a group member breaks the collusion, either by pointing to or expressing some of the pain that the group is denying, or by revealing something in himself or herself that might possibly question the strong, healing self-image. In the first case, there is likely to be a determined scapegoating, not dissimilar in force to the attack on myself for doing the same thing. I have already described an example of the second, a sort of moral condemnation and exclusion, of the man who acknowledged that he sometimes found his children a burden.

Now it seems to me that the desire to create a 'non-failing environment', to 'encourage' parents to stay in hospital with their children, or to do other things that we might think 'good for them' is in part the perception of these other people as part of ourselves. In this aspect, the desire to help, to do good, can involve not an understanding of the other person as a separate person, different from ourselves and with aspects that we can appreciate and learn

from, but an attempt to deploy the other person as part of
ourselves, in order to protect ourselves. There is something, I will
argue, about our society which draws on this tendency and which,
in its social implications, I see as totalitarian.

Chapter 5

The organisation of social life

WHAT IS SOCIETY?

In this chapter, and the two that follow, I want to look at social and cultural changes which have generated a world in which disappointment is denied, in which we seem to be turning increasingly to emotional management by experts, and which seems to produce personalities which not only deny disappointment but seek its opposite.

I am going to indulge myself in the sort of sociology of which I disapprove: vast general statements about what is happening to the modern world. So I will start with some reservations. Most of the processes I will discuss are only strands taken from our contemporary world, strands which at the moment seem to have some prominence in certain areas of social life, some of which *might* have a wider significance. Just as my 'we' does not refer to everybody, so what I have to say about contemporary society does not claim to be a complete picture. I am talking primarily about British and North American, and then Western European society, and some of these social processes might be important elsewhere; generally, I am talking about the social processes to which my 'we' are subjected.

Much of what I have to say concerns an increasingly rapid rate of social change and its effects on the way we experience ourselves. I like to think of this through the metaphor of a kaleidoscope. As we shake the kaleidoscope, we can see constantly changing patterns or changing cultures; it is as if the modern world is in a constant state of agitation and the patterns of culture seem to rearrange themselves with remarkable speed. At least on the surface; for example, the student culture when I took my first degree in the late 1960s is very different from the culture of my students today, and there are several intervening cultures in between.

Now the patterns in a kaleidoscope, however different, are always made from the same pieces of coloured glass (or more probably, these days, plastic), so there are always limitations on the possible patterns – if there are no green pieces of glass or round shapes, then the pattern will never include that colour or shape; on the other hand it might always include red triangles. If we are clever enough, we might be able to open the kaleidoscope and put some of our own colours or shapes inside. There are similar limitations on a culture – the ideas, feelings, ambitions, possi-bilities and people that make up our daily lives are usually limited, but can be combined in many ways. And periodically new elements may enter, old ones change.

But a kaleidoscope also has a structure; a round cardboard tube, for example, with a bottom made out of a material that will allow some light through and a top with a small hole in it. This sets much firmer limits on what we can do with it and see through it. A culture is always bounded by a social structure – a set of institutions and relationships which sets limits on what might be done, said and thought, what changes can be brought about. Whatever the changes in student culture over the past twenty-five years, it has existed within, with some modifications, the same set of buildings; there have always been first-, second-, and third-year students, postgraduates, teachers, administrators, and vice-chancellors, and classes and lectures following more or less the same format in the same rooms. Even if the personnel change, the structure in which it happens remains largely the same.

It is important to make a distinction at this stage between the society in one's head and the society outside one's head. At a guess, I would say it was not possible to be alive in our world without carrying around in our heads some idea of society. It might amount to no more than a vague and amorphous 'they'; it might, for a sociologist, for example, be a much more complex idea; indeed one that could only be contained in a number of books and essays. And we can relate to that idea, that 'internal object', in a number of very different ways. The society in our heads might be a persecutory figure, the 'they' who are always out to get you, watching your every move, always ready to take something away, to punish for no good reason. It might be a potential source of good, able to provide for everybody, get rid of poverty, ensure that everyone has a decent place to live and a fair chance in life; it might be a source of good ready to be plundered, something from which one should take everything that can be got whenever the opportunity arises. It might be something very close or very distant, something which can move around us, a protective container, a prison, a liberator; a source of authority that will guard the good and punish the evil, or an irrational, punitive and arbitrary authority. Perhaps for most of us, it is all these things at one time or another.

The society outside our heads is different. It is complex, very highly structured, full of aspects we don't know about as well as those that we do. The important thing about it is that it can be *known*, at least in principle. Some people know more about it than others, but even for those who know a great deal about it, this knowledge of external reality co-exists with the society in our heads, and is sometimes coloured by it. Our knowledge of society is always presented with a degree of imaginary colouring, but that does not mean that it is not knowledge. And sometimes our knowledge of the external society can challenge the internal society, something which can be a very painful process. If our internal society is a guardian of the good and true, and a punisher of the bad and false, systematic miscarriages of justice, such as those that have recently been established in Britain in relation to IRA terrorism in the 1970s, can provide not just external problems, but internal distress. We might find our internal society changes – comes closer to our new knowledge – or we might protect it: they were probably guilty anyway, and letting them go just encourages terrorism.

The important thing about the society outside our heads is that while it provides us with all sorts of opportunities, it must also provide us with disappointments. It does so in various and interesting ways which are important because they are beyond our control. There are many ways in which I can fail to get what I want because of something in myself: I do not work hard enough, I set about things the wrong way and so on. But other things happen to us by means of the outside world which can be disappointing through no inadequacy of our own. If I am black it is more difficult to find a job than if I am white, whatever my skill or ability; if I am a woman, then it is more difficult to get some jobs and more difficult to achieve promotion than if I am a man.

Changes in society can change my life without my having any understanding of how those changes come about. I might be made redundant, have to change career in mid-life; my house might suddenly lose a large proportion of its value; interest rate increases might force me to move home; inflation might eat away at hard-earned savings. There are any number of examples; sometimes these are positive, but the ones we tend to be most aware of are negative. The unseen is important here. We are only ever aware of the things around us, the people we know and work with, the streets we walk every day. We know we have local authorities and governments, churches and schools, but the sort of social change I am talking about is not brought about by any of these. Even those who have a knowledge of society do not know in any final, coherent way why a lot of things happen.

What I am concerned with here is what we *know* about the external society, the changes that it is undergoing and its effects on our ways of life, our culture, and the way in which we *experience* this society inside our heads. The two do not necessarily coincide; we might, for example, experience an increasingly abstract, centralised control over our lives as an increase in our freedom, our ability to become whatever we want to be. This in fact is one of my main arguments and I want to take it further: in the space between our experience and the reality, much modern psychotherapy, including the 'optimistic' aspects of psycho-analysis, serve to hide the reality and reinforce the internal experience of the world. We develop an illusion of our power over ourselves and find the normal reality of disappointment harder and harder to countenance.

It is not easy to separate what we know of society and our internal experience of society. Indeed there are some sociologists who would claim that it is not possible to know society at all, that we can only know the various things that people think and say about society – in effect, it is all in the head. Something that constantly strikes me is what I can only call a similarity between the sorts of problem that my patients talk about in trying to make sense of their individual lives and the sorts of issue that sociologists debate in trying to make sense of society. One of the arguments in sociology, for example, is how far the modern world is different from the traditional world, and whether that difference is a good or bad thing. Has the modern world grown out of the traditional world in some coherent way, or is it a radical transformation of the sort of society that once existed? My patients sometimes come to me wanting to make a radical break, wanting to get away from their childhoods, and part of the disappointment of psychotherapy is the realisation that it is not possible, that we are what we have become. We cannot retrospectively change our parents and our childhood experiences, although we might be able to modify their meaning. Others come feeling that there has been a radical change: before the accident, before the onset of depression, before the 'breakdown', their lives had been fine. Now they cannot recognise themselves, do not like what they are. Often they want to go back, and there is the same disappointment that this new and changed period of their lives cannot be erased; but there is, if they are lucky, a re-establishing of contact with what they had been, although it is usually discovered that the past was not as lovely as it was imagined to be.

Some sociologists too see the change that has produced the modern world as a change for the worse and look back to some past golden age or situation; others, it seems, see it simply as a radical change which in many ways is for the better, and they spend a lot of time insisting on its newness. It is as if the patient who wishes for a dramatic change has achieved it, and is furiously denying any connection with the past. My own view is the rather tedious one that there are continuities and discontinuities, changes and the absence of changes, much as we can see in our realistic perceptions of our own lives. And as in our own lives, there are contradictory changes.

'MODERNITY': EVOLUTION TO COMPLEXITY

One view, which has very few takers amongst sociologists today, is that we can trace social development from the simple to the complex. The more popular view is that history is full of breaks and reversals – that it cannot be seen as a more-or-less steady evolution. Again, a more mundane compromise is that there are certain strands in social development which can usefully be seen in evolutionary terms, or at least that the conception of evolution has a certain metaphorical value, and points to something that has really happened. The basic image is that of a cell dividing, the two parts joining together and then dividing into four and so on. The basic 'cell' in society is the kinship system, which in 'simple' societies fulfilled all the functions which in our society are fulfilled by specialised institutions. Each time a new specialised institution appears it then has to be reintegrated into the society as a whole, and this occurs through a change in the society's value system to a new, more universal, level.

What this gives us is a picture of a society steadily increasing in complexity, held together by shared values which become more universal – effectively more abstract – as development takes place. Thus in most Western societies we can find values of democracy (one person one vote, freedom of speech, etc.) which cover everybody in that society irrespective of their personal qualities. Indeed the personal qualities which we perhaps might think of as being most important – our personality, our feelings – are confined to their own specialist institution, the modern family. Whereas the family might once have been responsible for creating – bringing up – what we might call a whole citizen, it is now primarily responsible for the vital period of early socialisation, up until the age of four or five, when the state begins to take over through the education system. As this period of early socialisation becomes more specialised, so it too becomes a form of professional activity. It is surrounded by the 'proper' professions: doctors, nurses, midwives, health visitors, social workers, psychologists, etc., and what we might call the 'unofficial' professions, amorphous groups of experts such as the National Childbirth Trust. Parents themselves become a sort of amateur professional, there to be educated into what to do, how to behave, as different groups vie for there attention. When Talcott Parsons (1951, 1971; Parsons and Bales 1956), the sociologist who has portrayed this whole approach most thoroughly, talks about the modern role of parents, he uses as his model the role of the psychotherapist, just as psychotherapists often use the parenting role as a model for what they do. One interesting feature of the current period, as established professions such as doctors seem to be coming under attack and arguments are heard for taking, for example, childbirth out of the hands of professionals, is that the attacks come from 'unofficial' professionals and experts. It often seems as if there is no way out of this particular circle: all we can do is choose between experts, or become experts. What might be disappearing is the idea of bringing up children as a normal part of life, with all its messiness and contradictions, pleasures, satisfactions *and* deprivations.

I use the word 'might' deliberately. I think that this way of looking at the process is likely to be neither completely right nor completely wrong, but it is happening to a degree and much psychoanalytic work can be seen as part of it. Even if we don't take this view of social evolution seriously, there is behind it what was, until recently, a fairly familiar assumption: that our society is, perhaps slowly and unsteadily, getting better, that we are discovering the causes of misery and eliminating them.

THE SPECIALISED FAMILY

There is a link here with what Kohut claims to be happening in the modern family, the distancing of family members from each other. This has been taken up by Christopher Lasch (1977, 1980) into an intriguing criticism of modern society. There is at least a logic in using parenting as a model for psychotherapy – it is not the same thing, but what goes on in psychotherapy is clearly related to what goes on, or went on, in the period of early parenting. But to take psychotherapy as a model for parenting is a different matter. Lasch's argument seems to me to imply that there is a contradiction in the role assigned to the modern family. The industrial revolution meant the beginnings of a separation of home and and work, one that has continued to the present day. The external world of work has become steadily more impersonal whilst the home and the family have become the place for feeling, for strong feelings of love and hatred; but as the family has become more specialised, so the way we view the ideal of family relationships is less directly emotional; if we see the parent as the psychotherapist, then the parental role is not one of expressing direct emotion at all. I was struck recently when watching a British television chat show (*Wogan*) on which Robin Skynner (a British group and family therapist) and the comedian John Cleese appeared. They collaborated on a popular book, *Families and How to Survive Them* (1983), and had presented a series of radio programmes around the same theme. Robin Skynner commented that perhaps the model for an ideal family was the Cosby family from the television series; they were able to handle conflict and hostility through teasing, joking, etc. Wogan commented, without receiving any reply, that he found such a family insipid or anodyne.

I find I'm in complete agreement with Wogan. The model being held up is one in which the direct expression of difficult family feelings is inhibited or sublimated, although there is expression. I will talk later about why I think this might be an 'unhealthy' model; for the moment I simply want to point out that it seems to be one ideal model family current in our society, mainly amongst what might be called the 'liberal middle classes'.

As the family's early socialisation function has become more specialised, so the later functions become marginalised. School and friends take on a greater importance – and I suspect that any parent is aware of the conflicts that can and do arise. The strength of the peer group (as well as of the advertising industry) is there in the mass crazes for teenage mutant turtles and computer games. There comes a point, which I think is now noticeable each half-generation, when it is apparent that parents have to learn from their children – whether it be new information or new ways of thinking in mathematics. My own son was six when he showed me how to work with the graphics function on my computer.

As our children get older, the culture itself changes and what we ourselves have learnt about how to live – not to mention what we do – becomes inappropriate. In areas of morality and practical skills, parents seem to have less and less to hand on to their children. This has been accompanied by an increasingly long period of adolescence, the period between the point where our children mature physically and become able biologically to set up their own families, and the point where they have matured socially, completed their education and found jobs, become financially and psychologically able to move away. In emotional terms, I suspect that this period often lasts on into the thirties. But from school age on, the central focus is on the role of the outside, 'proper' professional teachers, child-guidance clinics, adolescent units, student counsellors, etc. There is less of an attempt to professionalise parents.

THE MANAGEMENT OF EMOTIONS

In a recent issue of the *Guardian* (31 October 1992) Susie Orbach, a psychoanalytic therapist, writes 'We are as a culture terrified of emotions. We find them messy, arbitrary and difficult.' It might be more true to say that our culture is obsessed with emotions, from soap operas through chat shows to an apparently endless series of self-help books dealing with anxiety, stress, assertiveness and relationships. There are regular articles in the press, including those written by Orbach and her colleagues in the

Guardian. They are concerned with the management of emotions and the attempt to make emotions 'safe'. The truth is that emotions *are* often terrifying.

Sociology as a discipline is as much a symptom of the society it studies as it is a way of producing knowledge, and it is significant that the last decade has seen the establishment of a 'sociology of the emotions'. The classic work is a study of air hostesses (Hochschild 1983), of emotion management and self-presentation. There are many professions where we have to package and sell ourselves and which require the display of certain types of emotion, and these include, it often seems, psychotherapy and counselling. The leading American humanist psychotherapist Carl Rogers (1951) places great emphasis on qualities such as empathy and unconditional regard and acceptance of the client; it is refreshing to find in psychoanalytic literature regular references to the importance of hatred in counter-transference and therapists remaining puzzled over long periods. In Rogers's work especially, I can sense The Great Therapist lurking behind every corner.

More recently there have been attempts to explain why emotions and emotional control should be the centre of attention. In an interesting paper, the sociologist Cas Wouters (1991) has argued that a cultural change towards valuing equality has, over recent decades, involved a different attitude towards emotions and emotional life. He illustrates this by referring to an interview with a pilot during the Gulf War, in which the pilot was quite happy to acknowledge fear. Wouters points out that during the Second World War such an acknowledgement would have been impossible; then a combination of authority and peer pressure was aimed at suppressing the experience of fear. The expression of emotion, in fact, seems to be intimately linked with hierarchy; the more hierarchical a social structure, the more important it seems to be to suppress the expression of emotion, in action and in talk, and in fact the absence of such expression was taken, certainly during my childhood and young adulthood, as a mark of social superiority.

On the face of it, the move towards egalitarianism and more freedom in expressing emotions is a 'good thing'. However, nothing is ever simply a good thing. Wouters argues that what is now socially impermissible is the direct expression of social superiority. In fact we seem to be seeing the deliberate development of a language geared to deny inequality, deny social superiority, whether of men over women, whites over blacks, the healthy over the unhealthy or whatever, although the real inequalities seem to remain or even grow. Wouters argues that in such a situation the management of emotions, the possibility of admitting but not acting upon feelings (as for the modern fighter pilot), has become a mark of status; the ability to admit to emotions without necessarily acting on them he calls 'authenticity'. Emotion management, then, becomes a matter of status competition. A further piece of evidence for this, perhaps, is the way that emotionality and the ability to talk about feelings, in my childhood and now, are often regarded as a feminine quality, but in my childhood it was considered a mark of inferiority whereas now it is often claimed to be one of superiority.

This process can be placed in a rather broader historical context than that of the last decades. The sociologist Anthony Giddens (1990, 1991, 1992), for example, sees it as a consequence of what is sometimes called 'modernity', a long process in which relationships are no longer 'guaranteed' by tradition or by the simple fact of there being a blood relationship or belonging to the same social group, by notions of honour, obligation and duty. Now, relationships have to be based on the satisfactions they offer here and now: sexual attraction, emotional intimacy and authenticity have become central, and again the management of emotions comes to the fore. Once more I repeat my reservation: this might not be happening everywhere and to everybody in our society, but it is happening to many; its roots can be traced back over a number of centuries, and at the moment, the process seems to be speeding up. Psychoanalysis is implicated in this in a fundamental way: the emphasis on symbolisation carries at its centre the notion that if feelings can be expressed, they can be better handled, better managed. This is true, but my point is that if we take from psychoanalysis simply an idea that it is good to put feelings into words, then we become blind to the effect of these cultural changes in one of several ways.

For example, in the first place Kohut's work on the narcissistic patient shows that we can find both a tendency to 'act out' powerful feelings and an ability to stay in analysis for a very long time, without undergoing any change. In other words, such a person can and does talk about feelings until the cows come home. But he or she also acts on emotions and thus fails to manage them. There are psychological reasons which can explain the inability, but it seems to me that they are complemented by a sociological reason: being in analysis, intellectual speculation and talking about feelings are signs of status. It is possible to develop and modify Wouters's argument. In some areas of emotional life, experiencing emotions without acting them out is socially approved – as in the fighter pilot example. In others, however, the tendency is towards both acting them out *and* talking – this is particularly true where sexuality is concerned. In the early 1970s, I once heard a student commune described as 'one of those places where everybody goes to bed with everybody else and then spends the rest the time talking about it'. And now, it seems, writing about it, if we take the many lifestyle magazines, daily papers – broadsheet and tabloid – and books on sexual etiquette into account.

The two can be seen to come together in a case reported recently by a Brazilian psychoanalyst, trained in Britain (Figueira 1991), In Britain, psychoanalysis is still a minority culture – it is not normal for people of a certain class and status to be in analysis. In the city where he returned to work, however, it was normal. The patient in question had had other analysts and came to him for the status reason that he had been trained in Britain, the home of psychoanalysis. She talked about herself in psychoanalytic terms and seemed often to want to implicate or to gain the approval of the analyst, particularly when it came to her sexual activities, and it took a long time before she began to talk about herself in other ways.

I have become aware of another type of patient: a person not usually in danger of 'acting out' but for much of the time someone who seems to have few or no strong feelings. All the defence mechanisms with which psychoanalysis has made us familiar are employed: denial, rationalisation (often at length), splitting, projection and so on. By and large, such people seem to be managing quite well in their everyday lives – not only are they reasonably successful in their jobs, but they are also able to maintain long-term relationships and cope with crises in a more-or-less adequate way. The reason they present themselves for therapy or counselling seems to be that they feel they ought to be 'more in touch with their feelings', perhaps at the suggestion of a partner. In therapy, they become more fluent in the language of feelings and to a degree achieve what they come for, but I always feel that it is learning the language that is most important when they decide to leave. Some feelings remain denied altogether: it is as if there are fashions in emotions and such people come to talk about the fashionable ones. At the moment, vulnerability and fear seem 'in' for men, anger 'in' for women.

The status dimension of being able to talk about feelings often seems to carry with it an idea that talking can resolve or remove feelings – especially those that may be unfashionable. I think this is implicit in my earlier quotation from Orbach. I have sometimes heard people condemned for being angry or jealous *even though* they have had years of therapy – when in fact it is their years of therapy which have enabled them to feel angry or jealous; my guess is that it is permissible for the fighter pilot to acknowledge fear verbally, but if he were visibly trembling and stuttering, the status aspect would be lost.

If we return to the longer-term processes of modernity that Anthony Giddens described, the way in which our relationships become centred on sexual attraction, emotional intimacy and authenticity, we can see also the reasons why ideas about the 'true self' appear in psychoanalysis and move to the fore, and the way in which these ideas come to be taken in the wider society into what might be called 'ideologies' of counselling and therapy.

PROCESSES TOWARDS THE ORGANISATION OF EVERYDAY LIFE

What I have described so far has to do with what might be called the professionalisation of everyday relationships – something which to begin with I described as a long-term evolutionary process. Contemporary sociologists offer different ways of looking at this, all of which are useful. Anthony Giddens points to the real increase in state power, through in particular an increased capacity for surveillance, brought about by the development of increasingly complex computer networks; this capacity makes totalitarianism a permanent possibility for modern society. Others argue that the state is becoming less important, squeezed, as it were, between the growth of multinational companies and that of local organisations. I suspect that both processes are occurring on different levels, but whether that is the case or not, what is clear is another process that Giddens points to: the increasing dominance of abstract systems and the standardisation of experience throughout the modern world. Who can tell what city-centre shopping precinct they are standing in if they don't know already, and who knows the elaborate structure of ownership and control that lies behind the shop fronts they are looking at? These processes undermine our sense of dependency on others, whether psychological, social or economic. There is the system, myself and a floating population of others.

We are aware of the immensity of the risks of being in such a huge system, in effect a system of global interconnections; if the system is global, then the disasters – ecological, military and economic – can be global too. Yet we have to trust the system, if for no other reason than that there is no alternative; but such trust cannot be as satisfactory as the trust of personal relationships, and to seek that satisfaction we are pushed more and more into the world of intimacy, the world of sexuality and emotions.

The German radical social philosopher, Jürgen Habermas, (1984, 1987, 1989, 1990a) argues too that it is now impossible to conceive of changing the elaborate political and economic system in which we live. Accepting this is perhaps the major disappointment with which the left has to come to terms at the moment. The main task for the left, he argues, is the attempt to modify and control the most dangerous aspects of the system. Most important amongst these is the way in which the system itself tends to 'eat' into our personal lives. The 'system' works according to what he calls a 'functional rationality': the various parts are undergoing constant modification to 'fit' into each other and maintain their existence in a mutually supporting way – the various economic and political changes we are witnessing at present are one of the results of this process. This entails the state, directly or indirectly, intervening in personal relationships to control them in such a way as to facilitate the 'functional rationality' of the system. This it does through policies of economic welfare and social services: training programmes become linked to social security and unemployment benefit; in Britain there is the attempt to create a significant low-wage sector in the economy; family relationships, the responsibilities of members of the family to each other and to the state, become increasingly delimited by legislation. What this does, he argues, is eat into the 'substantive rationality' of interpersonal relationships, our ability to communicate with, understand, and arrive at our own agreements with those around us. Welfare services are of course an important part of this. Indeed, it is now customary to see the history of modern society in terms of increasingly elaborate systems of control, from the need, during the early industrial period, to segregate and incarcerate those who did not fit easily into the new industrial labour force, through to the more sophisticated – on some levels – notions on community care.

The French philosopher-historian Michel Foucault (1967, 1977, 1984) has contributed much to understanding this process. The last century in particular has seen the growth of professional groups whose *raison d'être* is to 'know' increasingly intimate areas of human life: sexuality and sexual desire, feelings, the psyche – the soul – itself. The growth of this knowledge is also the exercise of power over people to a degree that was not exercised before – although the church went some way towards it through confession. Foucault's work argues that the exercise of this sort of power is not simply the function of the state – in fact we do better to envisage a multitude of power centres, with no one Centre, at which this knowledge is exercised.

Seen in this light, the psychoanalyst in private practice, with no contact with the health service, social work, etc., is as much a centre of power as any other. Giddens points out that in a situation where surveillance is so highly developed, keeping part of oneself back is part of the struggle, and this is as true in the psychoanalytic consulting room as elsewhere – I suspect the statement 'It's none of your business', whether said implicitly or explicitly, is a promising sign. Radical critics of psychoanalysis and psychotherapy tend to use this sort of argument to arrive at a blanket condemnation of the whole enterprise, but I will be arguing later that this is too easy – the existence of blanket condemnations is a symptom of what they criticise, part of a power struggle between professions. The process I am describing is much more ambiguous and problematic than they allow for, a mixture of good and bad.

I want briefly to try to sum up these processes which come to us, as it were, from above. There is, first of all, an increasing differentiation of institutions, and an increasing specialisation, in which the family – the place where the heart and the hurt are – is assigned the world of the emotions, and the raising of children itself becomes a sort of professional work. This coincides with centralised and amorphous systems of surveillance and control, in a world in which large-scale systems increasingly produce a need for intimacy. All of these focus us on gaining knowledge of, managing and controlling intimacy, feelings and personal relationships; and involve many of us spending our working lives engaged in such activities. Giddens talks about psychotherapy itself as an abstract system governing ways of life in contemporary society.

MODERNITY AND 'POSTMODERNITY'

Two contradictory themes can be found interwoven in much late nineteenth- and twentieth-century sociology. One points towards the increased centralisation and/or the increased organisation of economic, political and social power. The other, which has become more prominent over recent years, has pointed to the fragmentation of social life, seeing it often as a process of increasing freedom. In the latter tradition a number of theories of 'postmodernity' have appeared, claiming that we have entered a new historical period which has seen the end of the processes to centralisation and organisation, if indeed they were ever there in the way that was once thought. A dramatic presentation of the changes can be found on the cover of a recent book on the subject (Crook *et al.* 1992):

> The collapse of culture into a collection of packaged styles; the erosion of the state in the face of the development of both multinational and local organisations; the fragmentation and multiplication of familiar class and gender categories of modernity; a decline in allegiance to traditional political parties and the emergence of new social movements emphasising nonmaterial values; the development of flexible manufacturing systems which reprofessionalise labour and reduce the scale of bureaucracies; a decreasing confidence in the capacity of science to solve human problems, which delegitimates it and raises the possibility of its absorption into technology.

Now there is no doubt that these changes are happening, although whether they are as all-embracing as claimed is another matter; it is possible to see them as primarily affecting those whom Scott Lash (1990) identifies as the 'bearers of postmodernism', those of the middle classes involved in the arts, the media, the service industries, and other forms of self-packaging. What interests me, however, is the way that the two processes – increasing organisation/centralisation of social life and fragmentation – can be seen not as alternative but as complementary processes, like the two sides of the same coin.

Returning to my kaleidoscope analogy: if 'postmodernism' is a radically new form of society, we are left with the ever-changing patterns and with the structure that contains them, and I am suggesting that though the patterns are changing more rapidly the structure is more highly organised and complex than before; it is perhaps more difficult to see, and therefore we are left with the impression that there are only rapidly changing patterns. If we employ the conception of evolution that I discussed earlier, the levels of integration of the many social systems have become more and more abstract and general and the more practical limitations on our day-to-day lives seem to have been removed. We no longer have our families watching our every move, but there are a number of invisible limitations on what we do.

In our everyday lives, we are simply not aware of the structures of ownership and control of industry and finance capital, of the ways in which decisions are made, of underlying tendencies in the markets which push people into these decisions; we cannot see any underlying pattern. If, however, we give up the idea of such a social structure existing out there somewhere, it is like letting go of a proffered lifebelt in a strong-flowing river, leaving us only to be carried along with the current. The same is true in our personal lives: we need to try to hold on to some idea of ourselves as maintaining some consistency beneath the multitude of things that we do, that happen to us, that we experience, or our world will feel as if it is collapsing.

In fact many of the processes that are identified as postmodern have been around for some time. Perhaps the most notable 'new' development over the last three decades is that identified by David Harvey (1989) as a change to 'flexible accumulation'. Very crudely, the argument is that the established forms of large-scale production came under threat from the sixties onwards from a number of sources. One was increased competition from Third-World countries where labour was cheaper; another, with the growth of computer technology, was the increased flexibility of money capital – huge sums can now be moved around the world at short notice to where the gain is greatest. Large-scale production with strong trade unions and elaborate state control could no longer be maintained. The nature of the workforce has changed accordingly: the numbers engaged in full-time, semi-permanent jobs, the 'core' as it were, have declined; there have been increases, on the other hand, in self-employment, part-time work, short-term contracts, government-sponsored training schemes that take people out of the job market for short periods, sub-contracting, temporary workers and so on.

I particularly like this explanation because it contains the idea of a possibly global system, abstract and distant from everyday life, which none the less affects our everyday lives – as the global system becomes more abstract and organised, so our everyday lives become more problematic and fragmented. Although people are aware of the 'system' of control and it can still provide a focus for political action, it seems the process of fragmentation is often much closer to consciousness.

One area where we can see these contradictory processes coming together is in our sense of time and space. Anthony Giddens makes much of the development of standardised time and space; whereas in traditional societies, both were intimately connected with our social lives – when and where we were would be defined by who we were with and what we were doing – they are now measured in abstract quantities that are the same everywhere: an hour or a kilometre is the same in the middle of London or the middle of the Brazilian jungle. We can package up both into bundles and buy and sell them. What goes on in a particular space is determined by social forces that have their location thousands of miles away or no clear location at all: 'where exactly *is* the economic crisis which threatens my job?' – the only answer is everywhere and nowhere. In the Western world, one space is becoming much like any other: there is not much difference between the shopping precinct in Inverness, Colchester, Croydon or Brighton or any other town in Europe or maybe now even America. There is little left to give a place any specific identity, although we might try all the time to find something to make *our* place stand out – but what we find is not some organic feature of our social life but an image, often a historical and geographical pastiche. Giddens talks about this as 'disembedding' and it creates the necessity for the emotional work of 're-embedding', of establishing trust in the individual representatives of large organisations, and the emotional work of intimacy in finding attachments for ourselves in day-to-day life.

Whereas a century ago, it seemed to make sense to understand and feel one's identity to be bound up with the particular place where one was born and/or lived, it now makes little sense; I spend most of my life in and around Colchester, but for all the difference it makes to my sense of my self, it could be Sevenoaks or Norwich or Inverness. It seems to be the case that there is now no clear source in our social life that provides us with an identity for the self, although we frequently try to find one – in belonging, perhaps, to a particular nation, or a particular sex, or a particular colour or race.

On the other hand, it is becoming increasingly clear, and increasingly recognised, that we live in a number of different times; there is the time that belongs to the development of our bodies, the time that belongs to our social transactions, the time of social change around us, which I have just been talking about, and internal times: the time it takes us to adjust psychologically to events in our lives, to internalise, introject what happens to us. This process has its own time, and it seems to me this does not match the pace of my external life, and the inner rhythm is encroached upon, distorted by my adjustments to the pace of the outer rhythms.

Now it is possible to imagine a world, which I doubt ever existed in any perfect form, in which there is a coherence between our social activities, the cycles of nature, and the life cycle, when to everything there was a season. With the advent of modernity, and at ever-increasing pace over recent decades, this coherence is increasingly disrupted. We seem all but to have lost contact with natural cycles, and attempts to regain contact often seem forced and rather precious. Childhood, adulthood and physical maturity seem to have a flexible relationship; children act a sexual maturity before physical maturity, but the advent of physical maturity does not mean the end of childhood, let alone the end of social dependence on the family of origin, which might still go on for a period longer than childhood itself. This too means that being a person, experiencing oneself as having an identity, is more difficult. In the next chapter I will pursue the theme of fragmentation and the way it affects our self-perception.

Chapter 6

The fragmentation of everyday life

In the previous chapter, I suggested that there were large-scale, systematic social changes at work which led to and involved the notion that our emotional life could be managed and organised – an idea of which I am highly sceptical. I also suggested that at another, more immediate level, there seemed to be a process of fragmentation at work, and I tried to relate both processes as different sides of the same coin. Now I want to look more closely at the process of fragmentation and argue that this too can generate phantasies of organisation and control of the personality – phantasies (or fantasies) which are bound to be disappointed. Over recent decades, such phantasies have perhaps been the major subjective consequence of social change, but I want to argue here that other subjective consequences are emerging – among them the appearance of the phantasy of the all-powerful self, which I will look at more closely in the next chapter.

EXTERNAL AND INTERNAL FRAGMENTATION

I will begin with simply describing my normal working day. It begins with my wife and whatever children or stepchildren happen to be around. My early mornings are utilitarian – the main aim is to pull myself out of bed, put myself into a reasonably hygienic state and get some food inside. Rows are likely as everyone is tense. I travel a round distance of some thirty miles each day – possibly further than my ancestor of a couple of centuries or even a century ago might have travelled in a lifetime. In the space of two weeks, I will have travelled more distance than the longest journey my mother (now in her seventies) has ever undertaken. During that journey, I might have contact with neighbours, ticket collectors, fellow travellers, a schoolteacher, a nursery nurse, a shopkeeper, a taxi driver and so on. The chances are that I will speak to several people I have never before spoken to (and even if I have I will be unlikely to remember them) and will never speak to again. During the day I might go into several shops and interact with strangers, I might have casual and polite conversations with unknown people in corridors or at bus stops. I will also lecture a group of students and meet some of them in classes; I will have a slightly more intimate relationship with the latter than I do with the former; some of the students in my classes will also be my personal tutees, and I will know them to a greater – but rarely considerable – degree of intimacy.

During the day I will interact with colleagues, some of whom will be friends, some of whom I might be meeting for the first or second time; if it is a day on which I work as a therapist, I will be spending time with a group of people whom I might know very well, but who will know very little about me. In the evening, which might only be an hour or two, depending on the demands of my work and my wife's work, I will again be a member of a family, with luck more intimately so than in the utilitarian rush of the morning. Or, if the evening is a longer one, I might spend time with a friend or friends with whom I do not work; or I might spend it working – marking essays, writing, etc. On some days I make love to my wife; other days seem bereft of any sexual activity.

The processes I will discuss here go on outside of us, in the world *and* inside our heads in our experience of ourselves. The broader context of this process of fragmentation has to do with the emergence of individuals in the modern sense. It is too easy for sociologists to overestimate this change, but it is clearly there. There have always been individuals, and the change seems to be from a general perception of the individual as part of a wider, but quite concrete network of relationships – the tribe, the family, the village, etc. – to a perception of the individual as unique and somehow special. There have always been individuals with problems, but once these would have been seen as moral choices in the context of the community or as struggles with forces of destiny; the change has been to seeing them in terms of individual morality with individual solutions and in terms of mental illness, psychological problems. Our conception of the individual has become one of a unit, at first increasingly isolated from the wider society, then as internally divided, and now, in postmodernist philosophy, almost written out of existence.

If we stay with the way in which individuals have been conceived of in philosophy and psychology, we can see the way in which psychoanalysis with its increasingly complex conceptions of the psyche is part of this process. With the appearance of what has become known as postmodernist philosophy, the theme of fragmentation has become explicit, and the individual is often seen as no more than an intersecting point of social forces or discourses. For me, the problem in all this is recognising that something might be true without it being the whole truth. It seems to me that what has happened over the centuries since the Enlightenment, when the individual as we now think of it began to emerge, is that (a) a real complexity of the psyche slowly became visible, (b) that real complexity has been accentuated by changing conditions of life, and (c) the apparent complexity and speed of that change itself is now hiding the underlying reality of the complexity of the psyche.

In sociology, we find the theme of fragmentation emerging at the end of the last century, often in connection with the analysis of urban life. In the early part of this century the German sociologist Georg Simmel (1950) was putting forward an argument very similar to my own; whereas I am trying to place the process in a long-term context, Simmel used a simple contrast he had taken from another German theorist, Ferdinand Tönnies (1955), a contrast between rural and urban life, the former based on feelings and emotional relationships, the latter on something else. There was, he argued, something rational and calculating about urban life: it is so varied that we are constantly bombarded with different stimuli, and the only way we can deal with all this is through a constant monitoring, through thinking about what we are doing rather than working through feeling and habit and tradition. We deal at a distance with large numbers of people, cultivating the distance and thinking about relationships primarily in a calculating way.

Now that is only part of what goes on in my working day, and it is likely that the bombardment with different stimuli is greater than it was in Simmel's time. I did not mention what I might hear on the radio or watch on television, what I might see in the street, all the unexpected and sometimes powerful interactions that might occur in a class, or, even more likely, in a therapy group.

Nor did I mention the family events which surround the day – the emigration of my stepdaughter; problems about my son's schooling; my wedding anniversary; worries about whether one stepson will make a habit of visiting war zones as part of his career as a journalist and whether the other will manage to stick to his college course; worries and guilt about my mother who lives alone and recently had an operation for stomach cancer; worries about areas of conflict in my marriage, my career prospects and so on. The list of events and concerns is potentially endless. A few years back it seemed fashionable to say that people become involved in television soap operas because their own lives are so boring, but I suspect that most of us could unravel our lives into a soap opera if we had a chance. Perhaps we become involved in watching soap operas because they offer the opportunity for a degree of emotional catharsis in a manageably short period of time, before we have to get on with the next thing.

One part of this fragmentation that Simmel noted clearly is the multiplicity of roles that we are expected to play. We could lump my account of the day together to see it in terms of just a few central roles: husband, father, teacher, friend, colleague, psychotherapist. But any one of these can be broken down further: lecturing involves me in a different role to teaching a class and that in turn is different from being a personal adviser; marking essays and exam scripts puts me in yet another role. As a husband I am a friend, colleague, lover, and an enemy, a presenter of problems for my wife to overcome. Each of these roles draws on some different part of my personality and that part must remain dominant for most of the time I am playing the role – although all the other parts can be drawn on as and when necessary to ensure that I carry out this particular role: this is the use of a phenomenon that sociologists refer to as role distance.

It is very difficult for me not to think of myself as made up of different parts, manipulating them as I move through the day; there is nowhere in the day where they all come together as a whole person. I might like to think that this happens when I am with my family, but if I started to try to therapise my wife or lecture my son, I would soon be in trouble (and rightly so), Home is certainly the place where I experience my strongest emotions, whether of love or hatred, but they disrupt my other activities; I know a number of colleagues who feel relieved every Monday morning, when they can get away from the messy emotions of the weekend and 'be themselves', although, of course, they are no more themselves at work than they are at home.

Psychoanalysis is a child of this now rapidly accelerated process. It could only develop in an urban environment, where the anonymity of the analyst could be maintained, and where a degree of reflective, distancing thought was already established as a normal and essential part of everyday life, where our lives were already experienced in terms of personal difficulties. What is interesting is that its wisest practitioners never envisaged it as a solution to the conditions that produced it.

MODELS OF FRAGMENTATION

Later sociologists, particularly the American Peter Berger and his colleagues (Berger and Luckmann 1966; Berger *et al.* 1973), have talked about this process as a 'pluralisation of life-worlds'. It is as if, during the day, we move through a number of different worlds, full of different objects and different people. They also note the disappearance of any one, generally accepted set of overarching symbols by which we are all embraced, and which give some wider meaning to our lives and our place in society and the world. We might at various times try to embrace such a set of symbols which in principle cover everyone – Christianity, for example, or (at least until recently) Marxism or the ecological movement – but we will find these only accepted amongst a particular group, and we will spend a lot of time trying to avoid contamination by those who do not agree with us, or trying to convert them. Sometimes we try to find some meaning in a group that is explicitly sectional – women or homosexuals or blacks or the nation – with which we can identify. This is a course of action which involves an interesting contradiction: the more we commit ourselves to a particular group, adopt its symbols, beliefs and theories, the more we separate ourselves from other groups and the more we become aware that we are only part of the world, that our particular meaning cannot become that of everybody else. I suspect that it is possible to gain a sense of our own identity through such movements only temporarily or to do so at the expense of sooner or later becoming a sort of historical anachronism, like those few who keep going in the Communist Party of Britain.

There is another contradiction here as well. Some such commitments are products of systematic structural inequalities in society: feminist or ethnic commitments, for example, with the aim of transforming an inequality. Questions of identity, of selfhood, inevitably have some part in this, but it seems to me that there is always a danger that the issue of identity takes primary place and outweighs the wider social changes that are sought – it is as if the more narcissistic aim of finding a sense of oneself becomes more important than the more altruistic aim of bringing about a desirable social change. In my experience, left-wing politics can rapidly become a matter of being right rather than being effective. I will be looking at the 'politics of identity' in relation to masculinity, and the disappointments that are involved, in a later chapter.

Counselling and psychotherapy too can be seen as solutions. In a recent debate over the politics of psychoanalysis (Dryden and Feltham 1992), David Pilgrim claims that new trainees are somehow *expected* to idealise the profession and its founders; this was certainly not my experience in training, but idealisation goes on – over and above the commitment that might reasonably be expected in a profession that is also for many a vocation. However, I suspect that it is not so much idealisation *per se*, but the wider belief that we can find, in whatever school of therapy or counselling that we adopt, a system of overarching values that provides us with our place in the world and gives a meaning to our lives which transcends the personal. I suspect this accounts for two things: the number of radicals from the 1960s' student movement who have been attracted to psychoanalysis over the last two decades; and the disillusion and bitterness with which psychotherapy and psychoanalysis are sometimes attacked by ex-adherents. Most gods that fail soon become devils.

Given that no such overarching symbols exist, given that the modern world is incurably pluralistic and we cannot find our place in it, Peter Berger *et al.* (1973) suggested that models for our selves were taken from the two central 'life-worlds' of modern society: bureaucracy and technology. From the world of technology, we come to see our selves as made up of different components that can be put together into abstract packages; we come to adopt a problem-solving attitude to our selves and others. Just as we might repair a car engine or a television set by replacing a component, or modify it by adding some new component, so we tend to think we can deal with ourselves and our relationships in the same way. Sometimes it is other people who are the components: with somebody else as my wife, I wouldn't have these difficulties.

Alternatively, we may think of some part of our selves as the problem. We seek to change that part: people present themselves for therapy with a sexual problem, or a problem with jealousy, or with a phobia, a fear of going out, or a fear of spiders, often with no conscious idea that there might be some wider meaning to what is happening to them. The health service and independent professionals offer repair services, garages for the personality: stress clinics, training in relaxation techniques, assertiveness training, sexual therapy. Some garages deal with the larger vehicles: marital therapy, family therapy. In some uses of the word 'counsellor' – 'career counselling' or 'dietary counselling', for example – the problem-solving aspect is clear, and the more that health professionals have to establish themselves by results, the more we are likely to see all sorts of services focusing on problem solving. Sometimes, in experiential groups of trainee counsellors when one talks about difficulties, the others spend a lot of time seeking childhood causes, as if they were looking for the source of the oil leak, and they are vaguely surprised that when the 'cause' is found, nothing happens. Often experienced people talk of supplying the missing component: 'So-and-so needs some mothering.'

Imagine my description of my day as a problem: all this changing around is too much for me; what shall I do about it? It could be treated as a technical problem: perhaps I could find a better form of organisation, spending some days as a therapist and some as a teacher. I could try to ensure that the time I spend with my family is, in current jargon, 'quality time' – a phrase which I suspect wards off the guilt that we do not want to deal with because we have so little time for our family, and begs the question of whether or not it might be a good idea for our children to get used to spending normal, everyday, average time with us. On a deeper and rather more useful level, my day and my busy-ness might be considered as a defence against the depression I might have to feel if I were to allow myself time to feel it; the solution would be simply to cut down on the work I do.

Now I am in no doubt that I could organise my time better, and I could choose between financial and spiritual sacrifice and give up, respectively, either my university post or my work as a therapist; this in turn would bring a depressive pain which would be in addition to the depressive pain I might be avoiding by doing so much work. In other words, there is no 'engineering' solution which does not entail depression, disappointment or frustration. Moreover, such a solution ignores (and psychoanalysts tend to be good at ignoring such factors) the extent to which the social pressures will, whatever I do, keep me in a fragmented life – it is part and parcel of living at this moment in history in the Western world. I can think about packaging it up into its component parts and juggling with them, even dropping some of them, but this is not a solution; there will still be fragments, roles and sub-roles with a varying range of expectations which I should fulfil.

The technological approach to emotional difficulties is, I find, more explicit amongst counsellors than the bureaucratic model, but behind both we can find the same phantasy: that somehow emotional upheavals, conflicts and flux can be organised away. The existence of large-scale bureaucratic organisations creates expectations of orderliness and predictability, so we come to expect the same from our selves. This is a dream of emotional management, in the sense of expecting a stable and ordered emotional life, and if that does not occur, the assumption is that something is wrong. The two models come together in the expectation, often voiced by trainees, that an ability to articulate and understand feelings should mean that the feelings do not occur, just as somehow finding the causes of the feelings should mean that they disappear. It is often the case when seeing patients for the first time that I hear 'It does no good to talk about things.' What this usually means is that they are desperately afraid of being overwhelmed by feeling if they put a name to it, and they are trying very hard to keep the feeling suppressed. It is possible that in the course of therapy they learn that it is a help to talk about feelings: they *do* become manageable in a way they weren't before, and the energy used in keeping the feelings suppressed can be put to other, more productive purposes.

Then, it seems, a new illusion can appear; that we can talk about the feelings instead of having them, that the talking itself solves emotional conflicts and leaves us at ease and peace with ourselves and others. This kind of illusion is often bound up with a kind of counselling or therapeutic evangelism: the not-quite truisms of 'its good to get things off your chest', 'it's important to have somebody to talk to' and so on. Talking can clarify, can replace impulsive and possibly destructive acting out, it can be a medium for making decisions, but it is not an alternative to conflict and suffering.

Anthony Giddens (1990), drawing on the German writer Beck (1992), points to a change in unpredictability in the modern world. It is no longer the unpredictability of fate, of nature or of God with which we have to deal, but the unpredictability of human beings, the large-scale *human* systems which employ us, provide us with money, buy our houses for us, look after our savings, take care of our children and so on. We have to work to create a trust in our points of contact with these large-scale organisations, which again involves management of emotions. I recently spent about half an hour with an estate agent, during which he fully convinced me on one level that he was experienced, able, honest, realistic and thoroughly to be trusted; he would make himself available any time of the day to answer my questions and deal with my anxieties, and he even acknowledged that the fact that he was only just over half my age might make it difficult for me to believe this. By the end, it was only a sceptical intelligence that prevented my being convinced – despite the fact that I share all the public's prejudices against estate agents.

Now he had worked very hard to elicit my trust in the – possibly immense – organisation of which he was at the sharp end; I sometimes wonder whether those in the caring professions, particularly the large hospitals, or the health service, are engaged in the same activity. Yet our very suspicion of such trust-inducing activity, even if we might allow ourselves to be fooled by it, indicates that we know we are taking a risk. It is this consistent state of risk that is denied by those counsellors and therapists who see a life in terms of components, causes and effects, and possible orderliness. Adam Phillips makes my point much more clearly than I can:

> The patient is cured in psychoanalysis when . . . among other things, he continues to plan for the future knowing he is unable to do so. This conflict between knowing what a life is and the sense that a life contains within it something that makes such knowing impossible is at the heart of Freud's enterprise.
>
> (Phillips 1989: 22)

There is now a new model for thinking about our fragmentation, combining technology and bureaucracy: the computer. This is most apparent in developments in cognitive psychology, but in sociology it is there in the emphasis on the importance of the control and flow of information in the postmodern world, and it is there in 'models' of the social actor. Earlier I talked about roles and the fragmentation of roles; implicit in this, there is some idea of a self that can be be fragmented. In a lot of modern theory, this fragmentation is taken as normal and the idea of a coherent self behind the various roles is disappearing; what is important now, for many sociologists, is that we have routine, taken-for-granted ways (Giddens 1984; Goffman 1974; Garfinkel 1967), Giddens, for example, argues that we learn these implicitly, through the 'hidden agenda' of socialisation, of moving through our various roles. We are programmed during our childhood, and in our adulthood we can draw on the right programme at the right time to get through this situation into the next. These programmes become therapeutic devices for enabling others to get through difficult situations: there is a programme for grief and mourning, a programme for dealing with incest, a programme for overcoming marital difficulties, a programme for ending a relationship in a creative and productive way, and the job of the therapist or counsellor is to teach, explicitly and implicitly, such a programme. To quote Phillips (1989: 22) again: 'It begins to seem that having a life could involve not making a mess.'

THE DESIRE FOR FRAGMENTATION: A DIFFERENT RESPONSE

Returning to Harvey's (1989) analysis of flexible accumulation, it is arguable that the labour market has changed in such a way that it is difficult for many people to look forward to a working life in one career or job or place. The move has been away from large-scale production based on (comparatively) long-term planning towards small-scale, short-term production in which producers are not likely to find themselves stranded with large stocks of unwanted goods. In this context, the ideal product is one that only lasts until it is used for the first time, that is consumed as soon as it is produced: meals, hairdressing, window cleaning; in sum, the 'service industries' – of which, of course, psychotherapy is itself one. Even with more substantial products, the turnover time from production to marketing has decreased rapidly, and the competitive demand for constant innovation, constant change, which has been present as long as capitalism itself, has increased dramatically. In Harvey's terms, it emphasises 'the new, the fleeting, the ephemeral, the fugitive'. It changes, and speeds up, our perception of time. When I was younger, it was common to talk about a century as a period of time during which we could identify some overriding common features; the shortest such periods would be several decades, marked by dramatic events, such as the 'inter-war years' between 1918 and 1939. Recently, however, it has become common to talk about decades as significant and discrete periods, the 1960s, 1970s, 1980, 1990s as very different from each other, each marked by its own culture, dominant themes, way of behaving and so on. Nothing significant or dramatic marks the boundary between these periods; it just means that nothing new can conceivably last for more than ten years. If one maintains a sense of one's own continuity as a self through these periods, it must be at the expense of feeling significantly outdated.

We are pulled forward into the future and away from the past in such a way that it becomes very difficult to take things with us – internal things, an awareness and an *understanding* of our experiences; instead they often seem to lie jumbled up inside us, and we find we have an inner world like a rubbish bin. This is a different sort of mess to that I was talking about earlier, the flux of the inner life and our emotions, about which we maintain the illusion that it can be made orderly and predictable. We might think that the rubbish bin can be sorted out, but it seems to me that the push is towards emptying it and starting afresh. If we go back to my description of my day earlier: in any situation that arises during the day, my attention is focused on the next one and what I might have to do to prepare myself for it. All the emotion and problems of the present situation can only be stored because the imperative is to move to the next one. So the debris of the day piles up, and it is easier to imagine that I can just leave the day behind, that each day I can become a new person.

We can find these ideas elaborated by some of the theorists of postmodernism. Fredric Jameson (1991) talks about dominant metaphors of pastiche and schizophrenia. Pastiche involves the putting together of unrelated images, taking images from their 'natural' or normal place and putting them together where they don't belong. He uses Lacan's psychoanalysis for his model of schizophrenia: basically, a loss of the 'fixed' points which provide our language with something we can treat as definite meaning. We are left sliding from word to word, and meaning appears and disappears, never stable for long enough to be grasped.

Now I believe I listen sometimes to something like this from trainees in experiential groups. What happens is that a person will talk, about a difficulty, an event, a feeling or whatever. The emotional charge of what is being said will be high, but in the process of the talk there will be a movement from one issue to another, from one story to another, one feeling to another, leaving listeners frustrated, puzzled and then confused; attempts to intervene, to bring clarification, or to 'help' tend be discounted by the person telling the story. A request for clarification will bring a further tumult of stories; attempts to understand will be explained away, leaving the person who intervened feeling helpless. Although the anxiety is there, I often feel that the confusion, the inability to understand, is paraded for its own sake, and I feel as though I am being asked to endorse the confusion, accept and value the random and sometimes powerful and dramatic expressions that occur. Interpretations or interventions on my part are likely to be rejected not just by the person concerned but by the group as a whole. I am not heard properly, or there are immediate responses along the lines of 'I don't understand', or 'that's got nothing to do with what is going on here.' It is possible to understand this rejection as a refusal of the order that may be brought by understanding.

In the experiential group the confusion seems to me to be a schizoid defence against a threatening bad object, represented by myself, often no more than my presence in the group, and this is bound up with a father transference, often confirmed by the way in which my intervention will, apparently spontaneously, bring forth material about members' fathers. In this context the fragmentation seems to be a desired state, so that the whole group will become caught up in the process. What seems undesirable is the implication of bringing order and understanding and the discrimination that follows: 'order' means the ability to make judgements about some things being more important than others, some things being right and some things being wrong, both in a factual and a moral sense. These discriminations are precisely those attributed to the father-figure in much psychoanalytic theory, and they certainly involve the disappointment of not being able to be everything. It is reflected in the oft-remarked feature of much postmodernist literary theory: the insistence that it is not possible to discriminate between good and bad works of art and literature.

This seems to be a different choice in dealing with life to that expressed in the desire for order and predictability, perhaps one more clearly on offer after the developments of the last twenty or thirty years. But the two can go together, and to understand how this happens I want to go back to another point that Berger *et al.* (1973) make about bureaucracy as one of the fundamental models by means of which we see ourselves. A central feature of the way in which bureaucracy is organised and the way in which it deals with its clients is *anonymity*. In the most rational forms of bureaucracy, the office-holder is not in his or her position by virtue of wealth, or religious or political beliefs, or his or her personal characteristics or race, but by virtue of possession of a relevant set of knowledge and skills tested by public examination. If this is not the case, then we suspect discrimination, corruption or political tyranny. In carrying out his or her duties, the bureaucrat simply puts into process his or her skills according to a set of rules that is laid down; and the client too is dealt with not in terms of personality or belief, but according to a set of criteria laid down in advance. It should be evident that the sort of personality required for work in a bureaucracy seems almost opposite to the sort of personality required for work in a 'postmodern' society: one requires consistency, control, an absence of initiative, the other requires flexibility, an ability to tolerate flux and change, and a constant search for new responses. What is common to both in terms of my group examples, however, is the absence of internalised personal authority; the authority in a bureaucracy is anonymous, and I do not have to 'restrict' myself by taking in another real person and making that person part of myself; the rejection of authority (as I personify it) in the group is a rejection of just such a personal authority – whether it be of the father, or for some people the mother, or myself as therapist. It is therefore quite possible for people to think of themselves as ordered, or wanting to be ordered, in an abstract bureaucratic way and maintaining all the fragmentation of their experience. It sometimes seems as if the theories of psychotherapy and counselling are used 'internally' as bureaucratic rules laying down procedures for dealing with feelings and fantasies, but the advantage of these rules is that they do not require internal discrimination between good and bad, right and wrong. As long as we talk about it all, express it all, our internal life will remain orderly and predictable *and* stay fragmented; we will not have to give up anything. It is one the features of Kohut's narcissistic patients that they seem to be candidates for interminable analysis without undergoing any real change.

CONCLUSION

What I am suggesting is that more and more people are finding themselves in lives which are 'overfull' of experiences and that experiences are themselves highly variegated; they are difficult to cope with, to organise and keep inside. They carry with them the permanent possibility of 'falling apart', the end point that comes from the whole process of emotional overeating and consequent indigestion. At the same time, this flood of experience is attractive. It is attractive in a negative sense, in that we might feel that if we try to reduce it, we will have to withdraw from the world and perhaps sink without trace – it is as if this type of life offers us the choice of being in or out of it, with no half-way positions. And it is attractive in a positive sense, in that it can seem to offer a huge range of possibilities and pleasures, and if we do not feel that we are making the most of them, if we are not getting our share, not getting what we want, then something is wrong, with ourselves or with the world. It comes to seem that we can't live without this type of life and its possibilities, but neither can we live with it.

In such a situation, all sorts of therapy, including psycho-analytic therapy, seem to offer possible solutions; it is as if, as inner conflict and turmoil increase, so the phantasy of being integrated and whole grows proportionately; as the possibility of lasting, but incomplete, satisfactions decrease, so the phantasy of immediate and complete satisfaction increases. The various therapies become caught up in this, and therapists themselves move from one school to another in the search for something which works more quickly and more completely. The paradox is that as this fragmentation is the product of increased organisation, it seems to me that psychotherapy becomes a form of social control in the bad sense – that in effect it *does* try to mould gingerbread people, the sort of people who can maintain their phantasies in such a way as to live with the fragmentation, without threatening or questioning the level of organisation, the domination of what Giddens calls abstract systems. Above all, the necessity of disappointment is denied in all this – we can be everything we want to be, life is constant excitement: all we have to do is be open to it all. Danah Zohar tries to relate it all to quantum physics:

> the quantum world-view stresses dynamic relationship as the basis of all that is. It tells us that our world comes about through a mutually creative dialogue between mind and body (inner and outer, subject and object), between the individual and his personal and material context, between human culture and the natural world. It gives us a view of the human self which is free and responsible, responsive to others and its environment, essentially related and naturally committed, and at every moment creative.
>
> (Zohar 1990: 220)

Wow!

Chapter 7

The powerful self and its illusions

In my account of the conflicting trends of late modernity I have referred several times to Anthony Giddens. Giddens (1991, 1992), is the sociologist who has gone furthest in systematically exploring contemporary notions of the self, drawing on the ideas and prescriptions of various types of psychotherapy. Although he identifies a number of problems and contradictions in what is happening to personal life, and he is aware of the double-edged nature of late modernity, he seems to see these developments primarily as a 'good thing', involving an increasing freedom and autonomy and intimately bound up with the possibilities of a democratic society. I want to reverse his emphases: there are certainly elements of increased freedom in current developments, but there is much that is illusory and socially dangerous. My argument is that psychotherapy, to the extent that it is an 'abstract system' of social control, can prescribe a 'false self', in effect an illusory self, an illusory way of living. On the one hand, this illusion takes the form of making a virtue out of a disturbing necessity, turning fragmentation into a 'good thing'; on the other, it suggests, often implicitly and against its own explicit statements, that there are certain areas of our existence where we can find a coherent or real identity. The statement 'I have a right to do what I want to with my own life', for example, carries elements of both – I can control my self (identity), and I have a right to do what I want to without restriction, to 'actualise' myself in all the ways I desire (fragmentation),

NEW CONCEPTIONS OF THE SELF AND RELATIONSHIPS

To begin with I will simply present Giddens's arguments. Some of the therapies he employs to illustrate his argument are closer to psychoanalysis than others. The crux of his argument is that in the modern world, the self is not something that is consistently rooted in the surrounding community; we each have to find our self, and given the speed of social change we have to do so regularly. Relationships have to be rationally justified; they are no longer sanctified by tradition. We have to have a reason for what we do. Giddens refers to this as *reflexivity* – we are constantly justifying and reworking ourselves. In this context, he offers two views of the role of therapy: one he calls the 'negative' view, in which psychotherapy is an attempt to compensate for the loss of community; the alternative is that therapy is intimately bound up with the opportunities offered by the modern world for self-reconstruction and change, and it is with this latter view that I take issue.

The modern self is engaged in a constant exercise of self-construction and reconstruction, the alternative to which is despair. Giddens quotes, approvingly, Wallerstein and Blakeslee's study of divorce: 'They [the divorcees] sense that life gives hard knocks and is essentially unpredictable; they conclude that the best laid plans go awry and become discouraged about setting long-range or even short-range goals, much less working towards these goals' (Wallerstein and Blakeslee 1989, quoted in Giddens 1991: 11). To avoid this, the authors argue a period of mourning is necessary in which the self is reconstructed, perhaps through going back over all life experiences and finding new resources.

Drawing on a book, *Self-Therapy*, by Janette Rainwater (1989), Giddens further illustrates the way in which late modernity enables the construction of the self. The idea behind the book is that whilst therapy with a professional works and is often necessary, we only really become able to realise our full potential when we become our own therapists. To do this, we have to watch ourselves all the time. There is a list of questions that we should ask ourselves:

What is happening right now?
What am I thinking?
What am I doing?

What am I feeling?
How am I breathing?

(Giddens 1991: 76)

It is fairly easy to see how this sort of self-monitoring can become a requirement of modernity. If we think about my account of my day, the movement from one role to another, from one set of relationships to another, dealing with all the contingent events that might occur within any one of those roles does require a constant monitoring, and a set of guidelines for such monitoring is useful. It could become a little catechism that I use on myself regularly during the day, to keep control of myself, keep the right distance from feelings, give me the status of being able to talk articulately about myself and so on. The point of this self-observation seems to be not, as one might at first think, simply a matter of living for the present. The idea seems to be that by constantly asking oneself what one is doing and where one is going, it becomes possible to plan a future according to one's real needs, ambitions or self. It involves also the familiar rewriting of one's past through writing an autobiography and keeping a journal. The aim, in the familiar counsellese, is 'taking charge of one's life', which, in the same language, is a 'risky business'. Giddens quotes Rainwater directly:

> People who fear the future attempt to 'secure' themselves – with money, property, health insurance, personal relationships, marriage contracts. Parents attempt to bind their children to them. Some fearful children are reluctant to leave the home nest. Husbands and wives try to guarantee the continuance of the other's life and services. The harsh psychological truth is that there is no permanence in human relationships ... this clutching at security can be very discouraging to interpersonal relationships, and will impede your own self-growth. The more each of us can learn to be truly in the present with our others, making no rules and erecting no fences for the future, the stronger we will be in ourselves and the closer and happier in our relationships.
>
> (Rainwater 1989, quoted in Giddens 1991: 73)

For Giddens, this means being open to all sorts of possibilities and ready to make a complete break with the past, ready to contemplate actions other than the habitual. It is easy to see why such a way of living can make relationships problematic: not only are they no longer guaranteed by tradition, kinship or the simple fact of marriage; partners are likely to be involved in constant processes of self-reconstruction. Giddens describes our culture's response to this as the development of the notion of a 'pure relationship'. He starts with a long quotation from a book, *Women and Love*, by the American Shere Hite (1988), of which I am going to reproduce the first half here, in order to refer to it later. The speaker is a woman involved in the early stages of a relationship:

> I have a constant feeling of never being satisfied for some reason. Either he's not calling, or when he's calling, it's not romantic, and so on . . . When I try to talk to him, really talk to him, I feel like I just can't get through . . . It seems to revolve around a constant question of should I be asking myself 'Is everything all right in terms of him (does he still love me)?' or 'Is everything all right in terms of *me? How am I?*' If I am unhappy a lot and he won't talk to me about the problems or resolve the issues, should I say, 'Well, everything is really OK because he's OK and he's still there and he still loves me'? Or should I say, 'This relationship is terrible and I will leave it because he is not making me happy'? Loving him makes it difficult to leave him.
>
> (Hite 1988, quoted in Giddens 1991: 88)

There are a number of features of the 'pure relationship' in this. It is pure because it is not rooted in external conditions, whether of kinship or work. We tend to think of relationships that are based on kinship or work as *only* kinship or work relationships – the special relationships in our lives depend on something more than that, even if they are with kin or colleagues. Motivations other than established social ties and simple social proximity are behind the pure relationship – it has to stand or fall on its own terms. Giddens argues that 'Other traits – even such seemingly fundamental ones as having children – tend to become sources of "inertial drag" on possible separation, rather than anchoring features of the relationship' Giddens 1991: 89).

A relationship, then, must depend on its own rewards, and dissatisfaction of any sort is experienced as a threat to it, rather than being taken as normal, as might have been expected in the past. It is more difficult to coast along or make do in a relationship. The rewards become a matter of constant questioning. 'Is everything OK?' is the crucial and familiar question implying that we need to think about what is going on and we can do something about it. Simply being in a relationship is no longer possible – we *make* relationships. This has given rise to a new conception of 'commitment': it is not a matter of belief or conviction; it is what replaces the external social ties that might once have kept a relationship together. The committed person is:

> someone who, recognising the tensions intrinsic to a relationship of the modern form, is nevertheless willing to take a chance on it, at least in the medium term – and who accepts that the only rewards will be those inherent in the relationship itself.
>
> (Giddens 1991: 92)

Commitment buys time and emotional support through the 'peturbations which the relationship might undergo' and is part of a bargain: a return will be demanded for what is received. Giddens calls it an 'effort bargain', and commitment doesn't spontaneously appear with love or lust, it needs a conscious decision. The quotation from Hite illustrates the tentative and fraught nature of 'effort bargaining' at the beginning. Giddens points to the way in which a relationship in which the 'effort bargain' is unequal or not working, and one or both partners are unhappy, but which neither partner can leave, has become known as a 'co-dependent relationship' – a term originally applied to individuals in relationships with others dependent on drugs or drink. We can be addicted to relationships and that is assumed to be absolutely wrong.

The focus of the 'pure relationship' is intimacy; Giddens argues that rather than intimacy being a retreat from the impersonal nature of the modern world, it is made possible by the modern world, together with the psychic satisfactions that its achievement offers. Intimacy requires secure individuals able to balance autonomy and sharing; therapy manuals are the source of these ideas. It depends upon trust which has to be worked at and won; within the relationship, each has to trust and be trustworthy. Here he summarises another therapy guide:

> One 'should take time to listen to each other daily' since communication is so central to intimacy. Such talking and listening should not always be limited to the trivial events of the

day. Where there are substantive issues to be faced, they should
be seriously discussed. Partners should 'stick to one issue until
resolved and then be done with it', for 'rehashing the same
issues lessens trust and creates new problems'. Old disputes
that fester unresolved are often more likely to destroy trust
than new difficulties, which may be easier to face. One should
'get to the feelings behind issues', because surface appearances
may hide the true dynamics of a situation, and communication
which is not 'in depth' cannot get at these. Other recom-
mendations include nurturing an atmosphere of caring,
aiming for a variety of recreational pleasures mutually engaged
in, and learning to express anger in a constructive way.

(Giddens 1991: 97)

Finally, through all these activities, a self-identity and a shared
history are negotiated – it seems to be not just a process of mutual
recognition, but a process of mutual self-construction. The
relationship, like the self, is constantly constructed and
reconstructed.

THE ILLUSORY SELF AND ITS RELATIONSHIPS

The ideas and experiences described by Giddens are, I am sure,
familiar to many people; we *feel* as though we should be constantly
reconstructing our selves, examining and justifying our
relationships in a search for intimacy and commitment. What I
want to argue is that these are illusory tasks and goals set by late
modernity, carrying on the myth of self-control and of the
all-powerful self that can control itself.

There is little place for disappointment in such a view, yet it
seems to me that the view of the world in the quotation from
Wallerstein and Blakeslee (a view which they see as to be avoided)
is basically right: life *does* give hard knocks, plans *do* go awry, there
is no guarantee that our efforts will bear fruit. It might be that the
best that psychotherapy can offer is the opportunity to be sadder
but wiser, not some realisation that the world is a wonderful and
trustworthy place. The idea that we can somehow reconstruct
ourselves by rewriting our history is one that I often hear in
experiential groups when members are therapising each other.
There are a couple of examples that come to mind. In one case a
person was talking about a break-up with her partner, and the

depression that had ensued – although she did not perceive it as a depression, since depression was seen solely in terms of what she had felt in the relationship. The group's response was entirely in terms of all the encouraging things that she might look forward to; nearly all the interventions were in 'counsellese', about her 'discovering new parts of herself', how she must feel better for taking decisive action and so on. In all discussions of this sort, the term 'resolution' is frequently used.

In a second case a woman began talking of her guilt about the way in which she had treated one of her children. The group responded in two ways. One was emphasising the normality of what she had done, in terms of generalisations about the social isolation of mothers, and the other was to seek the psychological origins of her action in the way she herself had been treated by her parents, to show how she was an improvement over her parents and to show her that there was a cause for her actions that relieved her of guilt. Now I suspect that anyone who has suffered from guilt will recognise that extenuating circumstances and explanations of an action do not of themselves relieve the guilt, and there are actions which, in any civilised person, *ought* to result in guilt. The explaining away of guilt, in my experience, only works in the context of a usually short-lived manic reaction, in which one believes that one has found *the* answer to problems; the same goes for the explaining away of depression. The attempt to explain it away is an attempt at a rewriting of the self, a reconstruction of the self that is thought to enable growth, change, development, self-realisation.

The advocating of a constant self-awareness is also different from what it claims to be; my use of the word 'catechism' in relation to Rainwater's list of questions was not accidental; my first association with such instructions was learning as a fairly young child that God could see me wherever I was, and sitting on the toilet feeling both embarrassed and slightly excited by the idea. The idea of watching myself all the time is not quite so embarrassing or exciting but seems a suitably mature version of the same thing.

What this exercise seems to require is a sort of splitting that momentarily we might make when we are very frightened, the moment when we leave our bodies for a safe place to watch what is happening to us. I always remember one frightening incident from childhood – playing and falling on to an open fire – from above, as if I were sitting on the ceiling watching it; such experiences are often reported by people after a traumatic incident and for some such a separation becomes a permanent condition of their psychological life: Winnicott talks of a patient who experienced herself as above her body and attached to it through strings. Now Rainwater isn't suggesting a psychotic split, but she is certainly suggesting a split which I would see as neurotically obsessive, a way of guarding against nameless inner fears, and all too nameable outer fears: that I might do something wrong and lose control. 'Becoming one's own therapist' seems to entail such control and suggests that psychotherapy offers a support we need all the time. Compare this with Winnicott's cheery comment that 'life is the best therapy' – nothing there about watching oneself all the time.

Janet Malcolm's book *Psychoanalysis: The Impossible Profession* (1982) takes us a bit further. The analyst she writes about, a fairly orthodox Freudian she calls Aron Green, says that the patients he regards as having used therapy most successfully are those who, a few years later, hardly ever think about it. He does not regard those who constantly think about him as successes (however grateful they might be). To become one's own therapist in Rainwater's sense is, in such psychoanalytic terms, a failure. I think that theoretically Green's successes could be said to have integrated their experience in such a way that it has become a real part of themselves, modified by and modifying what was already there, rather than carrying or creating an internal therapist as some separate part. Now there is no doubt that the therapist enters his or her patient's head in some way; in our most omnipotent moments, it might be gratifying to think of ourselves as sitting there directing the patient's life, helping them through their conflicts and the rest of it. The reality more often – thank goodness – is that we enter our patients' heads and become something else to what we are; we are transformed there, if we have done our job well, into something we might not recognise, agree with or even like – if psychotherapy is able to set people free, then they must be free of the therapist as well.

It seems that what is on offer from Rainwater is a rather obsessive attempt at self-control, in the face of a clearly uncertain future. The future *is* uncertain, as Rainwater states, and there *is* real pleasure to be gained from being in the present with others. But it is the unreality of it that I want to emphasise first, and then

the implications of trying to live like this. We are instructed to
deny any determinism in the past, yet everything we know about
individual development indicates that it is the past experiences
that are determinant. Not in any absolute way: change is always
possible, although sometimes it might take years of hard work; but
the 'break' does not and cannot come, unless we are to do the
inconceivable and become another person, and then that other
person would have his or her own determining past. If the future
is unpredictable, then that is a good reason to be afraid of it. Not
to fear for the future is, simply on an animal level, giving up one
of the abilities that has enabled us to survive as a species. Fear of
the future means that we take care, that we look both ways before
we cross the road, that we keep our babies warm at night, that I
don't throttle my wife even when I feel like it. All these are
attempts to secure the future and to secure relationships,
necessary attempts for both the individual and the species.
Bowlby's work on the need for attachment shows quite clearly the
necessity of a secure base for our children; it is that which will
enable them to leave, and it involves doing our best to guarantee
the future at least up to that point. Rainwater is of course quite
right that some parents try to hold on to their children; but
children leaving home is also a real loss, and to experience that
loss, feel the desperation and barrenness that goes with the loss of
somebody important, is not the same thing as holding on to one's
children.

More important, perhaps, is the evidence that an attachment
need continues into adult life; the most glaring evidence for this
is the cultural emphasis on relationships which Giddens also
identifies and about which I will be talking soon. I think what
Rainwater is getting at is that what we should look for in a
relationship is the immediate pleasure of the moment: I am not
actually sure that closeness and happiness go together – more of
this later – but Rainwater assumes that they do and that this is the
aim of a relationship. Now there is, as she recognises, a
contradiction between this sort of immediate satisfaction and
security, but it is clear in the way that she presents it that the
former is impossible to achieve. In *Fear of Flying* (1976) Erica Jong
plays with the fantasy of a 'zipless fuck', an act of pure sexuality
with no complications or meanings beyond itself. Rainwater seems
to be envisaging the 'zipless relationship', and of course that must
remain a fantasy. What would a relationship in which there are no

rules be like? In the recent Woody Allen film *Crimes and Misdemeanors*, the hero visits his sister whom he finds traumatised after being abused by a partner met through a computer dating service. He returns home to announce to his wife 'A strange man defecated on my sister'; if we all had relationships without rules, of course, such behaviour would be unproblematic. I think a similar argument could be made about fences for the future. Rainwater does not use the word 'trust' in this quotation, but a relationship which yields intimacy requires trust, and trust is always setting down rules – or fences – for the future; minimally there are such 'fences' as 'If I tell you about my sex life, I don't expect you to tell my boss about it tomorrow morning, next week or next year'; 'If I tell you about this shameful deed, I do not expect you to blackmail me.'

It seems to me there is a similarity between living for the immediate satisfaction to be gained from another's presence and what people of my mother's generation used to call 'keeping one's eye on the main chance'. They both mean being aware of what one wants, and seizing opportunities to get it as they present themselves. The person who kept his or her eye on the main chance would be able to change opinions and loyalties radically if it suited; he or she would only maintain relationships as long as was necessary for whatever satisfaction he or she was seeking. The phrase was associated with the post-war 'spiv' – the operator on the borders of legality, out to make as much money as possible from deals on the black market. It is perhaps a tribute to the power of the modern market economy that such a model should now colour our personal relationships. Of course, if we are really going to be in charge of our own lives, then we are going to need to manipulate others into giving us what we want from them.

The emphasis in all this, from surviving divorce, through being one's own therapist and reconstructing one's past, to living in the present for the satisfactions one can gain from being with others, is on control. Such control spreads to a concern with the body, eating, smoking, drinking – anything that seems to take away our complete power over ourselves and leaves us dependent on something or someone else. I recently heard a woman who described herself as a 'recovering therapist' talk about our addiction to relationships, by which she seemed to mean any relationship upon which we depended. This is an immense act of denial – covering not only our real psychological dependence on relationships with other people, both inside and outside our heads, but also our social dependence on everybody who is engaged producing our clothes, food and everything else that we do not make for ourselves. It is sometimes like hearing children furiously deny that their parents are more powerful and able than themselves. If this is the way the self is perceived, then children *will* be experienced as 'inertial drag', and thus perhaps people have to be trained and even legislated into good-enough parenting.

If we should not be dependent, even on satisfactory relationships, then the 'pure relationship' is going to be in constant trouble. My argument is that as a false ideal of late modernity it offers a particular type of regressive satisfaction, but in doing so recreates all the pressures from which we might be seeking relief by engaging in it. The possibility of intimacy both is a relief from the impersonal institution in which I spend my working life, and holds out the possibility of satisfactions that were not available even to my parents' generation, but in practice both the impersonal institution and the intimate relationship demand selves that are as false as each other.

The centre of the 'pure relationship' is that, separated from its previous social cement, it depends upon 'emotional satisfaction'. Now this is absolutely clear in the quotation from Hite, which begins with the statement that the speaker never feels satisfied. Now, if there is such a thing as emotional satisfaction, then it is of a rather transient nature. In fact it is rather like the satisfaction of hunger: I might have a good meal tonight and feel thoroughly and happily satisfied, but sometime tomorrow morning I will be hungry again. In this sense to seek emotional satisfaction from a relationship is to be making constant, renewed and daily demands on the energy and ability of one's partner, and to experience those demands from one's partner. My first thought about this is that if I have a partner like this, why do I need my workplace? The answer is that there will certainly be times when the latter is less demanding and a more comfortable place to be, a haven from intimacy.

The idea of intimacy requires further thought. If it is the case that each us has conflicting emotional needs, then the satisfaction of one group of needs can have the effect of emphasising the dissatisfaction of another. If we think about the simple opposition of a need for autonomy, an experience of being one's own person, and a need for attachment, and in some circumstances dependence, then the point becomes obvious. It makes sense of the fact that many relationships that do last can be seen as a dance, with the partners becoming closer then moving away, then becoming closer again, perhaps punctuated by periods of moving forward along parallel lines. What this means is that satisfaction and dissatisfaction go hand in hand; a simple satisfaction is never possible.

Now satisfaction always remains as a fantasy, together with the possibility that it might last. This is bound up with the full force of unconscious phantasy in the state of being in love. In another quotation from Hite's book, a woman says 'Romantic love is the key to my identity.' This is what I called the regressive need. Whether a state where all our needs were satisfied ever existed, for any of us, might be debatable; what isn't debatable is that such a state disappears fairly early on in our lives. Some people attribute such a state to the womb, but even then there are the natural processes of growth that push us out; it might exist for a while in the understanding that our mother might find spontaneously within herself, in the process of good-enough mothering. But if we are to grow, such understanding must have its failures.

Again, I am not trying to say something simple and one-sided. Being in love with another person can be a wonderful state; it opens up depths of feeling and sensitivity to ourselves, to the person we love and sometimes to others, that we rarely reach in our everyday lives. It is easy to see why some people might be 'addicted' to it; the tragic, sad – perhaps at times unbearably sad – aspect of being in love is that it changes. We can imagine that with this person we have found our heart's desire, the understanding and the ability to understand that we have always wanted. In this sense, perhaps, it is a period of madness. Clulow and Mattinson (1989) suggest that it is a functional madness: it is what pushes us into pairing and setting up families, continuing the species when all the old social cementing of marriages has all but disappeared. But I do not think we should undervalue it as an experience, both for its own sake, and for what we can learn from the madness.

Now if we think of emotional satisfaction as the central basis for a relationship, our primitive fantasies of complete satisfaction are brought into play. This idea haunts the quotation from Hite. The simple question 'Is everything OK?' carries a whole impossible world of satisfactions, one loaded with so much feeling that the thought that things might not be OK is enough for the speaker to consider flying from the relationship. The demand for the impossible is at the centre of this type of intimacy; the tragedy is that it prevents us from seeing or learning from its impossibility. If everything is not OK, we do not learn but seek out another relationship in which it might be OK. If we fall in love, then the decline of being in love, whether slow or fast, is felt as a failure rather than a deepening of our understanding of the world and the reality of the other person. The speaker's sense of 'never being satisfied' is an accurate perception of internal and external reality, but it is experienced not as knowledge and understanding but as failure and deficiency.

Beyond this, emotional satisfaction is not always pleasant: it lies not only in receiving love, understanding and support, but in being able to triumph over that which we are envious of or afraid of, in destroying what we feel we can never achieve. There are times in close relationships when talking makes it worse, when my desire to get my wife to understand something is intimately bound up with my desire to destroy her composure or what I might perceive to be her serenity – which I might also perceive as her insensitivity, complacency, distance, coldness or whatever. I want to talk to her to convey how bad I feel by making her feel as bad as I do. I wonder how much of this is going on when the speaker wonders what to do when her partner 'won't talk to me about the issues or resolve the problems'. Emotional satisfaction involves the satisfaction of rows, attacks, hurting and being hurt; this is part and parcel of intimacy.

I want to be clear: I am *not* saying that emotional satisfaction is not an important part of any relationship that involves intimacy; I am saying that it is fragile, by its nature unstable and contradictory, and it can involve negative, destructive dimensions that might also be essential to the health of the relationship (more of this later). If emotional satisfaction is the *raison d'être* of a relationship, then the relationship itself must inevitably be volatile, unstable and probably short-lived. It takes on all the features of the late modernity from which we hope it might be a relief: it is changeable, never quite reliable, as volatile as our feelings themselves and demanding of constant vigilance. Dissatisfaction is thus a threat to the relationship – 'I will leave it because she or he is not making me happy.'

Another person's happiness is an immense responsibility, especially if the unhappiness is a result of internal conflicts in the person concerned. What psychoanalytic theory has to tell us about falling in love is that the person we choose is from the start intimately involved in our inner life (Skynner and Cleese 1983). We choose partners on the basis of our own internal processes, and the partner is chosen because he or she seems to provide some sort of solution to our own internal difficulties or conflicts. Thus I might have seen a particular woman as providing an understanding of my past history that no one else possessed; or I might have seen her as having solved the problems that I was still grappling with; or I might have thought that if I could solve her difficulties, mine would disappear. All these thoughts would have been unconscious at the time, although with the experience of failure I might be able to look back and divine them.

Now, given that the one certain thing about people is that they are different from each other, that they do not fit into each other like pieces of a jigsaw puzzle for any great length of time (at least not in a rapidly changing world), falling in love is bound to be followed by a degree of disillusion, and a likely sense of betrayal, possibly immense betrayal, when I discover that this other person will not play the role in my personality that I have assigned to her. In a homely and appropriate metaphor, Winnicott calls this the plate-throwing stage and suggests that the relationship will survive if the couple do not run out of plates. However, if we come to a relationship without the expectation of being unhappy for some of the time, then we are likely to get through our stock of psychic plates very quickly. In fact there is no need to build up a stock of plates to fight through the battles, since such battles should not occur. Once again, I am not saying that unhappiness should be borne or endured whatever; some relationships involve a clear, profound and mutually destructive unhappiness and would be better ended. This does not seem to be the case with the woman quoted; the simple appearance of unhappiness raises the possibility of ending the relationship. It is *always* a question of degree, of shades of grey. If I have a personal attitude on this, it is that if I can break even, I'm not doing too badly. But this involves tolerating unhappiness for periods, or perhaps in some aspect of my life all the time.

Returning to the Hite quotation in this context, we can tease out a further dimension to the notion of reflexivity. The tone of the quotation is one I find familiar, especially at the beginning of psychotherapy. I sometimes feel as a psychotherapist as if I am a sort of diary, in which the relationship events of the week, the various ups and downs and nuances of behaviour, are being written. It often seems that I am not needed for what I might say – indeed there is often a sense of fear that I might say something; rather my job is simply to listen and less obviously to accept it all. Behind this, there is sometimes – perhaps often – a sense of desperation, as if the speaker is very, very fragile, and is sitting there trying to glue the pieces together in the best possible way; any intervention that I might make would disrupt the pattern, possibly sending the pieces flying in all directions. If I sit and listen, the speaker might succeed in putting them together in the way that he or she wants, and might feel, for a short period, a relief from the worry and tension and fragility and danger that is bound up with the relationship.

The processes of trying to work out whether 'everything is OK' and the fear of falling apart, of fragmentation, if 'everything is not OK' point to a very fragile sense of self, and rather than something that actually makes the self, it is perhaps best seen as a symptom of a weakened self, holding itself together at the point of collapse. If being unable to leave a relationship in which there is real abuse is a sign of weakness of self, a lack of true autonomy, then so perhaps is leaving a relationship because of the confusion of feelings that it produces. The pain and sadness involved in accepting that the chosen one is not the person one thought, the failure of an enterprise that was undertaken to make up something missing or lost or damaged in oneself, is painful. Withdrawing from a relationship because 'everything is not OK' is an act of self-protection, but it can be the protection of a fragile self, one that cannot be risked in the reality of a relationship and one that cannot bear to know itself.

Now I imagine in all this it must sound as if I am engaging in moral criticism, and I am; but what I object to on moral grounds is not the fragility of the self and the inability to make deep connections with other people. It is our social world that makes that difficult, and there are certainly senses in which the inability to form deep attachments and the movement from one partner to another actually make it easier to live in such a world: it is easier to undertake the career moves and the changes in skill, the regular changes in the people around us, than it would be if we were attached to our partners in a profound way. My moral objection is the elevation of this sort of life into a 'good thing', something to be aimed at, in other words its conversion into an ideology – the making of an ideology, a virtue, out of a necessity which undermines the connections between people and an understanding of the world as it is. Yet often this is precisely what the activity of 'therapy' can seem to do.

The notions of 'commitment' and effort bargaining, although capturing the way in which people often think about relationships, manage to hide possibilities, particularly – and paradoxically – what could be seen as the more positive aspects of intimacy. They assume a coming together of isolated individuals who have no reason to stay with each other apart from wanting to do so. What I have said so far indicates that when two people come together in this way, what happens between them is less a matter of conscious control and planning (although that enters into it) than emotional attachment and interlocking that makes such control difficult: 'Loving him makes it difficult to leave him.' 'Commitment' in Giddens's sense is always to some degree a rationalisation, probably of conflicting emotions. The notion of 'effort bargaining' gets hold only of one side, the desire to protect the fragile self; the self that is strong enough to take the risk of losing itself is discarded. If we think in terms of effort bargaining, there is no room to say that it is better to have loved and lost than never loved at all – with the implication of having learnt all that that implies; and there is no room either for unrequited love, the sufferings of the young Werther. However hopelessly romantic, even melodramatic, Goethe's (1957, originally published 1774) tale sounds to modern ears, what is clear is that the suffering portrayed is more profound than the agony of wondering whether one's partner is going to pull his or her weight.

Implicit in the idea of effort bargaining is what might be called anti-effort bargaining: if I do not get from my partner what I want, then I will not give, I might even leave. In this way of thinking about a relationship, there often seems to be a built-in innocence: it is always the speaker who has been giving and has not been receiving in return; of course, if one talks to the partner, one finds that he or she is saying the same thing. Effort bargaining in this sense does not seem to allow for a sense of guilt and self-questioning. And it all takes place in the present; it is as if the speeding up of our time sense makes it difficult to think of a relationship unrolling over years – or sometimes even months – where the inequalities of effort might change and balance out. Over a period of years, partners will develop in different directions at different rates, and one or both will also stand still for periods. If commitment is to be a useful word, it seems to me that it should be seen in terms of a bargain only in the sense of an agreement to live with, allow and explore these changes, and in this there will be complex inequalities of effort. For it to work, both partners must be willing to exploit the other and be exploited for periods, or perhaps in one respect or another for most of the time. The patterns of arguments and peace that this involves are the story of the relationship, not the reason for ending it – as they become very quickly if we regard it all only as a trade-off.

The experience that seems to me to be lost in effort bargaining is the creative sense of love – that one actually creates something by putting the partner's interest in front of one's own for a while. This is connected with the sense of love that Klein talks about as reparation, the desire (phantasied to begin with) to try to make whole, to create where damage might have been done. And perhaps this is as important as the demand that one's own self be recognised in some way, and receive love. We might at times have to provide a punch-bag for the other person, as well as an object for love. A long-term relationship that is alive can be seen as an ongoing series of mutual projections and retractions, and therefore of self-discovery, where hate can play as big a part as love, and the relationship can contain passionate expressions of both. This too might, I suppose, be called effort bargaining, but the difference is between agreeing the price of a pound of apples, and working to build a many-roomed mansion.

The idea of effort bargaining also implies a fragile self: that unless it gets as much as it gives, it will be depleted; there is no sense here that an act of love can actually strengthen the self, reinforce one's own sense of inner goodness and the ability to do good; it is as if the supply of love were limited and cannot be produced within the self. I am not suggesting that love can be infinite, nor am I advocating that people make martyrs of themselves; I am saying that the ability to love does not depend on some one-to-one reciprocity with the love of another, but rather crucially depends on the state of one's own inner world. It is, I imagine, a fairly common experience to know that one is receiving love but is unable to find the inner resources to return it.

In Giddens's discussion of intimacy and trust, there is talk of the balance of privacy and sharing, but no clear discussion of what the two might mean. I have doubts about the word 'sharing' – it is well established in counsellese and is a rather delicate word which, in a counselling or therapy context, is usually used to refer to talking or telling somebody about something. Now this seems to me an inappropriate use of it. There are a number of dictionary meanings available; these can be reduced to two basic groupings – a sharing out and a sharing with. Now in the first case, a sharing out, a more or less fixed quantity is assumed and is divided out, not necessarily in equal proportions, between a number of people. Now if I tell somebody about something that is private, personal, I am not sharing in this sense. It is not like sharing out my box of chocolates; I don't end up with less than I had at the beginning – although there is a sense in which the other person ends up with more. Revealing an intimacy is more like a gift than a sharing, and can be experienced as such by both partners; I sometimes have a slight suspicion that the word 'sharing' is preferred by counsellors and therapists because it hides the inequality of the exchange. I believe the inequality is a necessary one, but it should be recognised for what it is.

Turning now to sharing with: the connotation here is that I undergo a similar experience of events with somebody else. Again this does not seem to me to be a matter of telling somebody else something that might hitherto have been private. Using a therapy group as an example, people do talk about their feelings, about events in their lives, about secrets. They often comment that they know the people in the group better than they know anybody else, including their spouses. But they do not *share* each other's private experiences – it is not the case that if, as a patient, I tell a group about my rows with my wife, they share my experience of that row. To do that they would have had to be inhabiting my body at the time of the row; we do not undergo the experience together. What we do undergo together, what we do share, is the experience of being in the group, listening to each other, reacting to each other, and it tends to be on this level that the therapeutic value of the group can be found.

In a relationship, whether or not we tell our partners what we are thinking and feeling, what is actually shared is the experience of being together in the same place, living together in the same home, undergoing the same events together. A relationship cannot but be shared in this sense. What we tell each other about ourselves is another matter. The paradox I noted earlier, that in a therapy group the levels of intimacy are higher than those outside, is interesting. A therapy group is a group of strangers whose only contact is that they sit in the same room for 90 or perhaps 180 minutes a week, and beyond that have no presence in each other's lives. If this were not the case, then they would be unable to reveal as much as they do in the group – an external relationship between group members always inhibits what goes on in the group.

The implication of this is that (a) sharing is always present in a relationship, however much the partners do or do not reveal to each other – it is not the opposite of privacy, and (b) the level of self-revelation in a normal relationship – sexual or otherwise – has to be limited to make it work. It can at times be a very deep intimacy, at others it will not. Privacy is not just a matter of autonomy but also a matter of making something work. If my wife told me every time she found another man attractive, or every time that she was irritable with something I was doing, if she always told me about what she could not stand about me (and vice versa of course) life would soon become intolerable. In a therapy group, these things can be said and explored; in a relationship this might be possible on occasions, but I suspect that for those occasions to be possible, a great deal of not talking is necessary.

Whether I am right about this or not, to imagine that it can all be settled by a series of directives such as those in the later quotation misses the point. Whether we are talking about intimacy, self-revelation, trust or whatever, the conflicts are as much internal as external, and often below our conscious perception, erupting in all sorts of unexpected ways. Making time to talk to one's partner is clearly a good idea, but sometimes it can be important not to talk. I think here of a patient who was struggling in psychotherapy with her constant unfaithfulness to her husband, upon whom she also felt very dependent. The two were clearly connected, but for a lot of the time, she saw the conflict as having to do with not finding him sexually attractive, which she felt really meant that the relationship was not workable; yet she also felt love for him as well as dependence on him. The only way in which she could begin to talk about it with him would have been by criticising, hurting him and endangering the relationship which she needed. In these circumstances it seemed to me that she was both morally and practically right not to talk about it – to let sleeping dogs lie, as it were, until she herself understood better what was happening. Now this seems quite reasonable: we need to be able to make judgements of, for example, when talking about ourselves is a form of unwarranted attack on the other person, when it is an attempt to project part of ourselves that we do not like, or when it is a demand that can never be satisfied. It is often, in my experience, precisely these drives that make it so urgent to communicate, to be intimate, and at the same time are destructive of intimacy.

Some of the other guidelines in the quotation seem to me simply unrealistic. Sticking to one issue until it is resolved is a lifetime's work in some cases and the only resolution – if that is the right word – is death; probably the death of both partners, since the surviving partner is likely to spend a lot of time reworking it all. Between any two people there will be differences that jar; some differences are so great and have such an immediate effect that we call them a personality clash. On the whole, I suspect we sensibly avoid such people if we can and go through a lot of suffering if we don't. But even with the people we love, we will find aspects that at one time or another, we simply cannot bear. If the relationship lasts for a long time we might find that we cannot stand the things we once loved about someone, and vice versa. But even in late modernity our character traits tend to be comparatively stable, and we have to make shifting compromises with what we do not like in the other person, and part of those compromises will be arguments about the same thing. The instructions go on to outlaw destructive anger – everything has to be made good rather than recognised as bad and contained – and insist on 'an atmosphere of caring'. This of course takes us to the professionalisation of personal relationships as well as parenting: life would be much better if partners were each other's therapists rather than each other's partners.

CONCLUSION

Now if all this does not fit the reality of the self, it is worth asking why people believe it, and what it does to warrant its existence. On a psychological level, it is a form of, I suspect often rather desperate, wishful thinking, a desire to get out of the mess of life. In terms of the way society works, however, something more is going on. One way of thinking about it is as what Marxists used to call an ideology, a systematically distorted set of beliefs that can be seen in two ways. One is that it is a set of beliefs produced out of the immediate experience of people but which hides a deeper social reality. A simple example would be the way in which an industrial worker might have some idea of what a fair day's pay for a fair day's work might involve and would be happy if he or she were getting that wage. Marx's argument was that even a 'fair' wage hid an exploitation that we cannot see, but could only discover through an economic analysis of the way in which capitalism worked.

The immediate experience of our lives, the fragmentation of our experience, does, it seems, lead to omnipotent conception of the self, but the attempts at self-reconstruction are constant failures, just as the attempted rewritings I described earlier failed. We can explain the persistence of the view, however, through a second dimension of the notion of ideology: that it serves our interests to hold a distorted set of beliefs. This happens, I think, when we realise we can ride the confusion of everyday life by making a career of counselling and psychotherapy; the psychological mechanism here is one I have discussed already – the phantasy that we can 'cure' our own mess by curing it in others. This leads us into a profession of social control, practised by those in the experiential group who try to explain away the pain, who therapise rather than understand, and the social structures of late modernity have an important place for such a profession.

My argument in this chapter has been that late modernity takes us beyond the notion of self-control to a conception of the omnipotent, self-constructing self, but the descriptions of such a self and the way it aims at emotional gratification indicate that it is in fact a very weak self employing an illusion of power and satisfaction, protecting its fragmented state because that seems to be the source of its power.

Chapter 8

The disappointment of identity
What sort of man?

I suggested as part of an earlier discussion that the politics of late modernity become bound up with our sense of identity, and I want to explore this through the sexual politics of masculinity. It seems to me that the attempt to find an 'identity' in any simple sense is doomed to disappointment, and that includes the attempt to find an identity based on sex and/or gender. Implicated in these disappointments are the notions I have been criticising – those of emotional management, the omnipotent self that can recreate itself, and behind that psychotherapy as an abstract system laying down the framework of the sort of people we should be.

Issues of gender are intimately bound up with the problems I have been discussing, not least in the frequently heard observation that women are more able and willing to talk about their feelings than are men. My own ideas about differences between the sexes have become much more complex over recent years. Perhaps the easiest way of putting it to begin with is that I now keep a much clearer line between what goes on in what I called 'society outside the head' and what goes on in personal relationships, which exist largely inside people's heads. There is no doubt that the two are connected, most obviously in the way that external social inequalities between men and women determine important inequalities in personal relationships – in terms, say, of property ownership, access to salaries, etc. The removal of such inequalities seems to me an entirely praiseworthy aim. Further, it is common-place – and right – to point out that in the division between public and private, women have been assigned to the subordinate, private sphere, whilst men have controlled the public sphere. Now on one level this is clearly and obviously true: the con-ventional division of labour has assigned women to the home and men to the outside world of work; men *have* dominated in what we call public life, and in many, many areas still do so.

However, the argument is taken further, to the point where we are urged to see the personal as political, and this is where I feel suspicious (see Craib 1988). All individuals, men and women, carry an internal distinction between what is private to them and what is open to public scrutiny. We can all say: 'That is none of your business.' Many of the developments I have outlined in the previous few chapters have led to an erosion of that private area, the maintenance of which, I shall argue later, is essential for the survival both of ourselves as individuals and of a democratic society. A feature of late modernity seems to be that each of us as individuals can experience himself or herself as immediately related to an entity which might be the state, or Giddens's abstract systems, with no mediation. The personality comes to be seen as part of the dynamics of that wider abstract system – what Habermas (1984, 1987) talks about as the colonisation of the life-world by the functional rationality of the system. It seems no longer possible to think of a private world – private to the personality, or to the family, or to the circle of friends – as a defence against the invasion of our lives by the dynamics of the wider system. The slogan 'The personal is political' makes that reality a virtue and reinforces the illusion of the powerful self which can control its make-up as politicians can supposedly control the make-up and direction of the state.

The argument that 'the personal is political' is an invasion of the 'private' by the world of the state. The question 'Who am I?' thus gets caught up in political arguments, another set of 'abstract systems' in addition to those represented by psychotherapy.

HATED IMAGES

I suggested earlier that one of the 'negative' themes in psychoanalytic theory emphasised the problems presented by dealing with our psychological bisexuality when most of us belong to a reasonably clear, single, biological category, and possess one of two possible sets of genitalia. The dilemma is complicated by the fact that both men and women have orifices and things to put into and stimulate orifices – this makes possible various forms of homosexual activity. The crunch of the difference seems to come with reproduction, and I sometimes think that the lasting scandal of human life is that we cannot reproduce by parthogenesis. To reproduce, men and women need each other, and therefore have good reason both to love and to hate each other – in much the same way that we need, and therefore love and hate, our parents. From this, it is possible to surmise that there will be moments when sexual difference is felt as a radical opposition; from my observation in therapy groups this occurs when hatred is the dominant theme, and very primitive psychological images of the opposite sex can be very near the surface.

Two such images seem to me particularly important. The image of the man is most commonly one of an absolute brutality, a man who gets what he wants by force, brooks no dissent and allows no freedom. The counterpart image of woman is all-powerful, irrationally uncaring, demanding obedience on threat of desertion – the mother who either s-mothers or abandons (see Winnicott 1988). Christina Wieland (1991) suggests that this primitive image of man is present for both sexes, and I suspect that is true for the image of woman as well. Some of the most tense moments I have known in therapy groups have been when these two primitive images seemed to face each other, each embodied in a man and woman whose previous histories had given a reality to their image of the opposite sex.

To go with these primitive, frightening and hateful images, there will also be ideal images – the ideal parents who never, of course, actually exist. Often, in my experience, these images are modified to fit one of several available social stereotypes – the independent woman, the submissive woman, the strong man, the new man and so on. Interestingly, the opposite of the moments of hate, those of falling in love, seem to free the internal images, so that for a while it appears possible to be a different sort of man or woman to the one one has been. In between the primitive images, the ideals and the comparative fluidity of falling in in love, there are all sorts of gradation in the way we may experience ourselves as a man or a woman and the way we experience members of the opposite sex. If there is an ideal for a relationship, then perhaps in the 'mansion of many rooms' that I referred to there would be rooms for each of the possible images, including the hateful and hated ones.

Now when the personality is brought into the political realm it is subjected to political arguments, which might be appropriate to politics but not to the personality. Politics can involve attacking, criticising and trying to eliminate, and when applied to the personality, the hateful and hated images become increasingly important as objects of attack and/or defence. They are not seen as necessary parts of life and relationships. The very real structural inequality of women becomes telescoped into equally real but very different aspects of the psyche, and perhaps for that reason, more intractable: social inequalities might be open to solution; primitive phantasies have to be lived with.

From the experience of ourselves as fragmented individuals in the face of 'something big out there' that we do not understand, we can believe that what goes on in our inner world is a direct product of what goes on outside, and/or we can begin to look there for sources of a firm identity that we can call our own. In either case or both, we can find ourselves seeking a sense of identity through a form of politics. It is in this context that I want to look at some contemporary ideas of masculinity. One of the earlier list of features of 'postmodern' society was the fragmentation of gender and sexual categories. There is a sense in which the stigmatisation of certain sexual practices, such as homosexuality, makes these practices central to one's identity – this has been a regular theme in the sociology of deviance. It is also the case that the systematically structured inequality of women provides a focus for attempting to find one's identity in one's sex or gender. Neither of these things seems to apply in the case of heterosexual men – to seek a sense of identity in masculinity is on the face of it apparently purely reactive, except in so far as falls into a more general pattern of 'identity finding' through sex, sexuality and gender.

THE PSYCHOANALYTIC SOCIOLOGY OF SEX AND GENDER

It is not surprising that psychoanalysis has had a fair amount to say about contemporary notions of sex and gender, and I want to work my way into the argument through looking at two very different approaches. One dominant strand of psychoanalytic feminism can be found in the work of the sociologist Nancy Chodorow (1978) and the psychotherapists Louise Eichenbaum and Susie Orbach (1985), which reproduces the telescoping of the personal and the political/social. There is a longish tradition in sociology that looks for a 'fit' between personality structure and

the wider society, the society 'working' in such a way as to produce
the personalities that it needs. Again Parsons (Parsons and Bales
1956) presented the most systematic version of this: women look
after the domestic and affective, men look after work, and
socialisation produces the right sorts of personality to do this. The
feminist psychoanalytic argument is, very broadly, that women
are left the task of 'mothering', and the way in which they mother
girl and boy children is different. In the case of little girls, there is
a strong identification between mother and daughter, and a
dilemma for the mother. The mother has been taught to suppress
her own needs and to gain her satisfaction from meeting the needs
of others. In her daughter she sees someone who must learn to do
the same but who is also herself tremendously needy – bringing
out the mother's own suppressed neediness. This is handled by a
fluctuation between a close identification with the infant daughter
and her neediness, and the attempt to suppress that neediness,
which leads to a sort of radical distance – a fluctuation in the
relationship which often continues into the daughter's adult life.
The argument also runs that because of the intensity and depth of
the relationship, the daughter is kept psychologically dependent
on the mother longer than is necessary; this is one of the ways she
learns to put her own needs into abeyance in order to satisfy the
needs of others. The little boy, by contrast, is pushed into
psychological independence earlier, and also learns that his needs
will be satisfied by women in a direct fashion. This leaves women
more open to emotional identification with others, and more able
to intuit and willing to satisfy the needs of others; whilst men
become more concerned with their own satisfaction and less open
to emotional identification with others. Hence women remain best
suited for the domestic sphere of emotions and caring, men for
the world of work.

The suggested solution is to bring men more into the world of
emotions and of child-rearing. This is an admirable idea, but what
I want to question is whether the problem its proponents point to
exists in the form that is claimed. There *are* very powerful
stereotypes of masculinity and femininity; these seem to exist in
most, if not all, societies, but they differ from society to society, and
within the same society they differ according to social class and to
geographical area. However, in our society, the general associations between masculinity and doing things, lack of emotion, etc.,
and between femininity and emotion, caring work, etc., have been

around for a long time. However, social change has been such that once the masculine was held up as a social ideal to which women, by nature, could not match up, whereas now, at least in some areas of our society, the feminine is held up as a social ideal, either to which men are unable to aspire or towards which they should try to change.

This sort of analysis seems to work if we remain at the level of accepted stereotypes; whenever I ask students – in mixed classes – to set out their conception of masculinity, they produce some variant of the stereotype: men are rational, aggressive, insensitive, etc.; but they always make qualifications. They point out that it *is* a stereotype, that they know men who are not like this. More importantly, from my point of view, I simply do not see any systematic differences of such a type between men and women in my therapy groups or my experiential groups. However, such differences are claimed when there is conflict and particularly when the more primitive images of masculinity and femininity are near the surface – and in such a situation, the stereotypes frequently seem to become true. They often appear in marital conflict, although again my experience has been that they are not appropriate when the partners are not in conflict or are separate from each other. It might be that the arguments about the different childhood experiences of men and women are broadly right, but most people of both sexes come through them with a more or less wide emotional register and ability for relating. If we think of it as a continuum, I suspect most people would be clustered around the middle range but that as we approach the ends of the continuum, we will find more men at one end and more women at the other.

The existence of social stereotypes, whatever their content, is, I suspect, a result of the necessity to maintain some sense of difference between the sexes in order to ensure reproduction. What matters is that there is a difference. As the American feminist, Gayle Rubin, put it:

> In fact, from the standpoint of nature, men and women are closer to each other than either is to anything else – for instance, mountains, kangaroos or coconut palms . . . though there is an average difference between males and females in a variety of traits, the range of variation of those traits show a considerable overlap . . . exclusive gender identity is the expression of

natural similarities. It requires repression, in men, of whatever is the local version of 'feminine' traits; in women of the local definition of 'masculine' traits.

(Rubin 1975: 179–80)

But as Rubin recognises, the repression is not complete; there is considerable overlap. The different socialisation processes of men and women, similarly, do not produce the cultural stereotypes – they leave each sex with a skewed but recognisable collection of common human traits, abilities, emotions etc. We are not formed in outline and in detail by cultural stereotypes or socialisation practices: they provide more or less flexible spaces or channels through which we move; in firm outline and detail we are formed by the specificities of our life – the raw material of our parents and situations and the myriad of cross-gender identifications that make each of us different and unique. What we then do is use these spaces and channels in various ways. Now there is no doubt that some of the social roles set out for us can be extremely restrictive, and that is a good reason for trying to bring about cultural and social change; but even as we do this, what actually happens, whether we are conscious of it or not, is that we protect ourselves from, use, comply with these roles. Any role which we occupy is going to involve some restriction, will only mobilise some part of ourselves – the question is always: what degree of restriction, what other sorts of restriction would we prefer?

What really happens, then, is that we use social roles, cultural practices, in different ways. To argue that there is a match between gender role and personality is mistaken; gender roles are tools with which personalities – a specific combination of 'masculine' and 'feminine' traits – struggle to communicate themselves. If sex/gender roles are more clearly demarcated, then the expression of men's 'feminine' traits and women's 'masculine' traits will be socially hidden, but there if we care to look. For much of the modern age, most people seem to have made do with this. With the impetus towards increased role fragmentation in late modernity, this now seems difficult and sex/gender roles themselves seem to fragment, and it is at this point that people begin to conceive of their personalities in political terms, to experience any role as a prison, and to seek 'solutions'. I want to look at three different reactions to this fragmentation as it relates to masculinity, each of which seems to seek a masculine identity and each of which would entail a more or less radical disappointment.

FIRST CHOICE: THE NEW MAN

One way of reacting to the fragmentation is to aim to become a 'new man'. As a basis I am taking a chapter from a book by David Jackson: *Unmasking Masculinity* (1990), an autobiographical work which is in many ways a symptom of the 'self' typical of late modernity as I discussed it in the previous chapter. In Jackson's case a series of life crises after a successful career in teaching brought him to question the sort of person he had been, to undergo a long period of therapy and counselling and to come out the other side as what I suppose we might appropriately call a 'new man'. He says at the beginning that he is not setting about the discovery of a 'real self' – he does not believe such a thing exists; rather identity or the self is necessarily divided against itself, a sentiment which on the surface is not very different from my own argument. He insists on the interlocking of social ideologies of masculinity and experience, phantasies and feelings, and of course these are interrelated, but not as directly as he seems to imagine. One way of looking at the book is as describing a change from a personality appropriate to a middle-class man some twenty to thirty years ago to one appropriate to such a man at the present time; the social changes that require such a transformation, the fragmentation of our experience of the world, of relationships and of the self have already been described.

I will proceed by setting out a number of quotations from his chapter on sexuality, and then discussing them in detail. In the first the author is talking about his feelings about his mother and his father – the latter often absent as he was growing up in wartime.

> I was so wrapped around in the folds of my mother's body that the boundaries of self and not-self didn't exist for me. The sense of complete fusion and oneness meant that I didn't have a sense of self apart from her. But simultaneously, I was also threatened by a fear of a possible withdrawal of that warm, protective nest. I was clingy around her because I was anxious, if she vanished, like in the peek-a-boo game, I would be annihilated. I didn't have a sense of who I was outside my

contact with my mother, so if she disappeared I became totally wiped out as well.

This partly explains my continuing ambivalence in trying to build a male gender identity and sexuality. Through all the reasons stated above (particularly my closeness to my mother and the sustained absence of my father) I found it extraordinarily threatening and painful to part myself from the seductive warmth of my relationship with my mother in order to build a separate, masculine sense of self through identifying with a distant father. The really painful thing was having to repress my closeness with and dependence on my mother in order to become 'masculine'. This led to a later over-straining to assert my 'masculine' identification at the expense of a feared softness or anything that could be interpreted as dangerously 'feminine'.

Therefore I wasn't able to experience myself as a male without a deep ambivalence, conflict and self-doubt.

(Jackson 1990: 116)

This seems to me to fit *too* easily with the theory I outlined earlier; it is an ordering of an experience rather than a questioning of experience. If we substitute 'men' and impersonal pronouns for 'I' and 'me' and cut out the odd personal detail, then we have not a memoir but a theory, and this is true of the chapter as a whole. Compare this with the way in which a therapeutic understanding of one's past is achieved; part of it certainly might involve an explanation, even an explanation of the sort provided in the quotation, but the explanation by itself is often anti-therapeutic. A patient who believes he has found an explanation for what troubles him can slip into a feeling that nothing need be done about it. A therapeutic understanding, however, is different. It is interesting to compare Jackson's account with Frank O'Connor's short story 'My Oedipus Complex' (1953). O'Connor's story deals with the identical situation – the return of a father from the War, being turned out of his mother's bed, dealing with the stranger in the house. It is a gentle and humorous story which tells of immense childhood rage and involves an acceptance of what was, surrounded by memories which are quite specific rather than illustrations of the theory. The forgiveness is in the story, not the self-conscious, almost political act that Jackson makes it, saying that he doesn't want to blame his mother, for she was doing what she could in a sexist society.

It might seem unfair to compare what is basically a work of psychological and sociological explanation with what is (probably) an autobiographical short story. But the work of psychological and sociological explanation is actually presented as an auto-biography, clearly one informed by the experience of therapy; and my main point is that the short story is a much better source for understanding the therapeutic experience. It seems to me that in the practice of psychotherapy, one of the therapeutic moments of the group process is the exploration of memories, some of which might have been suppressed, in which childhood feelings and actions are described and brought to life: they become part of the speaker, part of what he or she is in the present, rather than something lost or left behind, or internally discarded. When a group is seeking explanations, on the other hand, the speaker is at a distance from himself or herself, a distance which discards the experience rather than integrating it. Explanations are always to some degree a loss of self, when the aim of therapy is a finding of self. An autobiography written in these terms is a symptom of the penetration of the self by abstract systems. Jackson presents himself as a theory rather than a person.

The second point I want to make is that it deals with things that *had* to happen to the writer. The alternative to his course forward was to remain in an implicit or explicit incestuous relationship with his mother. And, of course, a daughter too would have to leave such a relationship. The pull of that early identification is strong, and I suspect that although separation can be made easier if, for example, the father is present, and present as a real person in all his complexity, it is still so difficult that it involves a degree of splitting. If one thinks of the problem, for the moment, as one not of becoming masculine but of becoming independent, then the feeling 'I am going out into the big wide world, and I cannot afford to be vulnerable and needy as I am at home' must be a common one for both sexes. Growing up is a matter of bringing the two together, of being able to be both dependent and inde-pendent, or, better, relatively independent or relatively dependent. If we return to thinking of masculinity, then the task of becoming 'masculine' for a man is bringing together the masculine and the feminine in the appropriate personal combination; the task of becoming a woman could be described in exactly the same terms. The difference between the sexes involves coming to the appropriate personal balance in relation to different sets of genitalia. Again, I want to emphasise the complexity of cross-identifications that become apparent; if I were to do a crude psychoanalysis of the quotation it would be in terms of emphasising the power of the feminine for this particular writer – something that Jackson himself takes up in his argument that the cultural fear of male inadequacy led him to suppress or repress his feminine side:

> This culturally learned, comparative fear of phallic/social inadequacy formed the basis of a lifetime's 'castration anxiety' in me. The fear that I was a weakling, a sissy, a 'half-pint' was experienced in my self-critical view of my own body. It was this anxiety and fear of not measuring up to the virile, heterosexual norms as represented by my father that produced an ambivalent striving in me towards a genitally-focused masculinity, in an attempt to distance myself from my 'sissy' traits associated with my mother.
>
> (Jackson 1990: 117)

It seems, apparently, that it was the size of his father's penis that he found particularly difficult to come to terms with. This was a perception of a real situation: little boys (and little girls) are not as big, as strong, or as capable as their parents (or at least I hope they are not). They will, in time, become all or some of these things. However, this means accepting a *de facto* inferiority that will last until some time in the future.

What Jackson is doing in these passages is confusing two aspects of a man's development that are confused in reality but need to be separated out when we think about it. By making masculinity the centre of self or identity, the two are hopelessly fused. The two processes are becoming an adult human being and becoming an adult male human being. Becoming an adult human being involves separation from the mother, from the seductive warmth and security of that early relationship; this involves a degree, possibly a high degree, of loss and consequent suffering. It also involves a recognition that one is not as powerful as one's phantasies would have it, as one would hope to be, as one probably imagined one was in that early relationship. This too involves disappointment, loss and consequent pain. These things have to happen if we are going to grow up. Becoming an adult male involves these thing as well, but also finding a compromise between one's femininity and masculinity, one's sexuality, the social expectations and definitions attached to gender, all of which tend to be run together in ways that make it difficult to sort out. It seems to me that the one indisputable fact about this latter process is that it is easier if one knows a male – a father or father-figure – in all his complexity and contradictions; a physically absent father, an emotionally absent father makes growing up as a male difficult.

But even with a good-enough father-figure, growing up is difficult, involving the sort of splitting, the fears and feelings of inadequacy that Jackson talks about. It is as if he lays all these difficulties at the door of our cultural definitions of masculinity, into which he had to be socialised; I am saying they would be there anyway and to rebel against these difficult experiences *per se* is to rebel against growing up.

Turning to the conclusion of the chapter, Jackson writes:

> The conflict between my need for masculine confirmation through sexual conquest and a desire for a grown up relationship has begun to be resolved over the years . . .
>
> At the centre of this process of reworking for me is the redefinition of what counts as male sexuality and a questioning of what seems most 'natural' in heterosexual relations. Dimly I have become aware that the 'natural drive' of my sexual behaviour – and especially thrusting, goal-oriented behaviour inevitably centred on penetration and orgasm – is a defensive carapace built to protect my fears of revealing my shaky grip on my masculine heterosexual identity . . .
>
> I now cannot experience myself as a man without deep ambivalence, conflict and self-doubt. That sense of my own emotional neediness has been difficult to admit and recognise in my own life because it eats away so voraciously at the foundations of my masculine identification and my power. As a result I have compensated for these eroding fears of emotional dependence, long-term involvement and vulnerability by clinging on to those ego-bolstering habits of activity and strength found in the 'natural drive' of masculine, heterosexual behaviour.
>
> I have now become aware that because of my need for self-affirmation and 'exercising power' in a world I suspect might be crumbling away at any minute, I have over-concentrated on my genital sexuality which has tended to stand

in for my whole masculine identity . . . and confused sex with
loving.

In trying to unlock a damaging split in me between a
traditional, fixed notion of masculinity/femininity, I've found
the attempt to relate to women in a warm, understanding but
non-sexual way important . . .

With difficulty, I've managed to build this kind of new
relationship with a woman friend over the last five years. What
it's helped me to do is to learn how to relate to women as total
personalities rather than sexual objects. Taking the sex out of
the relationship has enabled us to build an emotional and
intellectual understanding without being forced into the old
predatory or needy patterns.

(Jackson 1990: 133–5)

In this quotation I think we can see the underlying search for
a sex/gender identity. The confessional nature is clear, the sort of
confession that one might once have expected from someone who
has discovered Christianity – 'Once I was a sinner, but now . . .'.
Just as with religious conversions, what we are seeing is less
something which emerges from inside the person than something
which is taken from outside and imposed on what is inside. What
does seem clear is that the writer's experience has brought him
into contact with his internal complexity, particularly his
vulnerability and neediness. 'Brought him into contact with'
perhaps needs to be modified – it is clear from what he writes that
at some level he was always aware of these things and expressed
them, but now both contact and expression have changed. There
seems to have been an inversion in his evaluation of his self, and
a different set of qualities is now condemned and avoided. There
are comments about integration, but it is also clear what is good
and bad, and the self remains divided. From being one type of
man, the author has moved to trying to be another type of man,
but what is lost somewhere is what I might call, with some
trepidation, being himself – the 'real self' being precisely the
'ambivalence, conflict and self-doubt' that he comments on as if it
were the curse of his upbringing.

What, from the above quotations, can we deduce about the
nature of sex? It seems a highly serious matter, to be thought
about, struggled with and worked on; it is dangerous, involving
the exercise of power over other people, and particularly women;

it can, but shouldn't be, centred on the genitals; it seems to have nothing to do with producing children; and it needs to be complemented by non-sexual relationships with women.

One interesting feature of this list is that whilst the tenor of Jackson's discussion shares the concern, discussed in the previous chapter, with immediate emotional gratification, immediate sexual gratification seems to be another matter. On the whole traditional morality has condemned seeking immediate gratification in sexual relationships and emphasised their seriousness, and in this sense the morality of late modernity seems to concur with the morality of twenty or fifty years ago. In terms of the sexual act alone, seeking immediate gratification seems to me unproblematic if it is pleasurable to both partners, but it is also true that there should be some reciprocity between partners and this might involve one or both delaying gratification; and in a wider context, of course, the search for immediate gratification is likely to lead to an unpleasant chaos. Now it is also true that the sexual act always involves using the other person to achieve one's own orgasm; for a period at least, it only works if each partner becomes a sexual object for the other and uses the other for his or her gratification. It is to easy to talk about not using somebody and not treating somebody as a sexual object – it may gain the moral high ground but it makes the sexual act impossible. To treat somebody *only* as a sexual object is desirable only if that is what both partners want.

What is missing, however, is any idea that sex might be fun. Christopher Lasch (1980) identifies this as a feature of the narcissistic personality. In the context of my argument it seems a feature of a fragile self, and perhaps one haunted by primitive phantasies about the sexual act, tied up with the idea that the world might 'crumble away at any minute'. Whereas the 'thrusting goal-oriented sexuality' of Jackson's old self seems to have been a defence against such a crumbling away, now it is his avoidance of such activity. It is certainly 'bad', as if self-affirmation in sex will perhaps cause the other to crumble. This aside, however, his previous conquest-oriented behaviour and his way of writing about it now both imply a fragility of the self, as if closeness in the sexual act, the merging that takes place in the sexual act, might involve a loss of identity. His previous behaviour, as he describes it, seems to enable him to avoid intimacy, but strangely his present behaviour can also be seen as built around a similar avoidance of the complexity of an intimate sexual relationship. When he writes about non-sexual relationships with women, it is as if he is writing from an internal fragmentation of needs. Some needs may be met by his sexual partner and others may be met by non-sexual relationships with other women.

On the face of it, this is common sense: no one person can be everything we want, and most people have a range of friends. But if we ask what is being avoided in the sexual relationship, it seems to me to be the confrontation, even the conflagration that might initially occur if his whole personality were brought into play. What is not clear from what he writes is whether this 'spreading' of needs is a result of the conflicts and slow processes of mutual understanding that a relationship involves, or whether it is a way of avoiding those conflicts. My guess is the second, as the argument is one familiar to me from people who seem to need to keep at arm's length the depths of feeling that can be reached in a sexual relationship – an understandable reaction, but one which detracts from the richness that is possible.

Now sex as play in my experience can occur at the beginning of a relationship, where it is surrounded often by real passion, the straightforward, physical, lustful passion of exploring a new body and the passion of being in love. The process of identification with the other, the merging that goes on and the sorting out of a knowledge of the other person that is closer to reality than to phantasy, can make sex a serious business; as can the routine and familiarity that come later, when there is a need, in current phraseology, to 'work' at it; but if the work goes well, then the 'fun' aspect will be to the fore. Sexuality is certainly dangerous, and it is at times surrounded by all the conflicts, internal and external, of the relationship, and the invasion of the personal by the political now weighs it down with the problems of the good society. The possibility that at times it may just be fun, relaxation, and pleasurable is difficult to retrieve.

One of the political issues that surround us as part of late modernity is that of power, and the interpersonal dimensions of power seem to run directly into its political, social and economic aspects; the former can seem simply to be an extension of the latter. To a degree, of course, the two do interpenetrate – this is especially the case in terms of the way that economic inequalities are reflected in inequalities in a relationship between a man and a woman, and these can and do haunt the relationship. 'Money' is one of the most frequent reasons for quarrelling. However, the important point I want to make here is that inequality cannot be eradicated but it can be modified within the relationship. In other words, it can be fought over, and shifting compromises reached. The same is true of other social inequalities, although it is perhaps easy to overestimate how far this can occur – attempts to take on an equal sharing in child-care seem to have the odds loaded against them by the nature of the labour market and the almost complete absence, in Britain at any rate, of paternity leave. But there are always degrees of difference and degrees of inequality, there are always battles that need to be fought. The important thing about these battles in relationships is that within the limits set by the surrounding social structure, both parties possess what I would call 'interpersonal power' – the various strategies which we use to persuade other people to comply with our own wishes: they include trying to talk to a partner, remaining silent, bullying, adopting the victim role and so on. My point is that power is unavoidable, it is inherent in the very concept of action and we have it by virtue of being human, and to try to renounce one form of power is to exercise power in another way. There is a recognition of this in various jokes about, for example, the 'new man' finding it easier to make sexual conquests than the 'old'.

In the quotation the exercise of power is linked with genital sexuality and then with penetration. The form of sexuality which the author is working towards is later illustrated by him as taking turns with his partner to rub baby oil into each other's backs. In strict Freudian terms this is a return to a pregenital, polymorphous sexuality – not a return I would want in any way to condemn, incidentally, since such mutual massage is an extremely pleasant activity. What is open to question is the apparent favouring of this activity over genital sexuality. Freud though of genital sexuality as 'mature' for a very good reason – that it is necessary if the species is going to continue in existence; as I have said before, enough of us have to be heterosexual, have to achieve genital sexuality, for enough of the time to ensure reproduction. If power is undesirable, and is associated with penetration, then what happens at some level is the rejection of bearing children; there is nothing at all about parenting in Jackson's chapter on sexuality, and very little indeed in the book itself, although he fathered three children in his first marriage.

Power itself of course is not undesirable, nor is thrusting activity, nor, I hope, is having children. A systematically unequal distribution of power is undesirable; concentrating on 'thrusting activity' by itself might be desirable or undesirable – although if the sexual act is confined to thrusting activity, I suspect it will very soon become boring. Confining the sexual act to acts of reproduction is undesirable, and I suspect for humans impossible, but severing the act entirely from its reproductive function seems equally undesirable. My argument is that mixing up these levels of power results in a gross oversimplification of what goes on between people, and if as a man I seek to find my identity by taking the 'right side' in these personal political battles, then it involves an attempt to reject an essential part of my personality – or of *anybody's* personality – a sort of personality engineering.

I think this is most clear in the attempt to develop a non-sexual relationship with a woman. What Jackson has to say makes sense on the level of a relationship in which the sexual component is not acted out; the morality of a relationship lies in what one does, not what one is, and most people are involved in all sorts of relationship – especially with children and with parents and with siblings, but also with a range of other adults – where an acting out of sexual desires would be inappropriate. But this is not to say that the sexual desires themselves should not be there; indeed I suspect we have no choice about this. In some relationships, it is important that the desire be there but that the action should not be taken – the relationship between parents and children is an example of this. I suspect indeed that the best adult friendships – with members of the opposite sex or members of the same sex – involve precisely these desires which are not acted upon. In this sense all our important relationships will be sexual relationships. It is unclear from Jackson's account whether he is conscious of this, but the thrust of his argument indicates that he is engaged in an attempt to be different rather than to act differently – an attempt which is as doomed to failure as the attempt to be 'good' which most of us make as children.

SECOND CHOICE: THE 'MEN'S MOVEMENT'

A second false solution reverts to a more traditional conception of masculinity, not, however, that associated with patriarchy – the dominant, violent male. It is in this area that Jungian analysis seems to be contributing most to 'therapy' as an abstract system, drawing on mythologies as offering explorations of masculinity and guides to achieving it. I am thinking in particular of Robert Bly's work *Iron John* (1990) and the literature that has grown up around it, and the 'movement' that seems to have developed, especially in America.

I am actually unclear about many of the aims and ideas of the movement: they seem appropriately confused – an appropriateness that I shall explain later. One argument is rooted firmly in material that I have already discussed. It is that with the separation of home and work, father and son have become distanced – the theme of the absent father. Men grow up in our society without the older male guide, mentor, sage or what you will, to initiate them into masculinity, into manhood. Anthropological evidence is drawn on to show that societies other than our own seem to have clear gender roles, even where social and economic relations between the sexes are more equal than ours and even where the male gender role is not one we associate with our forms of male dominance. The achievement of success as a man is seen as satisfying the requirements of these roles. To achieve these roles, to achieve masculinity, involves a series of initiations, of tasks. It is this that has been lost in modern society.

Bly himself, rather like Jackson, takes '1950s man' as the model to be broken away from, and it is often argued that what we call 'patriarchy', strictly the rule of the father but more often the name for what people don't like, is a comparatively recent historical phenomenon, beginning with the separation of home and work. I have doubts about this, particularly since it seems to be tied up with the idea that men should take responsibility for the existence of patriarchy, as if it were a creation of men. It is as if the current fantasy that we have control over our lives is being read back into history. Against this I want to juxtapose the idea that people have never been in control of their lives and that the individual life is always a matter of struggling with conflicting internal and external forces that we do not control. We find ourselves placed in different social positions and we have no control over that placement; at different times in history, we might have a different range of choices about what we do about the placement, but that is all. At different times in history we might have different choices about dealing with the drives and emotions that render us recognisable as human beings, but again that is all. Thus to see patriarchy in terms of personal misdeeds and personal guilt is not very helpful – as a social system it remains not understood, unknown. Thus I am a little suspicious of Bly's notion that proper manhood must be regained through grief for past misdeeds, loss of our previous roles and the loss of the father–son relationship. I can grieve for *my* previous misdeeds, loss of *my* previous roles, the absence of a close relationship between *my* father and myself – these indeed are parts of any life. To transpose this onto a collective, however, makes no sense for me. I can see it in familial terms – that I might take on my father's or my grandfather's guilt, perhaps even further back; I might grieve that I will not occupy my father's position – a very important grief if we think of it in terms of the Oedipal complex – but this is probably as much as I can reasonably handle; I don't think I am strong enough to take on as well the grief for all men even through the period of history since the industrial revolution.

So something else is happening in Bly's writing – it is not, I think, a serious proposal that would enable men to lead more effective or comfortable lives, that would direct them to their own individual experiences. It is in fact a blurring of individual differences, of the specific nature of *my* life and the things I have done and the things that have happened to me. To seek my self as a man in the context of a man's movement involves taking on all sorts of experience which do not belong to me and substituting them for the experiences that do. It is much easier to feel guilty about somebody else's sin than it is to recognise and feel guilty about one's own – even if one's own is on a much lesser scale. When the women's movement first began forming itself on the far left, such a strategy was often noted amongst men: feelings were directed to the large issues at the expense of interpersonal relations. Feelings can also be directed to the large issues of interpersonal relations at the expense of how I live with this or that person.

Perhaps a slight digression is necessary here, because it might seem that I am arguing against any sort of collective commitment. I do not think that this is the case, but I think careful thought needs to go into political organisation in a way that perhaps it hasn't before. It does seem to be the case that, as the postmodernist theorists argue, traditional forms of radical, class-based, socialist movements are disappearing and movements around specific issues – ecological issues, gender issues, nationalisms – are taking the centre stage. The traditional class movements, of whatever form of socialism, did have a coherent way of life as their basis: the people involved would live in the same communities, work side by side at similar jobs, share an experience which could enable the Communist Party, the trade union, the socialist party to provide the relationships necessary to a sense of one's own identity. This is indicated for me by the fact that deliberately setting out to find one's identity through such a movement was never commented on and there was, it seems, a dialectic of commitment and withdrawal from the party which was largely unquestioned in terms of the 'self'. Now at least with the gender-based movements, the establishment of a self seems intimately tied up with the politics of the movement, and the self that is sought seems to be sought through discovering identities with others – hence, I think, the fragmentation of such movements: straight men, gay men, different types of gay men, etc. The problem for a collective political commitment seems to me not that of finding the organisation in which a self can be established and maintained, of seeking a basically narcissistic gratification, but that of finding ways of co-operating with people who are different, and as in the case of relationships between the sexes, this involves a degree of self-sacrifice.

But back to my main argument. The 'dominant' male of the 1950s is regarded with suspicion by Bly, but so is the search for what, in cultural terms, is the more feminine side of men, of which Jackson is an illustration. Instead what men need to recapture are qualities of leadership and responsibility, the ability to protect the weak. For Bly, ritual is important, the 'socialisation' of younger men into masculinity by older men, and much of the activity of the men's movement seems to involve reconstructing rituals from more primitive societies: spending weekends in the forest making contact with more primitive feelings. The effects of such rituals seem at first glance to be striking: I have heard a colleague talk admiringly of men looking more upright, stronger, more alive as a result. There is in all this certainly a challenging of feminism; the implication is that under the impact of feminism, men have become too soft, and self-assertion is needed.

Now the rewriting of history, the absorption of the effects of social structural relations into personal relations, all seem to me to be symptomatic in being caught up in late modernity. Men too are now being drawn into the scope of abstract expert systems; it is perhaps the previous gender role of middle-class men in our society, which involved a suppression of emotion, a degree of assertive authority' etc., that makes these attempts – at the moment – look faintly ridiculous. Bly's rituals have been compared to Boy Scout activities and, with more sinister overtones, to those of the Hitler youth, and both comparisons are instructive. The Boy Scout movement belongs fairly firmly to the early twentieth century, an earlier example of an expert system taking over socialising activities from the family, but with a set of ideals that has been dated by very rapid social changes. The Scout movement aimed at a solidity of character, a sense of duty to something bigger than oneself, and a form of self-control that suppressed feeling. The world of late modernity requires a flexibility of character to which a control of feeling is put to service, and it requires loyalty to self rather than something larger than self. The abstract systems which govern our lives do not in themselves seem worthy of loyalty, and they work by drawing not on the loyalty of those who serve them so much as on their self-interest. Above all, of course, the Scout movement was aimed at boys who were in the process of becoming men, not at men who had never made it, and had grown up in a world that no longer required them to make it.

The comparison with the Hitler youth harks back to my earlier comments. The aim in any such social movement is to form the 'self' in such a way as to serve the larger purpose, and most interestingly it has an organic base – there is a history to the German nation, just as there are histories to the social classes that provided the basis of socialist movements. There is no history to men or masculinity in the same sense. Masculinity, of course, has a history: we can trace its various manifestations and developments from time to time and place to place; but it is only over recent decades that any significant number of people have tried to see themselves as 'men' rather than as German or British or American or working class or whatever. There is no organic social base for a men's movement, so what we end up with is simply another way of being men, amongst many others. The Bly rituals do not produce 'men' or enable men to achieve 'masculinity', defined in some ahistorical and transcultural way; rather they allow just one form of masculinity amongst others – and that, of course, is all that has ever been possible, however much men might have tried to persuade themselves that their particular form of masculinity was the 'natural' one.

Rituals are, of course, powerful events. Bly's rituals are not like the long-established ones of, for example, the Church of England, where the effect is the one noted by Durkheim in his discussion of primitive societies: they bring together people who spend much of their lives in separate pursuits in a way which emphasises what they have in common, and confirms the collective support that they might seek if they needed it. The effect of such rituals in my experience is to leave one feeling perhaps more comfortable, a little more secure, perhaps a little more able to be a 'good' person, but not usually transformed. Nor are Bly's rituals like my university departmental meetings, which seem to me to act both to reassure members that they have an opportunity to defend their own interests and have a say in the way the department develops, and to reassure people that they can handle their differences from and hostility to each other. My sense in coming away from a department meeting is often the supremely satisfying one of having participated in making decisions with friends and colleagues and of hating the lot of them and feeling that I have no place there. Both are essential to the working of the department. The first keeps us together, the second provides the grit that keeps us working.

Bly's rituals, however, seem to be distinctly late modern in their nature, in that they are not geared towards the maintenance of normal or routine life, of reinforcing a degree of social cohesion in a society or group that is threatened; men have never been a group in that sense. Rather they are aimed at producing the immediate emotional satisfaction that we have come across before; they are like revivalist and evangelical religious meetings. There are lots of immediate conversions, and perhaps some lasting effects (of which perhaps we ought to be suspicious, as we would of anybody who had found the truth), but most likely a gradual wearing off of the effect. Conceivably we might spend years of our lives trying to achieve a status that we are supposed to have achieved already. And like any other gender role, the individual must adopt a relation to it – one never becomes, except in moments of illusion, one's role; the internal divisions will always remain. This is illustrated by the fact that the pay-off of it all is hardly remarkable. Reviewing a popular version of Bly's work by

Sam Keen, *Fire in the Belly: On Being a Man* (1991), Diane Johnson comments on his encouragement of 'the practice of virtue' and adds: 'In short, there is nothing in this book that one would not enthusiastically wish men to take to heart, or that they could not have heard from their Episcopalian ministers in the Fifties' (Johnson 1992: 15). It seems to boil down to the idea that we should all try to be good people and do what is best, an entirely praiseworthy idea but neither original nor very helpful.

THIRD CHOICE: THE ACCEPTANCE OF PSYCHOLOGICAL BISEXUALITY

I want to look briefly at a third option which I find preferable, but which also illustrates the dangers of running the personal and political together. The first two options both clearly involve a 'false self', a suppression or repression of some part of the personality to mould it towards a social ideal which in turn would try to deny the disappointments it generates. The Jungian analyst, Andrew Samuels, is a lucid proponent of this third view. In his work on fathers and in particular on masculinity (1989, 1993), he argues that in the distinction between the 'old man' and the 'new man' and between 'good' and 'bad' fathers we find a cultural splitting which exists inside and outside individual men. As ever, the split is between two sides of the same coin, and he suggests that we can link the two through what he terms 'aggressive playback', the ability to move between different forms of aggression. He further suggests that the split involves the idea that once a man allows aggression in, he cannot escape from it: this seems to be where Jackson ends up.

When he discusses parenting, Samuels talks about the 'father of either sex' and the 'mother of either sex' and similarly about sons and daughters of either sex. Now this recognises clearly and suggestively the psychological bisexuality in what actually goes on: a woman can both 'mother' and 'father' a child; she can father the son in her daughter and mother the daughter in her son. A man can mother the daughter in his son, and father the son in his daughter. It also illustrates clearly the complexity that must be faced in public debates about parenting, single-parent families, parenting by gay and lesbian couples, etc. Yet if we accept this at face value, we run the risk of setting up another social ideal, one which does not require that we somehow get rid of part of ourselves, but demands that we try to be something that we might not be. I might think, for example, that I ought to be able both to mother and to father my children, and that I ought to be able to mother them as well as their real mother. Yet there is no reason why my own internal 'maternity' should be *as good as* their mother's even though it is undoubtedly there; there is in fact a good reason why it should not be as good as their mother's – that reason is that she is a mother. Now of course some men can carry out mothering better than some women, and vice versa, but we are still left with men and women, and with biological mothers and fathers, and with the simple arithmetical fact that two people will be capable of a wider variety of parenting functions than one. We are encouraged, in late modernity, to think of ourselves as capable of being whatever we want to be; we can be encouraged to think that we can be everything that we might want to be. Yet it remains a problem for me that, however good a mother I can be, I am still a man, I possess a penis rather than a womb, so some essential physical and consequently emotional aspect of mothering is not available to me. I can be a maternal man, but I can never be a mother.

Samuels runs the risk of denying this biological rooting of parenting, and perhaps our biological rooting is the ultimate disappointment: I will never be a mother, never a women. And, of course, it is my limited physical embodiment that leaves me vulnerable to death.

CONCLUSION

Being a man involves, then, a number of disappointments: I will have qualities that are not socially approved or valued (and the social valuation might change over time); I will also possess qualities that I might not like or value (and my valuation need not coincide with social valuation); at some level I will think of myself as a man as a monster; at a similar level, I will think of women as monsters; at other levels I will have a range of more or less realistic conceptions of what men and women are – none of which will match any really existing man or woman; I will possess all sorts of 'feminine' characteristics I might like or not like; I will encounter women who are better men than I, and women who are worse women than I; I will never have a womb and I will never give birth; I am dependent on someone else if I am going to be a father. Throughout life I will have to find shifting compromises between all these facts, but the one thing that is clear is that I can never be a man in any simple sense, nor in any sense that might be held out to me as socially and politically desirable. On the other hand I might spend a lot of time and energy attempting to mutilate myself to become such a person, quite possibly with the help of psychotherapy.

Chapter 9

The false self of late modernity

I launched into a discussion of death, grief and mourning in Chapter 2 because it seemed to me to highlight, in a startling manner, the way in which psychotherapy is implicated in producing an easy, 'optimistic' and, I think, rather glib view of life in late modernity. It is also, I believe, an essential key to what might be called the false self of late modernity, the sort of self that our contemporary society seems to require of us. Grief and mourning involve taking something inside, but not in order to be 'full up', to achieve emotional satisfaction. Rather they involve loss in the outside world and for a while at least they emphasise internal loss, internal inadequacy; our confusions and conflicts are emphasised. This tends to be hidden in our contemporary conceptions: cathartic release – grief, anger – is emphasised and of course cathartic release brings temporary satisfaction, a temporary filling. The complexity and conflicts of the psyche are denied and instead there is the offer of a fuller and more creative life at the end of the process. The mapping of mourning can, at the extreme, be considered a training in how to avoid the work by a deployment of cathartic release and manic defence. This means that it is difficult for an inner world to develop.

The narcissistic personality that Christopher Lasch (19), borrowing from the psychoanalyst Otto Kernberg (1975), identifies as typical of contemporary society is in part defined by an inability to mourn. This inability involves a difficulty in accepting depression, despair and conflict – in a word, disappointment – as part of life. It is an inhibition on the strength of the self which is then open to identification with models offered from the outside. The facts that therapy can take the place of our personal relationships, and that people so urgently seek a self through identification with a gender, for example, are a result of this weakening. The inability to mourn leaves us in need of and urgently seeking a false self. In this chapter, I am concerned with exploring the nature of 'false' and 'real selves' and attempting to specify what is dangerously different about the false self of late modernity.

REAL AND FALSE SELVES

Winnicott's (1965, 1986) conception of the false self refers to the very early relationship between mother and child, in which the mother is too anxious to be able to bear (hold or contain) the baby's anxiety. Instead of the mother being able to 'metabolise', give meaning to, the baby's gestures (movements, cries, etc.), these gestures are expected to reassure the mother. The child's own spontaneous, 'real' relationship to the world comes to be hidden away as he or she learns to calm the mother's anxiety. Winnicott and others talk about the possibility of a patient with a 'false self' remaining in analysis for a long time, without being touched by it, much of it proceeding on an intellectual level.

All societies, all institutions, require a false self. In my university work, for example, I am expected to put my students' interests before my own, rendering ideas intelligible rather than exploring the latest avant-garde development of those ideas for my own sake; I am expected to behave in a reasonably rational and civilised manner, co-operating with colleagues even when I don't agree with or like them. I am expected to be present at certain times, to keep abreast with the development of knowledge in my field, and to show a degree of commitment to my department and to the university as a whole – so, for example, there will be times when I attend meetings outside of normal working hours, and I regularly work at home in the evenings or at weekends.

The relationship between the self demanded by the university and my 'real' self is a complex one. Many of the things I am expected to do rest easily with me, and if I had a choice, I would choose to do them. These are at least consistent with a part of myself with which I am content (although not necessarily my real self). There are a number of demands with which I am happy to comply – a lot of the administration, some of the teaching, for example – but which I would not choose to do. In these areas, I make an internal compromise between my self and the institution.

I agree to carry out the activities as well as I can with reasonably good grace, and in return I expect not to put much of my heart into them. This is, I think, fairly close to false-self activity: I respond to the university in order to keep it happy.

There is a further level of activity which is different again; it is implicitly or explicitly required by the institution, but not only would I not do it if I had the choice, I would positively rather not do it. This includes, for example, meetings outside of normal working hours, and some types of administration. Sometimes I carry these out with more or less bad grace, sometimes I manipulate myself out of them; the more bad grace with which I do such things, the closer, I suppose, I am to my 'real self'.

Now all this is fairly normal, and many people could talk about their work in the same way. All my activities are open to internal and possibly external negotiation, and at one extreme I could resign, at the other I could be fired. There are, however, two pathological forms that my relationship to the university could take. The first would be if I felt internally compelled to do everything demanded of me and more. My internal perception would then be something like this: 'If I don't comply, then something disastrous will happen – either I or the university will fall to pieces.' The second form would be if I were expected to be a certain type of person, rather than act in a certain way. When, in *Asylums* (1968), Erving Goffman talks about the mental hospital's 'colonisation' of patients, I think this is what he means. The patient tries to become exactly what the hospital desires, the hospital tries to make the patient into a certain type of person. Most patients simply comply – they carry out the internal and external negotiations and reach a way of living in which they have something for themselves. But sometimes, if this is discovered, the institution demands colonisation. If a patient acknowledges that he or she is complying in order to get out, this can be taken as a sign of illness and a reason for keeping him or her in.

In the case of the university, this second pathology would occur if the very fact that I might want to negotiate my commitment, internally or externally, were to be taken as a sign that I was not sufficiently committed to the institution – if it demanded that my self and the institution be identified. Certainly such identifications might appear spontaneously; that is closer to the first form of pathology. The second form involves the institution's expectation of such an identification. One of the ways in which counselling can be drawn into such a demand was illustrated by a leaflet which arrived while I was writing this book. It was from an organisation specialising in offering counselling services to businesses, inviting me to join their list of part-time counsellors. The accompanying publicity offered to help businesses with their 'people problems', claiming to 'add value' by, amongst other things, 'increasing employee morale, performance and motivation'.

Now it seems to me that one of the things good counselling should do is *question* morale, performance and motivation. What is being avoided by work commitments? For what might a desire for good performance at work be a compensation? On what basis is morale maintained? A decline in these areas might actually be an appropriate reaction in the course of a person's life; looking back over my own life, periods of decreased effectiveness at work have been important periods in my own self-development, and help geared to increasing work effectiveness would have got in the way. The important thing is not increased effectiveness, but a freeing of the internal and external negotiation processes – which may affect work efficiency in a variety of ways, not necessarily in those desired by management. In this context, the term 'commitment' is often used, and Christopher Lasch (1984) argues that one aspect of the narcissistic character in contemporary society is an inability to commit himself or herself to an organisation, seeing the world in terms of what can be gained rather than what can be given. I think, however, that the important point is being able to negotiate commitment: a mindless commitment in this sense is as narcissistic as an inability to commit oneself.

The demand for commitment, for an employee to be a particular type of person, is likely to draw in the fragmented and isolated character of late modernity, but perhaps its strongest appeal is to those who demand it: just as a highly anxious parent might demand that the baby relieves his or her anxiety, so as adults we can impose our expectations on others to relieve our own anxiety. This is likely to be part of the psychodynamics of management, and to the extent that market criteria are used within a health service, it will affect the relationship between the 'carer' and the client or patient. But I think it has a significance beyond this particular relationship.

THE FALSE SELF OF LATE MODERNITY

I want now to suggest a number of ways in which late modernity makes it difficult to develop a critical commitment of the sort I have just been discussing. A critical commitment must involve at the very least an ability to embrace something which isn't perfect and to risk the loss of what has been embraced: it involves the past loss of an ideal object as well as a possible future loss. If the ideal is kept alive in the form of a manic defence, then a critical commitment is not possible; the only possibility is a mindless commitment or no commitment. A critical commitment means being able to embrace and employ a false-self aspect of the personality. Instead, late modernity seems to encourage the *adoption* of a false self, which maintains infantile phantasies of omnipotence and satisfaction that are bound up and expressed in one or another theory of the self, an employment to which psychoanalysis can readily be put. David Jackson (1990), for example, struggles to find his 'new self' through precisely such a theory.

Jackson's book contains a great deal of speculation about what he should be or about what he would like to be, all backed up with more or less elaborate theories. Such theories seem to replace an emotional awareness of internal multiplicity, often in the way that talking about something can become a way of not experiencing it. For example, Jackson talks a lot about postmodernist theories of the absence of a unified or 'real' self, but such fragmentation cannot be tolerated as an experience – it is stitched up with a theory and absorbed into his attempt to become a particular sort of person. That people should think about themselves in such ways reflects a real social change. It is not only a matter of the increased isolation and fragmentation of our experience, and the lack of containment that Kohut (1971) describes in terms of family relationships, and which I have pointed to here as the professionalisation of child-rearing and other relationships, but also the increasing abstraction of the systems which control our lives. At the level of the family, the specialisation and implicit professionalisation of parenting create a situation in which the spontaneous and diverse reality of the parent–container is kept at bay and it becomes difficult to relate to and internalise a whole person as a parent. The abstract social systems in which we live provide a distant and impersonal container, offering a vague threat but no clear boundaries. The speed of technological and economic change, reinforced by the movement towards 'flexible accumulation', undermines the boundaries provided by long-term employment, career structures, the possession of skills. Once, whilst listening to a patient, I had a very strong sense of a baby whom nobody had picked up and held, and who had thus not been able to discover where he ended and the outside world began. To a degree, perhaps such an experience is now a constant feature of our everyday lives. It is difficult to know our boundaries, our limitations, how far we can go. And it is difficult to feel held by the social structures in which we have to live: our family, our job, our friends are all very uncertain, perhaps too risky to trust. We are surrounded by distant social structures and unreliable, closer contacts with people. Because we cannot allow ourselves to rely on these contacts, we cannot risk losing them and we cannot take them in; we remain empty inside.

Such a situation is fraught with anxiety. We might try to deal with it by a constant push towards achievement and the security that we imagine achievement might bring, looking for something to hold on to that will provide guarantees, certain boundaries; but the space around us and inside us is so large that we can never achieve enough to fill it up: we have to move on to the next achievement, and the next, *ad infinitum.* If we stop, we fail. Alternatively, we might try to fill the space around us with other people, but if we have to deal with them as real other people, then the fear is that we might be too limited, too small to survive. Perhaps sometimes we can imagine we ourselves are large enough to fill the space and the outside world is really part of ourselves. We can be what we want to be and needn't feel threatened from the outside; but then, if everything is inside, there is nothing inside that will enable us to learn what we are, to find our boundaries in contrast with others. In this context the search for immediate emotional satisfaction makes sense: we are seeking the experience of being as full as possible, and if we can gain such an experience from another person, we can be full and be in contact in a way that provides, for the moment, a boundary.

I recently became acutely aware of this when I was teaching a short course on group processes for people in the caring professions who worked with groups. The day was built around a central conflict between students and teachers. The student demand was for a set of techniques or tools that would ease their anxiety when working with groups; the teachers were offering the experience of anxiety and some understanding of what the anxiety might be about. Simply being in a group creates a range of anxieties about boundaries, about, amongst other things, being too small or too big. The phantasy is that a recipe, a set of tools, might relieve the anxiety; in this sense the students wished to be filled up. If we had responded, we would have been offering a false self along the lines offered by the therapists that Giddens (1991) discusses.

If I can try to sum this up: the starting point is a social world which changes rapidly and which is organised for us by systems over which we have little or no control. Areas of life – from parenting to mourning – that were previously integral to the self become subjected to a form of professionalisation, sets of external prescriptions offered as a relief to anxiety – the anxiety of both therapist and patient, teacher and student, parent and child. The environment is both too distant and changing too quickly for a self to be established and maintained in any more than a very basic way. In such a context, psychotherapy as an abstract system offers an intellectual false self in its theories of the self, and in its prescriptions holds out a fantasy of maintaining infantile omnipotence and the achievement of full satisfaction.

THERAPY AND SOCIAL CONTROL

Now part of my argument is that psychotherapy and counselling are becoming or have become intricately bound up with forms of social control in modern society, and such forms of control are invidious in various ways. Social control is not necessarily a 'bad thing', although the notions of freedom and fulfilment current in late modernity tend to give it that flavour. Any society, in order to exist, needs to control its members; the state, where it exists, always plays a role in this, as does the immediate community and a variety of other institutions. Some control needs to be exercised over what people do, and this will always be the case. Most societies seem to attempt to control what people think, although in the liberal democracies of North America and Western Europe, the boundaries of what can be thought have been pushed back a long way, and there will inevitably be formal and informal restrictions on what thoughts can be expressed. The component of social control which seems to have emerged most clearly in late modernity is the control of feeling as well. Doubtless historically elements of such regulation have always been there, but now it has become public and organised, perhaps primarily through the growth of psychotherapy and counselling, which bring together action, thought and feeling.

The American sociologists Gagnon and Simon (1986) see this in terms of the breakdown of traditional sanctions on behaviour and a consequent social necessity to exercise control through producing 'internal scripts'. The notion of a social script is a popular and useful one for sociology, elaborating on the notion of a social role. There are positions within a network of social relationships, and each position carries with it a 'script' which we learn directly and indirectly. As the networks of relationships become more fragmented, so the social scripts have to be written for the 'depths' of the individual, the individual's inner life. In this context, there are two ways of reading Freud's work, both of which have some truth in them. The first is to see him as demonstrating the depth to which social scripts penetrate, the way in which they are intimately bound up with the unconscious, particularly in the case of the incest taboo and the development of our sexuality. In doing this, he also shows how these scripts become bound up with something else, with the language of the body and of the psyche and the ways in which they can become transformed. It is at this level that we can find internal conflict, the development of neurosis and psychosis, the difficulties that we have with boundaries, with accepting limitations, in a word, all the problems of disappointment. It is also at this level that we find the painful working out of the compromise between fate and destiny, the integrity of a divided self, and the possibility of creativity.

The second way of reading him is as a pioneer script-writer, providing the first draft of our socially necessary inner scripts – drafts which have come to be elaborated in ever more complex ways. If this is the case, then two reactions are possible. We can join in the elaboration, believing that it is leading to a better, human world; or we can reject the enterprise altogether. It is possible to say, from this point of view, that psychoanalysis is an enemy of freedom.

There is a third option: to recognise that both readings contain a degree of truth and both the acceptance and rejection of psychoanalysis have points in their favour. The problem, then, is the immensely difficult and disappointing one of examining the complexities of what we, as therapists, do, knowing that there will be no clear answer, and all answers will be double-edged. What I want to argue here is that if we can hold on to the idea that psychoanalysis takes us to the point where the social scripts enter into dialogue with something else, it is possible, if we are careful, to take elements of the script that do seem to make life better, to lead to a better world, *and also* to recognise that there is much more going on in the psyche than the learning of any script that we, as therapists or counsellors, might offer. It is important to recognise that area of life – and to recognise that it is a painful one. If we try to 'cure' that pain, then we are engaging in a form of manipulation – a form that goes deeper than that practised before, and one that is consonant with what is needed by the abstract systems that govern our lives.

One way of looking at this is in terms of Habermas's distinction between the functional rationality of the social system and the possibility of communicative rationality, the possibility that we can, in co-operation with others, and within limits, make decisions about how best we can run our lives. The 'false self' I have been trying to outline, with its fantasies of control and satisfaction, and the freedom to be what it wants, enables the functioning of rapidly changing and increasingly abstract systems and inhibits the development of relationships that might interfere with such functioning. What this seems to mean is the collapsing of the distinction between 'being' and 'doing'. Half a century ago, this distinction could be collapsed via work: we could 'be' our job – but then it was always possible to draw a distinction between the job and the self. Now doing seems to involve all our activities – the work we do, the things we buy, the way we run our sexual relationships; and all these come packaged as 'lifestyles' which can be changed. The possibility of *being* fades.

My argument is that late modernity produces a fragmented and isolated self and a fragmentation of our experience of ourselves; this is masked with a vision of the omnipotent, self-constructing self which maintains many of the phantasies of infancy into adult life. Many forms of therapy, including psychoanalytic therapy, try to realise this phantasy. Yet such a personality, in reality, finds autonomy difficult, rational discussion and choice difficult. It has to be a false self or nothing; the compromises of a critical commitment, the recognition of what we do to make life with others possible and to pursue our own interests, all become difficult. I will argue later that, apart from anything else, such characteristics undermine the possibilities of political democracy, but for the moment I want to go on to elaborate the characteristics, as far as this is possible, of what might be called not the 'true' self but the disappointed self.

Chapter 10

The disappointed self

To repeat, I have argued that the impetus of late modernity has been towards the isolation and fragmentation of individual experience of the self, and that this has been masked with a vision of the omnipotent, self-constructing self which maintains many of the phantasies of infancy into adult life. Psychotherapy of various types, including psychoanalytic therapy, has been implicated in this process, offering the false self that late modernity encourages: the self that denies or in other ways avoids the disappointments that are a necessary part of everyday life. In this chapter I want to explore the internal dynamics and the conscious actions of what I will call the 'disappointed' self, the self implicit in the 'negative' side of psychoanalysis. This is dangerous ground, in that I too will seem to be prescribing a self, setting down what people should be like. My response is that I am – like Freud, Klein and many others, but without laying claim to their abilities or distinction – trying to describe what people *are* like. Problems occur when this reality is denied.

First, I want to make a few comments on my earlier discussions of Giddens's notion of the 'pure relationship', and my arguments about masculinity. In both cases my argument was against the idea that we can actually construct ourselves, although we might want to and imagine that we can. Trying to do so is likely to entail a great deal of energy being put into changing the other person so that he or she lets us be what we want to be. Opposed to this is the implication that a relationship is best seen in terms of a mutual accommodation, involving not only a recognition that emotional satisfaction is occasional and temporary, but also a conflict between one's own desires and the ability to love, to put the other's interest above one's own. My argument also implied that it is important to recognise the value of 'sharedness', in the sense of a life undergone together. In adult life this, as well as the person, seems to me to be the equivalent of the secure base provided by the parent in infancy. The 'reflexive monitoring' that Giddens emphasises is clearly a part of any relationship – there has to be an attempt to organise life – but it equally clearly has a destructive dimension

To begin with, there is a contradiction to be negotiated in an intimate relationship. On the one hand, there is what I described as the sharedness of the relationship, the events that the partners experience together. These include, in the case of people living together, the straightforward, day-to-day routines of being in the same place, often at the same times. These can become the focus for reflexive monitoring from time to time ('How do we divide the housework? Shall we have a child? What do we do about the fall in house prices?'), but the sharedness of it all creates a firmer sense of solidity than would be there otherwise – a secure base. This is emphasised by the apparent demands for constant change and development that late modernity seems to present: if the 'sharedness' seems important to us, it can also threaten to hold us back, take on the feel of a burden. It is then that the 'reflexive monitoring' can undermine it. The best description I have heard of this is that it is like pulling up a tree to examine its roots to see if it is healthy. The result is that we undermine ourselves, producing the primitive feelings and actions that often accompany the breakdown of a relationship.

The 'programmes' for relationships that I discussed are essentially similar to 'traditional' programmes in which each partner had his or her role, in which the wife's position was subordinate, and happiness was to be found in fulfilling one's role. In each case, aspects of our humanity are ignored and denied and a view of the person, the self, consistent with a particular type of society is encouraged. The same process of denial is also at work in the conceptions of masculinity that I discussed. I argued against searching for an identity, a self or a sense of self on the basis of gender, more specifically masculine gender. It involves an illusion, that a gender role can provide a firm sense of identity, of self, when in fact a gender role is something we have to relate to; whether we like the role or not, we have to internalise and deal with it in terms of our own inner conflicts, abilities and inabilities. There is no doubt that gender roles are unclear and more complex than they used to be, and on the whole I suspect this is a good thing, but it carries the danger that primitive fantasies of the other sex are perhaps closer to the surface. All of the options I have discussed are trying to create a gender role as if it would solve something, solve the internal divisions and fragmentations that are a part of life.

Implicated in all this is a view of the personality which, on the one hand, emphasises the importance of aspects generally underrated in much contemporary therapy – our ability to think, our rationality and our moral sense – and, on the other, suggests a rather different conception of integration to contemporary notions of 'wholeness'.

THE THINKING SELF

It is now fairly common to think of Freud as combining elements of nineteenth-century romanticism and rationalism, the former involving an emphasis on the 'real self' and the power and authenticity of feeling. It seems to me that it is the rationalist side that has been underemphasised in modern psychoanalytic work and even more so in other modern therapies, and I want to explore ways of looking at our rational abilities.

Where thought has been seen as important, in the work of Bion (1967, 1976), for example, the focus has been the movement from feeling to thought, the primitive developments of symbolisation; higher levels of thought have been noted but not generally explored. On the other hand, in sociology, thought processes have been emphasised but largely taken for granted; their place and function in the psyche and in relation to feeling have not been explored. Here I am interested less in the more primitive levels than in our ability to employ symbolisation in relation to our emotional conflicts and real-world dilemmas.

The ability to think in the sense in which I am using it here involves a number of features. It involves the toleration of and ability to think about internal conflicts, to recognise the complexity of reactions and allow each side its thought. This is different from the reflexive rationalisation for which Giddens, for example, speaks. The latter is seen as reason-constructing and self-constitutive. The thought for which I am arguing is an articulation, rather than a construction, of what is there, and as far as possible it avoids the implicit projections of looking for reasons or causes of feeling. It is more the toleration of a play of internal arguments, out of which something new may or may not emerge. The most important aspect is the toleration of the arguments, the recognition that when I am thinking and feeling one thing, I will be thinking and feeling something different fairly shortly. Secondly, it involves an ability to recognise that some choices and some feelings are more valued than others; sometimes this might be a matter of a conscious choice based on experience: because I have spent a lot of time living alone, I do not act on my occasional desire to break up my marriage. Alternatively, I know enough about my background and my make-up to recognise that an absorbing interest in abstract theory will always be important to me, even if I often wish it were not.

There is, of course, a degree of construction going on in this – the constant play of what I can and can't decide about myself is part of the internal argument. The same play goes on in my thoughts about the outside world: what can and can't be changed, what I can and can't know. If it is an existential fact that we are condemned to choose, these processes of thinking have in some way to be related to actions, and judgements have to be made, sometimes fine judgements.

Such judgements are never purely rational, but they are surrounded by rationality: they need to be thought about, argued about internally and externally. The toleration of argument and the making of choices both require sacrifices and their attendant disappointments that prohibit the achievement of any straightforward emotional satisfaction. The difference between thinking in this sense and the ability to express and talk about feelings was illustrated for me recently in a one-year experiential group. The members had expressed and discussed their feelings throughout the year, and in the course of doing so they experienced becoming bound together – almost a merging – which made the ending of the group difficult, and it seemed to inhibit their ability to learn from their experience. In one of the final sessions, a shared sentiment seemed to be that if they talked about what they had learnt from the group, then the value of the experience would disappear. What *would* disappear, of course, would be the phantasy satisfaction of group solidarity – thought brings out individual differences. In some experiential groups, any attempt to link experience with theory is condemned immediately. I have sometimes noted a similar reaction in patients. For one man the group session itself would provide a satisfaction: the more intense the feeling in the group, the more satisfying it would be. He was noted in the group for having an apparently direct access to his feelings and an ability to express them. Yet for a long time, he repeatedly said that he didn't know how to use the group, and when it was over he went away and got on with his life without thinking about what had been talked about.

Now there are, in clinical terms, many layers of meaning to this; the one I am interested in is precisely the inability to think during the space between sessions; the session becomes an end in itself, and although something else is desired, the one thing – thought – that could produce something else would involve the modification of the satisfaction to be derived from direct expression. The people who seem to do best in psychotherapy are those who carry on the thinking in between sessions, sometimes, perhaps especially, when fighting against what has happened. This fight recognises the inevitability of internal conflict. Thinking in this sense involves the ability to think against oneself, to realise that whatever the present feeling, its opposite and many others will, in time, occur. To act on a gut feeling is sometimes the best thing to do and sometimes the worst – thinking involves a realisation that there are things in other people that I am blind to and things that are not there, but which I see too easily. In this sense it is different from the self-monitoring advocated by Rainwater (1989) – it is recognising that I might not actually know what I am feeling, and that even if I do, that is only part of the story. If thinking is a loss and a recognition of a loss, it is also a step back from the inner world, and an area for experimentation in thought, a process of waiting until I know better – at this level, perhaps, it can merge at the edges with free association, dreaming and reverie.

For Freud, the truth itself, as an outcome of thought, was a value, and if the scientific sense of truth that he sometimes espoused now seems rather naive, the idea of truth as the greatest possible absence of illusion is still important. This is clearest in his refusal to gain any comfort from religious beliefs. In this sense thought involves a constant doubt about the world and ourselves, and in its ideal form is combined with our ability to decide and act, and the ability to experience strong feelings without being driven by them; we must question and at the same time lay wagers on the certainty of our knowledge. This takes us back to another version of Adam Phillips's (1989) dictum: we must think and judge rationally whilst knowing that such thinking and judging can never be entirely rational. And it must be articulated with what we can know of our emotional responses: thought which is 'dry', which is not constantly linked to and mediating a range of emotions, becomes destructive.

THE MORAL SELF

There is also an implicit morality in all this, what might be called an internal 'procedural ethics', which focuses less on the moral decisions that are made than on the ability to arrive at them. Such an ethics has a number of dimensions. Quite clearly it involves the demand 'Know thyself', but this is only the start. My earlier argument adds the demand 'Think' as well. In classical terms, of course, the two have always been connected. The demand 'Know thyself' did not imply that a lot of goodies would follow; it was more a matter of avoiding foolishness and disaster. The emphasis in the modern world of counselling on 'self-awareness' seems to see it more as an end in itself, a source of satisfaction. Knowing oneself and thinking about oneself together represent the non-exclusive poles of Freud's romanticism and rationalism. Further depth to such a dual injunction comes from Kleinian psychoanalysis with its emphasis on the inevitability of human destructiveness.

In general, Kleinian psychoanalysis enables us to see unpleasant and often unfashionable feelings in a different light. As I noted earlier, jealousy, within reason, can be seen as a healthy emotion, and guilt can be seen as an appropriate response to destructive actions. Basically, however, Kleinian theory offers a morality of the inner world, concerning our ability to maintain and re-establish good inner objects in the face of anxiety and rage. In this sense it is an injunction to live with our feelings and fantasies, as opposed to projecting them, or perhaps even better, to avoid setting up another partial ideal, to tolerate the cycle of projection and internalisation that is a normal part of life, and as far as possible to recognise what we are doing. In practical terms, it seems to me to involve holding on to our ability to make reparation, to put the other's interest before our own, even when we are engaged in our most destructive rages and rows. In my experience there are times when this can only be held onto as an abstract idea; other people seem to possess the ability in a more integrated way. In either case, it is this which not only restores love after hatred, or maintains it alongside hatred, but enables the restoration of the good inner objects that enable stability to be regained.

To be able to achieve this entails the recognition that I myself can be as persecutory and destructive as I imagine other people to be. It is, I think, a fairly common experience in transference in psychotherapy for a patient to talk about a persecutory and undermining parent with whom the therapist is identified. The patient will often defend himself or herself from the perceived persecutory attack by the therapist by displaying his or her own persecutory, bullying or undermining side. It is as if the patient is showing the therapist how it felt when he or she was a child, what it is like to be faced by such a parent. This occurs inevitably because the parent becomes a part of the child, and it is perhaps very difficult to become aware of this. The victim role is a politically powerful one in our culture and it has become more so with the development of a naively egalitarian ideology in some areas of social life. Just as, to the child, parental figures can seem large, distant and immensely powerful, so as adults we are faced with social systems that seem to have similar qualities. In the face of both, we feel powerless and victimised. And of course there are senses in which we can be victims of parents and of abstract social systems, but we are never simply victims, and to see ourselves as such is to deny that part which is also the victimiser – a part which in the transference example emerges beyond our awareness.

On a wider level, I am suggesting that it is important in human life to identify not only with the victim but with the victimiser, and this too is a disappointment of our ideal self. It used to be argued by some liberals that increased understanding of political opponents would remove conflict. This is clearly not the case: an increased understanding of those who, for example, support apartheid might very well increase conflict. I am talking about understanding the other person, the powerful, abusing person, *in ourselves*, and I suspect that it is only when we can do that that we become less likely to act in that way. Again it is a matter of internal morality, of recognising internal immorality.

THE INTEGRATED SELF

I want now to elaborate on the notion of integration involved in the disappointed self. It seems to me that the term 'integration' is often taken to be synonymous with 'wholeness', an idea that the components of the self or of the psyche can fit together into a unitary whole, that we can know what we want, exist without conflict in a state of satisfaction. The form of integration I am talking about here involves both a growth and a limitation of the psyche, and both are, in effect, disappointments.

The growth involves the well-recognised process of taking in those parts of oneself that have been denied and projected. This is precisely what I have been talking about under the heading of morality, and the reasons for resistance are clear. The alternative involves some sort of recognition that the good and the bad inside myself, or, better, the good and the evil, the love and the hatred, are equally part of me, part of my self-substance and perhaps even dependent on each other. The parts I do not like have not been injected into me by some other, and although they might have been affected by my upbringing, they are not there as a result of my upbringing; they are there as part of my humanity.

I will try to follow this through in relation to my earlier comments about relationships: there is perhaps a continuous process of projection and withdrawal, and the question 'Is everything OK?' seems bound up with the projective part of the cycle. It carries as an implicit question: 'Is this person providing me with the wholeness I cannot achieve myself?' and carries also as an implicit statement: 'There is something about this person that leaves me unable to stay with them.' In both cases the 'something' is some aspect of myself with which I have difficulties. If these projected aspects are recognised as part of myself, then the question becomes something like: 'These aspects of our relationship are good, these are bad – why?'. The answer to the second part is frequently likely to be 'I simply do not like, have difficulty with this aspect of my partner, it clashes with something in me, or it exaggerates something in me that I do not like.'

Given that we both have reasonably stable personalities, I can set about trying to change my partner, emphasising the projections involved in the relationship, or I can set about the work of accommodation which allows the cycle to continue in a manageable way. This seems to me to involve recognising that there is what might be called an authentically bad aspect to a relationship, a recognition that in certain areas, perhaps because of individual history, perhaps because of something as intangible as psychic make-up, partners will clash, argue, feel hurt and frustrated. The issue of maintaining a relationship is then always a matter of balance, never of absolutes. Some relationships, generally, I suspect, those between some parents and their adult children, might conceivably be predominantly authentically bad.

Neville Symington (1986) suggests that it might be useful to think of a third position beyond Klein's paranoid-schizoid and depressive ones. This he calls the 'tragic' position, and it involves arriving at an understanding of the fact that one's parents and one's upbringing were what they were, and perhaps in one sense had to be. I am not sure that this can follow on easily from Klein's theory, but the point is important. The disappointed self is able to recognise what cannot be changed and learn from it; in fact such learning is part of the disappointment, and it involves the recognition of one's own shadow, the integration of the 'bad' parents and through this the recognition of one's own limitations. Such integration, it seems to me, carries the probability of recurring internal conflict; indeed I suspect that it is through the conflict that the integration is achieved; new but always temporary compromises are arrived at. It also involves an understanding that 'integration' and projection, splitting, etc. are two sides of the same coin. I cannot think of any easy way to express this except as a paradox: integration is the acceptance of a process of being unintegrated, of depression, internal conflict and a normal failure to contain these within the boundaries of the personality. Perhaps another way of putting it is that integration involves a madness, a disorder, an internal division that for most of the time remains within reason.

The second dimension of integration is perhaps best compared with what Winnicott (1988) terms 'unintegration', the early infantile state where the baby might experience itself as a different self on different occasions: when asleep and when awake, when hungry and when satisfied and so on. Winnicott seems to think that good-enough parenting maintains the continuity of the self until natural development enables integration to be achieved. From the beginning of integration, the fear of disintegration becomes important. Now I have noticed that some patients who enter group therapy will spend a lot of time talking about the events of the week. It is if they are using the group or the therapist as a sort of diary; what seems important to the patient is that the events are recorded, as if without such a record they would not exist, or – importantly – they would not belong to the same person. The desire seems to be for the form of holding that enables unintegration to move into integration, although, of course, for the patient to be there at all, a comparatively high level of basic integration must have been achieved. Nevertheless, there is not the high anxiety that comes with the fear of disintegration, and, interestingly, an attempt to do more than recognise the experiences, to link them together into a whole that makes some sense – bringing a higher level of integration – is often resisted.

Now it is as if a degree of unintegration seems important to such a person. In terms of the social conditions of late modernity it is perhaps easy to understand this: we are required to move from role to role very quickly, and it is increasingly difficult to find any one central role that can provide a core: partners change and so do careers; children grow up, neighbours and friends move away. It is interesting in this respect that modern sociological conceptions of the social actor tend to see the 'core' in terms not of personality but of taken-for-granted ways of getting through situations, whatever the content of those situations. The 'doing' is important, not what is done. The sort of patient I am describing seems concerned to know that he or she is the one who has been doing; to look at what has been done is resisted precisely because this level of integration seems, I think, to inhibit the ability to move from situation to situation. It restricts possibilities: if I have a personality structure, if I have specific qualities and abilities, then I will have to think in terms of limits on what I can do and I might not be able to do everything that I want to do. It is in this sense that integration involves a restriction, and a necessary disappointment perhaps in the most difficult sense of the word – because in this context it can most clearly mean the disappointment of ambitions that are dear to the heart. On a more mundane level it means opening oneself to the fears of not managing a rapidly changing world – the fear of disintegration. The paradox is that further integration brings a corresponding fear of its opposite.

There are, then, a number of aspects to integration that can make it a not-so-attractive prospect from the point of view of those who see psychotherapy as offering solutions, happiness and satisfaction. It means becoming aware of and suffering conflicts; becoming aware of and putting up with what I have described as the authentically bad aspects of relationships, and of the self; and it means coming up against and recognising the limits of one's abilities and the very real fear of disintegration that that can bring.

I have in the above suggested two different versions of integration: the acceptance of internal conflict, the necessity of projection, etc. on the one hand and the acceptance of limitations, boundaries on the other. Perhaps they are united by the quality of modesty – which seems to me well worth emphasising in the face of the ideas about the self I have been criticising – but it should be a modesty which can be amused by its own pride.

THE POLITICS OF DISAPPOINTMENT

I talked earlier of the implicit totalitarianism in the slogan 'The personal is political'; this does not, of course, mean that the two are not connected. It is possible, employing modern therapeutic notions, to construct a very naive political programme on the basis of ideas of autonomy, self-development, etc. Anthony Giddens (1991, 1992) does precisely this, employing anodyne notions of respect, equality and so on which seem to me to have the same effect on the personal level as social utopias may have for societies. If we take seriously what I suggested earlier, that the biological necessities of reproduction entail that men and women must both love and hate each other, then the guides for the 'pure relationship' attempt to suppress the dynamics that result from this. Jealousy, possessiveness, devotion, sacrifice, rage, brutality, respect, tenderness, understanding all have their part to play.

If my argument is right, then for the good side of the relationship to exist – for men and women to love each other, respect each other, co-operate as equals – they must also hate each other, despise each other and attempt to subordinate each other. I am suggesting in fact that we might as well try to cut off one side of a sheet of paper – we end up with nothing; a sort of sanitised, polite world that is brave and new. I am suggesting, in effect – and not just about relationships between men and women, for the battle is an internal one in each of us, whatever our sexuality – that the depth of hatred of which a person is capable is a marker of their potential to love, and vice versa; and the same is true for all the other qualities. The disappointed self can recognise these paradoxes and employ rational abilities to stand back (but not avoid them). With careful thought, proper, enforced legislation and other changes, we should be able to establish a real structural equality between the sexes. This will and should not stop men and women loving each other and hating each other and fighting the battles that this entails, sometimes enhancing each others' lives beyond imagination and sometimes – very rarely, one hopes – killing each other. If we try to stop this, then we are moving towards a totalitarianism, a demand that our innermost being be formed and controlled by institutions of social control.

Moving to a less dramatic level, I think this argument leads on to some of the problems that have been identified in Habermas's work. What I have called the false self of late modernity is the self demanded by the functional rationality of the social system; the disappointed self is able to stand back from the desire for narcissistic satisfaction and engage in the processes of thinking that can facilitate communicative rationality, the free negotiation and working out of personal relationships that can restrict or counteract the dynamics of the social system. Habermas, however, is frequently criticised for his overemphasis on rationality, for wanting to turn the world into a seminar. Certainly his discussion of psychoanalysis as an 'emancipatory science' (1971) sees it in terms of freeing the individual from the constraints of irrationality. My argument here has been that such a freeing is vital but can only ever be partial: if we are able to change ourselves it is in the direction of finding better ways to live with ourselves, within our physical, social and emotional limitations.

It seems to me that this does entail a guiding principle for political thought, but one full of paradox. One of the ways of interpreting my earlier comments about the moral self is to suggest that the question should not be 'How do I become a better person?' but 'How do I live in such a way as to avoid becoming a worse person?'. The second question recognises the power of what we do not like about ourselves and the limitations on our abilities to change. If this is moved to the political level, the question becomes less 'How do make our society a better place to live?' and more 'How do we prevent our society becoming a worse place?'.

The paradox of this is that it is the traditional conservative question about politics, yet I am proposing it here as a radical question. One way of looking at the changes instituted by late modernity is that they represent the possible triumph of abstract social systems over the life-world, over our world of everyday spontaneous experience and our ability to use that experience creatively. For most of its development, modernity has seemed to offer the chance of creating different types of society that would be better places to live, and my central question, in that context, *is* a conservative one – one rightly rejected by the powerful socialist and Communist movements of the left. But those movements themselves are now fragmented, and the right has become the 'radical' grouping, aligning itself with social change, with the development of late modernity, with the fragmentation of experience that it involves. Habermas (1990b) is, I think, right when he argues that in the foreseeable future the function of the left in politics is to defend the boundaries of the life-world against the demands of the social system, and in most contexts at the moment, this means defending it against the demands of the market. But it also means thinking carefully and critically about apparently radical demands associated with ideas of personal growth, individual autonomy and unproblematic equality, which can themselves be seen as market ideologies.

Chapter 11

The values of psychoanalysis

For much of this book I have been very critical of some psychoanalytic ideas and some developments in psychoanalysis; now I want to switch direction – there is much in psychoanalysis, not just as a general psychology or a method of treatment, but as a way of approaching the world and the task of living, that is useful. As a treatment and as a theory, psychoanalysis embodies a number of values which I think need defending – against critics not only from the new therapies and from outside psychoanalysis but also from itself, from its own desire to be popular and its tendency to get caught up in the social processes of late modernity precisely because it is unaware of them. What I will do in this chapter is suggest that many of the central accusations that are laid against psychoanalysis actually point to its most important contributions: its ability to identify and understand a reality of the self under the illusions of late modernity.

One way of characterising late modernity is as a time of growing knowledge but diminished understanding; there is an awful lot of information around but little critical organisation – in this sense late modernity is like the patient who uses therapy as a diary, but resists understanding why he or she should be using it in such a way. Many of the criticisms of psychoanalysis are in effect criticisms of understanding, of grasping and holding on to depth, complexity and contradiction. In what might appear to be its conservatism in the face of new therapies, and late modern concerns with self-expression, self-direction and a naive equality, psychoanalysis can find a radical potential.

THE CRITIQUE OF PSYCHOANALYSIS

There are a number of dimensions to late modern criticisms of psychoanalysis and psychotherapy. To begin with, it is perhaps useful to contrast them with the tendencies I have been criticising. There is often a similar emphasis on gaining rapid results and an underemphasis on thought – psychoanalysis takes too long, is too concerned with talking rather than feeling, etc. These criticisms seem to come mainly from the new therapies and they share the denial of internal complexity that has been my target throughout. Those who condemn the activity as a whole seem to carry over into the denial of the complexity of the external world as well. I will take as my source some comments from Jeffrey Masson (1985, 1988, 1991, 1992), perhaps currently the most vocal of the critics of psychoanalysis, and a recent contribution from David Pilgrim (1992), an English critic who takes up some of his ideas.

The ideas that I employed earlier often provide the basis for this critique, an implicit or explicit acceptance of Foucault's analysis of the development of the professions, together with what I have called the 'professional anti-professionalism' that tends to accompany the ideology of equality that Cas Wouters (1991) talks about. The image of the professions has changed in some ways rather dramatically over the past century. In the work of the French sociologist Emile Durkheim (1957), for example, we can find the profession held up as a model for a future society. The development of modernity, with its increasingly elaborate division of labour and individual differentiation, brings problems of conflict, and anomie, the lack of clear social norms, which are not inevitable. Durkheim suggests that such difficulties might be overcome through the emergence of professional associations, with their own clear morality and rules of conduct, enforced by the profession itself. Such a vision has affinities with guild socialism, a vision of socialism organised on the basis of associations of artisans, and, I would add, something in common with the visions of anarcho-syndicalism. Now such a vision sounds, I suspect, entirely utopian, and it might always have been utopian, although more plausible a century ago than it is now. The dominant contemporary view of the professions is that which informed my earlier arguments: the professions are always to some degree engaged in establishing and extending their own power over their clients and against other professions. This runs into arguments about the flexibility of the labour market, the undermining of specialist bodies of knowledge and development of a workforce capable of moving regularly to other jobs: the specialist professions hinder this. The left see them as inhibiting democratisation, the right as inhibiting the free play of the market.

David Pilgrim seems to see the profession of psychotherapy entirely in these terms. He argues that the claims to scientific knowledge that therapists sometimes make, and their case studies and arguments, are a rhetoric to justify their position, work and salaries. Pilgrim extends his critique to cover the use of diagnostic categories as a form of objectification of patients, and the use of the term 'patient' itself. Psychotherapists are engaged in establishing power over their clientele. Jeffrey Masson seems to think that psychotherapy is inherently exploitative and corrupt: the qualities are built in to the therapist/patient relationship. In so far as it is possible to draw out underlying assumptions behind his attack, they seem to be along the lines of: 'Nobody is free of the ability and desire to exploit others, therefore nobody should be put in a position where this desire can be realised; psychotherapists are worse than others in this respect because of the implicit claim to be specialists in living.'

Now it seems to me that the growth of the professions and the attack on them are both features of late modernity, contradictory processes occurring on different levels. Professionalisation is one of the means by which abstract systems establish themselves; there is a centralisation at the level of organisations, and, on the individual level, an apparently greater freedom. Somewhere in between, ideas about reasonable ways of living get lost. The choice seems to be to throw oneself wholeheartedly into the profession of therapy, claiming to cure, transform, save and the rest of it; or to attack therapy for its pseudo-scientific basis, which is the rhetoric behind which therapists seek to extend their own personal and professional power. Somewhere in between, there is a not ignoble idea of a self-governing profession which accepts its own limitations, and which does not try to pathologise whole areas of life, or insist on what it has to offer being essential if life's difficulties are going to be negotiated. There are, I think, strong political arguments in favour of self-governing, self-regulating professions: they provide another level of social organisation – another area of freedom – between the state and the individual and the market and the individual. The professions themselves should of course be subjected to the wider social interest through the laws of the land, but these intervening organisations are important in the same way that it used to be accepted that strong trade unions were important. They enable the involvement of more people more directly in the political processes that govern the nation, and they allow it, at best, in a way that extends collective (as opposed to individual) self-government. But such professions need to be aware of their own limitations and boundaries and be realistic about their expertise.

I think that what is behind this is a view of the world as either black or white: professions are either good things or bad things, not a site for struggle between contradictory forces. The same comment can be made about the notion of knowledge. Postmodernist philosophy in general emphasises the connection between knowledge and the exercise of power over others. This comes to be seen as the only dimension of knowledge, and knowledge itself is seen as rhetoric. The idea of a scientific knowledge, which always needs to be questioned, is rejected. Science is regarded as being fundamentally similar to any other type of thought: meanings are always a product of discourse, of language itself, deployed in an ongoing power struggle. I have examined what I regard to be the fundamental objections to such a position elsewhere (Craib 1992), and I will not rehearse them again. Such a criticism of scientific knowledge aims at something of a straw target: an implicit or explicit idea that science produces 'absolutely true' knowledge, against which it is argued that there is no such thing. The possibility of shades of grey, of the probable, or likely, or even possible, which it seems to me science is really about, is lost. The knowledge that science does produce is bound up with political processes in complex ways: it is implicated in processes of domination and of liberation, it can keep us alive and it can kill us. Our knowledge of the process of grieving can be the basis for an attempt to organise and control the process, or it can be the basis for allowing the uniqueness of each process to follow its course.

There are aspects of psychoanalytic theory that can be regarded as scientific – in one or another of various senses – and making statements of probable knowledge; a large part is more speculative, and this merges into technical and aesthetic dimensions of practice. What is clear is that psychoanalysis has a wider, more established and sophisticated body of theory to its credit than any other type of therapy (except perhaps those closest to cognitive psychology), and when other disciplines turn to psychology, it is usually to some branch of psychoanalysis. This concern with theory, with thinking and with knowledge, is itself an important value and must be contrasted with the suspicion of theory displayed by those therapies which emphasise emotional expression.

Psychotherapists can use this knowledge, and their professional status, to seek personal gratification and exercise power over others. Masson seems to see this as the only possibility, as if differences in knowledge and expertise can never be beneficial, at least where they concern human relationships. Behind this, I think it is possible to discern the same demand for innocence and the attempt to deny internal complexity that haunts the sort of therapy I have been criticising. A therapy which claims to cure, to enable self-realisation and growth, to be positively good, sets itself up for Masson's type of criticism simply because the therapists, like their patients, carry their own dark side, their own failings and inadequacies. In this connection, I sometimes find trainee counsellors who feel that payment for their work somehow devalues the goodness of their intentions and the worth of their concern; in other words, it threatens their own satisfaction. There are good reasons for some doubts: 'How good am I? Am I actually worth payment?'. But there is more to the doubts than this, and I suspect that it is the late modern fantasy of unproblematic satisfaction. The involvement of money in the relationship underlines an inequality, a difference between therapist and patient, which challenges the more naive political ideologies of equality and the therapists' fantasies of being perfect, understanding parents. Of course, in reality, the therapist is working, doing his or her job, in a broadly similar way to anybody else.

Masson's desire for innocence and simplicity – perhaps the innocence and simplicity that is so often projected on to children by therapists themselves – can be seen in his recent lament that, for the psychoanalyst, there can be no such thing as a 'purely external event', and no such thing as a straightforward, simple victim. He goes on to make the claim, which is, I think, self-evident, but from his point of view seems to be the major criticism of psychoanalysis, that: 'I think . . . it is in the very nature of psychoanalysis to ascribe greater force to internal factors than external ones, to slight the outer world in favour of the inner one' (Masson 1992: 38). This is rather like criticising a central heating engineer because he or she doesn't repair your car. The *raison d'être* of psychoanalysis is the inner world. The opposite is true for, say, sociology, and the denial of one is as pathological as the denial of the other. There *is* no such thing as a 'purely external event' any more than there is such a thing as a 'purely internal event'. There is, however, some need for an informed division of labour – we do not live in a world which can survive on renaissance people. Those who concentrate on the inner world will be as corrupt, as full of human failings, as those who concentrate on the outside world, whether they be sociologists, plumbers or estate agents.

One possibility that the profession of psychotherapy can offer in this context is the recognition that expertise, difference, and the power that that expertise carries can be put to beneficial *and* destructive use, and one of the things that appeals to me about psychoanalytic therapy is that it can be in a better position than many other professions to articulate this. It is in a better position because at its centre is some notion that we are 'all ill', of a common, imperfect humanity, and that this imperfection can only be negotiated; there are no clear paths, codes or sets of instructions. On the other hand, it is not all confusion; there is such a thing as morality, even if it is inevitably contested, such a thing as knowledge, even if it is not absolute; there are power differences between people that can be creative as well as destructive. Such a position is a disappointment to both sides. It means that psychotherapy can never do what it often claims it can do, that therapists never become the sort of people that they might want to become at the beginning of their training, but that they are not as corrupt, ignorant and unsuccessful as the critics would like to claim.

A point where all this comes together is in the use of the word 'patient'. In a recent exchange with David Pilgrim (1992), I deliberately used the word 'patient' throughout, pointing out that it carried implications of dependence and that I thought the temptation behind replacing 'patient' with 'client' was a desire to deny dependence, a dependence the reality of which is greatest when we are at our youngest and oldest, and the prospect and memory of which is frequently terrifying. I also commented that ·

the purpose of therapy was to enable a relative independence – or in this context I would prefer the term 'mature dependence'. In his response, Pilgrim commented that clearly I did not like dependence. What strikes me about this is that it is a cultural blindness to what I was saying – which was that dependence is inevitable, and, of course, it is inevitable not simply when we are very young or very old: it is necessary, and it is a fact, throughout our lives, economically, politically, physically and psychologically. Dependency, of course, is not the same as being a patient; we cannot avoid dependency even when we are not patients. But the word 'patient' itself is interesting.

Two meanings are given in the *Shorter Oxford Dictionary*. The first is somebody who endures or suffers pain and misfortune for long periods, the sense of the 'patience of Job'; the second is somebody who undergoes some sort of act by another – clearly the medical sense of the term is involved here. Both senses are relevant to psychotherapy. The first, perhaps, is the most obvious. Our patients are patient in the sense that often they have suffered for a long time and they endure the process of therapy, suffer the process of therapy, which is by no means always a comfortable experience. They are patients in the second sense when they agree to embark on psychotherapy, in that they agree, and of course agency is involved, to submit themselves to the skills and knowledge of another, even if the process will only work if there is a sense of co-operation. The period of dependency will not abolish dependency, although it should enable a more fruitful form of being dependent – mature dependence; and it involves, more often than not, a period of patienthood where the exploration of self is dependent on the knowledge and skill of the therapist.

There is something more profound in all this, and that is the value of the peculiarity of the individual, and the way in which this peculiarity is contained in the messy contradictions, 'strangeness' and ambiguities in ourselves and in other people. In the paper by Masson that I quoted above, he continues his argument with a quote from Anna Freud:

> I was impressed by the story of a boy who, at 4½ years, had escaped with his family from enemy-occupied territory. A subsequent analysis showed which elements of the experience had been singled out for traumatic value: He had suffered a

severe shock from the fact that the invaders had deprived the father of his car. This, to him, meant that the father had been robbed of his potency. Beside this all-important oedipal experience, everything else (loss of home, security, friends) paled into insignificance.

(A. Freud 1958, quoted by Masson 1992: 19)

Masson then goes on to comment:

This is a good demonstration of the incapacity of analysts to see beyond their theoretical constructs. It is typical that psychoanalytic interpretations avoid external reality and focus on predetermined events that *must* loom large in the child's psyche . . .

(Masson 1992: 19)

Now of course it *might* be the case that Anna Freud, or whoever carried out the analysis, was seeing what the theory said was there. But on the other hand there is no a priori reason why her account should not be accurate. It might be true that Masson expects the wider set of losses to be traumatic, because, presumably, *his* theory tells him that they should be, and in fact that they were, although of course he can have had no contact with the child concerned. If we go back to the Anna Freud quotation, we can see that it is the nature of the external reality contrasted with the boy's interpretation of that reality that impresses her. There is in the quotation a recognition of the trauma in social terms – its depth is what makes the boy's reaction remarkable. At the same time there is a recognition that no event is purely external, that to be aware of an event at all is to make it internal, to interpret it through previous experience and our current constellation of relationships and purposes. Even amongst sociologists, who might be expected to prefer the external, this has been regarded as a truism for most of the century. It is part of the disappointment that psychoanalysis has to offer: there is no simple world of villains and victims (which is not to say that there are no villains and victims); there are no such things as undifferentiated and pure traumas; and there is no easy or straightforward way of dealing with what has become known, in a simplistic way, as post-traumatic stress disorder.

The nub of the value of psychoanalysis lies here; it is its emphasis on the individuality and specificity of meaning and of the individual life, and from the point of view of late modernity this seems unacceptable. Therapy as a system tries to set out general ways of behaving and acting and being; the external reaction denies the sometimes odd and even shocking nature of our individual reactions to events; and those who endorse the fragmentation of late modernity can no longer see the individual at all, merely a collection of selves.

In an obscure and typically difficult way, the German philosopher Theodor Adorno (1974) made a similar point in his later work: the totality, he argued, the concept of which had once been a source of truth, was now victorious and a source of confusion and untruth; we lived in what was in essence a totalitarian system in which truth, if were to be found anywhere, might be found in the fragmented experience of the individual. In this context, I have been arguing that the very experience of the individual is being penetrated by that totalitarian system and that one of the instruments of that system can be psychotherapy. Yet at the same time the straightforward rejection of the insights of psychotherapy does not help, for it denies one of the few areas where a separation from the system can be achieved: the complex internality of the individual, comprehension of which can enable him or her to take a critical and analytic distance from what is happening, and can enable the formation of relationships based less on the illusion of common identity than on the reality of individual separation, difference and dependence. But this achievement means recognition of the real internal pain of fragmentation, of internal conflicts and of our manifold limitations. This, perhaps, is the most important message of psychoanalysis.

THE DEFENCE OF DIFFICULTY

One way of putting all this is that the central value of psychoanalysis is difficulty. It would be hard for the Chancellor of the Exchequer to say that he or she had only a limited understanding of the economy; that there were no policies that could be guaranteed to overcome the recession and no good reasons for preferring one policy over another; that cycles of recession and expansion were normal and so on. Yet the analytic psychotherapist must say something like this to prospective patients. Neville Symington writes:

> My own opinion is that it is always a mistake to tell a patient that he or she needs psychoanalysis. It is a very God-like judgement to make. How can I know that someone needs psychoanalysis? How do I know how his or her life will be without psychoanalysis? How can I know that psychoanalysis is going to benefit this person?
>
> (Symington 1986: 203)

He goes on to point out that to make this judgement, to assert the benefits of treatment to a patient, is likely simply to bring about resentment.

I certainly make a point never, as far as I am able, and however much it is demanded, to make promises. I point out that in no way is it a miracle cure, that it takes a long time, that there are no guarantees of success, and that in the context of group therapy as much is taken out as is put in; and I also add that during therapy, the patient is likely to feel bad, perhaps even to feel worse than when he or she enters therapy, that it is an anxiety-provoking and often painful process. I do sometimes allow myself to go as far as saying that if the pain can be tolerated, then change might occur. People often come with anxieties about group therapy in particular; they might fear, for example, that they will be attacked by the group; or that they will find it easy enough to try to help others and not be able to seek help for themselves; or that they will have to bear the others' pain and it will double their own; that there will be somebody in the group they cannot stand, or who cannot stand them. All these fears are quite realistic – all these things can and do happen in the process of group therapy, and it would be wrong of me to offer reassurance; rather my task is to explore the anxieties, to recognise and understand their truth.

Now truth is not necessarily a marketable commodity. Psychoanalytic therapy cannot be offered as a guide to 'the good life', or as a cure that is bound to work, as a bringer of relief from pain and anxiety, or as a way of achieving personal change, although something of all or any of these might result. It can only work in any of these respects if the patient has an idea of what it is about and is prepared to undertake the exploration. If the 'prescription' of psychoanalysis produces resentment, then the promise of a cure turns it into something like a medicine: the patient is constantly looking for improvement and instructions as to how to pass the therapist's exams.

I have had one group in particular where there was a 'prescription' of psychotherapy by GPs or psychiatrists, where a constant theme for a long time was the expectations of parents, and how a failure to live up to those expectations was experienced as an attack on the parents and carried implications of the loss of parental love. In terms of what was going on in the group there was both an underlying resentment of me as the person or the representative of the persons who put them there, and also a desire 'to get better' to please me, to avoid the loss of love and attention and support that might follow the absence of change. I suspect that such feelings would be around in any therapy, but promises of effectiveness reinforce them, and paradoxically limit the effectiveness of therapy. In the face of such expectations, it is a hard struggle for both therapist and patients to allow themselves to feel bad, hopeless, despairing, yet often the real experience of these feelings is the first sign of change.

It follows from this that there will always be some ambivalence and complexity in the psychoanalytic relationship itself – indeed this will be a central aspect, appropriately brought into focus at various times during the course of the therapy. This ambivalence, the complexity and paradoxical nature of the therapeutic relationship, is so integral that it seems difficult to deny, yet the use of therapy cases in popular writings manages to hide it. The sort of example is familiar to anyone who reads what might be called the 'emotion' columns in the press: 'David was having bitter arguments with his wife; in therapy he realised it was his own fear of intimacy, a result of growing up with a possessive mother and a distant father. After a while he began to realise that he needn't be scared of his wife's love.' If only . . .

There are a number of forces pushing therapy in the direction of hiding its problems. The first is quite straightforward: the pressure of the market. Quite independently of recent changes to the British National Health Service, the popularity of psychotherapy generates a proliferation of therapies and therapists who *de facto* compete, within health services and on the private market. Anxiety and conflict do not have an immediate appeal. Self-knowledge can be more attractive, at least until we move into the darker regions of the self. Cure, growth, self-actualisation sound much better in an advertising brochure. Behind the operation of market forces, however, there are all the dynamics of late modernity pushing us in the direction of the false self, and in the face of this it is important that psychoanalytic therapy hold on to some of the principles for which it is so often criticised.

One area in which this stands out clearly is to do with the length of the treatment. There are therapies around that promise results in weeks or months. The introduction of internal markets in the health service and the dynamics of private health insurance are likely to emphasise this. My undergraduate students most frequently comment in a puzzled or disapproving way on time when I give them a case study to read: the eight-year treatment of a borderline patient. Can anything that takes that long be any good?

Time is central to our experience of late modernity. It is arguable that over recent decades our lives have become measured in more and shorter time spans; speed has come to be associated with efficiency and effectiveness. This can be seen from my discussion of group therapy for bereavement, and perhaps from the increasing popularity of short-term therapy altogether. One distinctly late modern feature of our sense of time seems to be not only the deliberate catering for, but encouragement of, our difficulty in focusing attention. The organisation of news in 'sound bites', the ability to graze through many television channels and the attempts to catch the grazer are another aspect of the speeding up of time and of change – our attention changes as rapidly as our world. In this context, careful and critical thought, which requires standing still mentally and an effort to think issues through, becomes more and more difficult, and it becomes important that somebody, somewhere is maintaining the importance of long-term work and thought.

I have suggested that there is a case to be made that we have become divorced not just from the rhythms of the natural world, but also from what might be called our natural psychological time. The psychological processes of learning to love another person, and of grieving the loss of another person, are the areas where this is most apparent: in the comparative brevity of many relationships and in social and professional expectations of what mourning should be. Bion commented many times how much resistance there was to learning from experience, and I am constantly surprised by its difficulty. For an adult it means beginning to experience what has hitherto been too threatening to experience, and what will probably never be easy to experience. Emotional learning requires a modification, and a loosening of these defences – in Bion's terms an opening of the thinking process from the bottom up, the translation into thought of bodily and emotional sensations that have hitherto been denied. This does not happen quickly.

One possible result of such learning is that we begin to feel the fear and pain of loss. The ending of therapy is a very painful enterprise. It always needs to be handled carefully, and of course psychotherapists can handle it badly. It seems to me, however, that any therapeutic process will involve a degree, possibly a high degree, of dependence on the therapist, and although this lessens as the process continues, the ending will always be difficult: it will be frightening ('What will I do without this person?') and it will always be painful – whatever might be gained from therapy, the process as a face-to-face relationship will be lost. It will involve grief that can last a long time, like any important grief. I have heard a report that amongst the various consumer groups that spring up around therapy there is one for people who have become dependent on their therapist and suffered through the ending of therapy – as if this could somehow be avoided. There is a sense in which the process of psychotherapy reproduces the problems of the patient's everyday life in relation to the therapist. It is not, and cannot be – if it is to do more than offer an illusion – otherwise, and psychoanalytic therapy, perhaps above all others, is aware of this: it must be honest about it.

If I put a hand in the fire and it is burnt, I will not do it again in a hurry; psychotherapy says, in one sense, put your hand in the fire and keep it there. Psychological development depends on 'staying' in the fire, to the point where we begin to understand the pain and find that it is bearable, and that it might even be used in some way. This is a process which perhaps in other ages might simply have been called 'life', and it certainly has to do with being, not with doing. Perhaps one way of characterising psychotherapy is as a process of learning to be, when neither the process nor the being itself is necessarily a comfortable experience. They are experiences that are not encouraged by modern forms of life, where the emphasis is always on doing, or on being only in the limited sense in which it is equated with immediate satisfaction.

And of course the results of such learning are always ambivalent. This is why I think psychoanalysts' ambiguity about a successful treatment is important. This is captured in an everyday sense by a story told me by a colleague that throughout her childhood, adolescence and young adulthood, going to the dentist was a routine activity about which she had no fear. After a year or so training as a counsellor, she found herself terrified of these visits and realised that this would be the case for the rest of her life. The movement towards external and internal reality makes life both easier and harder; energy involved, in this example, in denial is released (and of course it was not just denial of the fear of the dentist but also of other fears) and can be put to other, more productive purposes. The price is experiencing a real and appropriate fear; perhaps the best description of this dimension of psychotherapy is of learning how to suffer.

References

Abraham, K. (1927) *Selected Papers on Psychoanalysis*, London: Hogarth Press.

Adorno, T.W. (1974) *Minima Moralia: Reflections from a Damaged Life*, London: New Left Books.

Beck, U. (1992) *Risk Society: Towards a New Modernity*, London: Sage.

Becker, E. (1973) *The Denial of Death*, New York: Free Press.

Berger, P., Berger, B., and Kellner, H. (1973) *The Homeless Mind*, Harmondsworth: Penguin.

Berger, P. and Luckmann, T. (1966) *The Social Construction of Reality*, Harmondsworth: Penguin.

Bion, W. (1959) 'Attacks on linking', *International Journal of Psychoanalysis* 40: 308–15.

—— (1967) *Second Thoughts*, London: Heinemann.

—— (1976) *Learning From Experience*, London: Heinemann.

Bly, R. (1990) *Iron John: A Book About Men*, Reading, Mass.: Addison-Wesley.

Bollas, C. (1987) *The Shadow of the Object: Psychoanalysis of the Unthought Known*, London: Free Association.

—— (1989) *Forces of Destiny: Psychoanalysis and Human Idiom*, London: Free Association.

—— (1992) *On Being A Character: Psychoanalysis, and Self Experience*, London: Routledge.

Bowlby, J. (1953) *Child Care and the Growth of Human Love*, Harmondsworth: Penguin.

—— (1960) 'Grief and mourning in infancy and childhood', *Psychoanalytic Study of the Child* 15: 9–52.

—— (1961) 'Processes of mourning, *International Journal of Psychoanalysis* 42: 317–40.

—— (1971) *Attachment and Loss. Vol. 1: Attachment*, Harmondsworth: Penguin.

—— (1975) *Attachment and Loss. Vol. 2: Separation, Anxiety and Anger*, Harmondsworth: Penguin.

—— (1981) *Attachment and Loss. Vol. 3: Loss, Sadness and Depression*, Harmondsworth: Penguin.

—— (1988) *A Secure Base*, Harmondsworth: Penguin.

Brown, G. and Harris, T. (1978) *The Social Origins of Depression, A Study of Psychiatric Disorder in Women*, London: Tavistock.

Castoriadis, C. (1991) 'Cornelius Castoriadis interviewed', *Free Associations* 24: 483–506.

Chamberlain, D. (1987) 'The cognitive newborn: a scientific update', *British Journal of Psychotherapy* 4: 30–71.

Chasseguet-Smirgel, J. (1985) *Female Sexuality*, London: Karnac.

Chodorow, N. (1978) *The Reproduction of Mothering: Psychoanalysis and the Sociology of Gender*, Berkeley: University of California Press.

Clulow, C. and Mattinson, J. (1989) *Marriage Inside Out: Problems of Intimacy*, Harmondsworth: Penguin.

Craib, I. (1988) 'The personal and political', *Radical Philosophy* 48: 14–15.

—— (1992) *Modern Social Theory: From Parsons to Habermas* (2nd edn) Hemel Hempstead: Harvester Wheatsheaf.

Crook, S., Pakulski, J., and Waters, M. (1992) *Postmodernisation: Change in Advanced Society*, London: Sage.

De Mare, P., Piper, R., and Thompson, S. (1991) *Koinonia: From Hate through Dialogue to Culture in the Large Group*, London: Karnac.

Dryden, W. and Feltham, C. (eds) (1992) *Psychotherapy and its Discontents*, Buckingham: Open University Press.

Durkheim, E. (1957) *Professional Ethics and Civic Morals*, London: Routledge & Kegan Paul.

Eichenbaum, L. and Orbach, S. (1985) *Understanding Women*, Harmondsworth: Penguin.

Figueira, S.A. (1991) 'On being a psychoanalyst in Brazil', *Free Associations* 23: 423–46.

Fine, H.J. (1991) 'Looking for Hegel', *Contemporary Psychology* 36: 804–5.

Foucault, M. (1967) *Madness and Civilisation: A History of Insanity in the Age of Reason*, London: Tavistock.

—— (1977) *Discipline and Punish: The Birth of the Prison*, Harmondsworth: Penguin.

—— (1984) *A History of Sexuality. Vol. 1*, Harmondsworth: Penguin.

Freud, A. (1958) 'Child observation and prediction', *Psychoanalytic Study of the Child* 13: 112–6.

Freud, S. (1984a) 'Beyond The pleasure principle', in *Collected Works* Vol. 11, pp269–38; Harmondsworth: Penguin.

—— (1984b) 'Mourning and melancholia', in *Collected Works* Vol. 11, Harmondsworth: Penguin.

—— (1985a) 'Civilisation and its discontents', in *Collected Works* Vol. 12, Harmondsworth: Penguin.

—— (1985b) 'Moses and monotheism', in *Collected Works* Vol. 13, Harmondsworth: Penguin.

Gagnon, J.H. and Simon, W. (1986) 'Sexual scripts: permanence and change', *Archives of Sexual Behaviour* 15: 97–120.

Garfinkel, H. (1967) *Studies in Ethnomethodology*, Englewood Cliffs, N.J.: Prentice Hall.

Giddens, A. (1984) *The Constitution of Society*, Oxford: Polity Press.

—— (1990) *The Consequences of Modernity*, Oxford: Polity Press.

—— (1991) *Modernity and Self-Identity: Self and Society in the Late Modern Age*, Oxford: Polity Press.

—— (1992) *The Transformation of Intimacy: Love, Sexuality and Eroticism in Modern Societies*, Oxford: Polity Press.

Goethe, J.W.von (1957) *The Sufferings of the Young Werther*, London: Calder.

Goffman, E. (1968) *Asylums*, Harmondsworth: Penguin.

—— (1974) *Frame Analysis*, New York: Harper Row.

Gorer, G. (1965) *Death, Grief and Mourning in Contemporary Britain*, London: Cresset.

Gould, S.J. (1989) *Wonderful Life: The Burgess Shale and the Nature of History*, London: Hutchinson.

Habermas, J. (1971) *Knowledge and Human Interests*, London: Heinemann.

—— (1984) *The Theory of Communicative Action. Vol. 1: Reason and the Rationalisation of Society*, Oxford: Polity Press.

—— (1987) *The Theory of Communicative Action. Vol. 2: A Critique of Functionalist Reason*, Oxford: Polity Press.

—— (1989) *The Structural Transformation of the Public Sphere*, Oxford: Polity Press.

—— (1990a) *The Philosophical Discourse of Modernity: 12 Lectures*, Oxford: Polity Press.

—— (1990b) 'What does socialism mean today? The rectifying revolution and the need for new thinking on the left', *New Left Review* 183: 3–22.

Harvey, D. (1989) *The Condition of Post-Modernity*, Oxford: Blackwell.

Hinton, J. (1967) *Dying*, Harmondsworth: Penguin.

Hite, S. (1988) *Women and Love*, London: Viking.

Hochschild, A.R. (1983) *The Managed Heart: Commercialisation of Human Feeling*, Berkeley: University of California Press.

Jackson, D. (1990) *Unmasking Masculinity: A Critical Autobiography*, London: Unwin and Hyman.

Jameson, F. (1991) *Post-Modernism, or the Cultural Logic of Late Capitalism*, London: Verso.

Johnson, D. (1992) 'Something for the boys', *New York Review of Books* 16 Jan.: 13–17.

Jong, E. (1976) *Fear of Flying*, London: Panther.

Kastenbaum, R. (1982) 'Dying is healthy and death a bureaucrat: our fantasy machine is alive and well', in M. Dimatteo and H. Friedman (eds) *Interpersonal Personal Issues in Health Care*, London: Academic Press.

Keen, S. (1991) *Fire in the Belly: On Being A Man*, New York: Bantam.

Kernberg, O. (1975) *Borderline Conditions and Pathological Narcissism*, New York: Jason Aronson.

Khan, M. (1974) *The Privacy of the Self*, London: Hogarth Press.

Klein, M. (1937) 'Love, guilt and reparation' in M. Klein and J. Riviere (eds) *Love, Hate and Reparation*, London: Hogarth Press.

—— (1957) *Envy and Gratitude*, London: Tavistock.

—— (1975) 'The importance of symbol formation in the development of the ego', in *The Writings of Melanie Klein. Vol. 1*, London: Hogarth Press.

—— (1986a) 'Notes on some schizoid mechanisms', in J.Mitchell (ed.) *The Selected Melanie Klein*, Harmondsworth: Penguin.

—— (1986b) 'Mourning and its relation to manic-depressive states', in J.Mitchell (ed.) *The Selected Melanie Klein*, Harmondsworth: Penguin.

Kohut, H. (1971) *The Analysis of the Self*, New York: International Universities Press.

Kristeva, J. (1989) *Black Sun: Depression and Melancholia*, New York: Columbia University Press.

Lacan, J. (1968) *Speech and Language in Psychoanalysis*, Baltimore: Johns Hopkins University Press.

—— (1977) *Ecrits*, London: Tavistock.

—— (1979) *The Four Fundamental Concepts of Psychoanalysis*, Harmondsworth: Penguin.

—— (1988a) *The Seminar of Jacques Lacan. Book 1: Freud's Papers on Technique* (ed. J-A. Miller), Cambridge: Cambridge University Press.

—— (1988b) *The Seminar of Jacques Lacan. Book 2: The Ego in Freud's Theory* (ed. J-A. Miller), Cambridge: Cambridge University Press.

Lakoff R.S. and Azim', H.F.A. (1991) 'Society's changing views on mourning', *Group Analysis* 24 (4): 355–62.

Lasch, C. (1977) *Haven in a Heartless World*, New York: Basic Books.

—— (1980) *The Culture of Narcissism: American Life in an Age of Diminishing Expectations*, London: Sphere Books.

—— (1984) *The Minimal Self: Psychic Survival in Troubled Times*, London: Picador.

Lash, S. (1990) *Sociology of Postmodernism*, London: Routledge.

Lewis, C.S. (1961) *A Grief Observed*, London: Faber and Faber.

McCallum, M., Piper, W.E., Hassan, F., Azim, A., and Lakoff, R.S. (1991) 'The Edmonton model of short-term group therapy for loss: an integration of theory, practice and research', *Group Analysis* 24 (4): 375–88.

Malcolm, J. (1982) *Psychoanalysis: The Impossible Profession*, London: Pan.

Masson, J. (1985) *The Assault on Truth*, Harmondsworth: Penguin.

—— (1988) *Against Therapy: Emotional Tyranny and the Myth of Psychological Healing*, New York: Atheneum.

—— (1991) *The Final Analysis: The Making and Unmasking of a Psychoanalyst*, London: HarperCollins.

—— (1992) 'The tyranny of psychotherapy', in W. Dryden and C. Feltham (eds) *Psychotherapy and its Discontents*, Buckingham: Open University Press.

Milner, M. (1969) *The Hands of the Living God*, London: Hogarth Press.

Mitchell, J. (1975) *Psychoanalysis and Feminism*, New York: Vintage.

O'Connor, F. (1953) *The Stories of Frank O'Connor*, London: Hamish Hamilton.

Osterweis, M., Solomon, F., and Green, M. (1987) 'Bereavement reactions, consequences and care', in S. Zisook (ed.) *Biophysical Aspects of Bereavement*, Washington, D.C.: American Psychiatric Press.

Parkes, C. Murray (1987) *Bereavement: Studies of Grief in Adult Life*, Harmondsworth: Pelican.

Parsons, T (1951) *The Social System*, New York: Free Press.

—— (1971) *Societies: Evolutionary and Comparative Perspectives*, Englewood Cliffs, N.J.: Prentice Hall.

Parsons, T. and Bales, R.F. (1956) *Family, Socialisation and Interaction Process*, London: Routledge & Kegan Paul.

Phillips, A. (1989) 'Making a mess', *London Review of Books*, 2 Feb.: 22–3.

Pilgrim, D. (1992) 'Psychotherapy and political evasion', in W. Dryden and C. Feltham (eds) *Psychotherapy and Its Discontents*, Buckingham: Open University Press.

Piper, W.E. and McCallum, M. (1991) 'Group interventions for persons who have experienced loss: description and evaluative research', *Group Analysis* 24 (4): 363–74.

Rainwater, J. (1989) *Self-Therapy*, London: Crucible.

Raphael, B., (1984) *The Anatomy of Bereavement: A Handbook for the Caring Professions*, London: Unwin Hyman.

Rayner, E. (1991) *The Independent Mind in British Psychoanalysis*, London: Free Association.

Rogers, C. (1951) *Client-Centered Therapy: Its Current Implications and Theory*, Boston: Houghton Mifflin.

Rose, N. (1990) *Governing the Soul: The Shaping of the Private Self*, London: Routledge.

Rubin, G. (1975) 'The traffic in women: notes on the "political economy" of sex', in R. Reiter (ed): *Toward an Anthropology Of Women*, New York: Monthly Review Press.

Salzberger-Wittenberg, I. (1988) *Psychoanalytic Insight and Relationships*, London: Routledge.

Samuels, A. (1989) *The Plural Psyche: Personality, Morality and the Father*, London: Routledge.

—— (1993) *The Political Psyche*, London: Routledge.

Sartre, J-P. (1957) *Being and Nothingness*, London: Methuen.

Segal, H. (1991) *Dream, Phantasy, Art*, London: Tavistock/Routledge.

Simmel.G. (1950) 'The metropolis in mental life', in K.H. Wolff (ed.) *The Sociology of Georg Simmel*, New York: Free Press.

Skynner, R. and Cleese, J. (1983) *Families and How to Survive Them*, London: Methuen.

Symington, N. (1986) *The Analytic Experience*, London: Free Association.

Tönnies, F. (1955) *Community and Association*, London: Routledge & Kegan Paul.

Turkle, S. (1990) 'Dynasty', *London Review of Books* 6 Dec.: 3–9.

Verney, T. with Kelly, J. (1982) *The Secret Life of the Unborn Child*, London: Sphere.

Wallerstein, J. and Blakeslee, S. (1989) *Second Chances*, London: Bantam.

Wieland, C. (1991) 'Beauty and the Beast: the father's unconscious and the riddle of femininity', *British Journal of Psychotherapy* 8: 131–43.

Winnicott, D.W. (1958) *Collected Papers: Through Paediatrics to Psychoanalysis*, London: Tavistock.

—— (1964) *The Child, the Family and the Outside World*, Harmondsworth: Penguin.

—— (1965) *Maturational Processes and the Facilitating Environment*, London: Hogarth Press.

—— (1971) *Playing and Reality*, London: Tavistock.
—— (1986) *Home is Where We Start From*, Harmondsworth: Penguin.
—— (1988) *Human Nature*, London: Free Association Press.
Witham, Anna (1985) 'The idealisation of dying', *Free Associations* 3: 80–91.
Wouters, C. (1991) 'On status competition and emotion management', *Journal of Social History* 24: 699–717.
Zohar, D. (1990) *The Quantum Self*, London: Flamingo.

Index